RESEARCHING REAL-WORLD PROBLEMS

A GUIDE TO METHODS OF INQUIRY

ZINA O'LEARY

SAGE Publications
Los Angeles • London • New Delhi • Singapore

First published 2005

Reprinted 2007

 SAGE Publications Ltd
1 Oliver's Yard
55 City Road
London EC1Y 1SP

SAGE Publications Inc.
2455 Teller Road
Thousand Oaks, California 91320

SAGE Publications India Pvt Ltd
B 1/I 1 Mohan Cooperative Industrial Area
Mathura Road, New Delhi 110 044
India

SAGE Publications Asia-Pacific Pte Ltd
33 Pekin Street # 02-01
Far East Square
Singapore 048763

British Library Cataloguing in Publication data

A catalogue record for this book is available from the British Library

ISBN 978 1 4129 0194 9
ISBN 978 1 4129 0195 6 (pbk)

Library of Congress Control Number: 2005901271

Typeset by C&M Digitals (P) Ltd., Chennai, India
Printed on paper from sustainable resources
Printed in Great Britain by TJ International, Padstow, Cornwall

Summary of Contents

Contents

Contents

Acknowledgements

First and foremost I want to thank all of the students, colleagues, and friends I have worked with over the past ten years at both the University of Western Sydney and further afield. I have learned a tremendous amount from our shared experiences. A special note of thanks to Brent Powis for his willingness to review each and every chapter of this book.

I'd also like to thank Patrick Brindle and Vanessa Harwood at Sage. Their professionalism, responsiveness, and belief in my 'down to earth' approach is appreciated more than they might realize.

My parents also get a mention. Thanks dad, for being the inspiration for the start of Chapter 5 as well as being an inspiration in so many other ways. And thanks mom, for being a hell of a role model when it comes to knowing how to cut to the chase and get to the heart of an issue.

Finally, I'd like to acknowledge my daughters, Dakota and Scout, who give me tremendous joy every day, and also don't mind seeing their names in print.

Part One
Orientation to Researching Real-World Problems

1   **Researching Real-World Problems**

This introductory chapter argues the relevance and need for research that grapples with real-world problems. It discusses the practical and 'applied' nature of most research projects and highlights the challenges and payoffs associated with research that attempts to address significant real-world issues.

1

1

Researching Real-World Problems

'We are at the very beginning of time for the human race. It is
not unreasonable that we grapple with problems ... Our
responsibility is to do what we can, learn what we can,
improve the solutions, and pass them on.'

- Richard Feynman

GRAPPLING WITH PROBLEMS

You've probably already picked up on this, so I don't think I'm telling you anything new, but in case you hadn't noticed – the world is not a perfect place.
Problems abound.

Governments are riddled with problems – in fact, governments themselves
are a problem! The environment's a mess. Our planet is turning into one giant
greenhouse, there's salinity in the soil, and we don't have enough clean/safe
drinking water to go around. In fact, we can't find a way to distribute money,
food, or medicine so that everyone with a need can get a share. Health care and
education are far from adequate and/or equitable, and from the global arena to
the local playground we can't seem to overcome racism, sexism, prejudice or discrimination. Domestic violence and child abuse occur daily in every corner of
the world, and child pornography is a multi-billion dollar industry.

We also have to deal with the threat of terrorism as well as our fear of that
threat. We poison ourselves daily with toxic chemicals – from alcohol, cigarettes,
factories and automobiles. Children are starving – some due to war and political

upheaval – some from mass media-induced anorexia. Meanwhile schools struggle with violence, drugs, sexual and racial tension.

And don't get me started on the workplace … Did you know that more than 5,000 people die every single day due to work-related accidents and disease (International Labour Organization 2005)? Meanwhile, we 'survivors' deal with significant stress from the boss, massive bureaucratic inefficiencies, gross inequities, and the need to balance work with a thousand other responsibilities.

Yep – there are a lot of real-world problems we can grapple with.

From problems to problem solving

Now that may sound pretty depressing, but don't despair. We may live in a world plagued by problems – but we also live in a world dedicated to learning, changing, improving and evolving. Yes, problems abound – but so does problem solving and problem solvers. We are part of a world surrounded by people who work in government, in education, in health care, in big business, in small business, in the community, in academia etc., all dedicated to doing their part to ease, fix and alleviate problems. In fact, we live in a world where most struggle on a daily basis to solve problems in order to make the world, or at least their world, a better place. So okay, we may never live in a problem-free world, but at least we can say we live in a world where alleviating problems will always be high on the agenda.

THE ROLE OF RESEARCH IN PROBLEM SOLVING

So what is the role of research in problem solving? Well, research is the process of gathering data in order to answer a particular question(s); and when researching real-world problems the questions asked generally relate to a need for knowledge that can facilitate decision-making, thereby aiding problem resolution.

Does this then make research the answer to our problems? Well unfortunately no – but research can be an instrumental part of problem resolution. Research can be a key tool in informed decision-making. It can be central to determining what we should do, what we can do, how we will do it, and how well we have done it. Research may not be the answer to our problems, but it can supply some of the data necessary for us to begin to tackle the real-world problems that challenge us all.

Take change management literature as an example. It will clearly tell you that in order to make change happen – in order to solve problems – you need to:

- *understand the problem* – including all the complexities, intricacies and implications
- *be able to find workable solutions* – vision futures, explore possibilities
- *work towards that solution* – implement real change
- *evaluate success* – to find out if problem solving/change strategies have been successful

4

If you think about it, all of these activities can be, and should be, informed by research. Research can be the key to finding out more, that is, uncovering and understanding the complexity of real-world problems. It can also help us in our quest for solutions. It can be key to assessing needs, visioning futures, and finding and assessing potential answers. It can also allow us to enact and learn from change through use of 'action research' strategies. And finally, evaluative research can be central to monitoring and refining our attempts at problem solving. In short, research may not be the answer – but it's certainly a tool that can help us move towards problem resolution.

Researching practical problems

Precisely because (1) there are so many 'problems' out there, (2) there is a true dedication to problem solving from global to local scales and (3) research is recognized as central for effective and informed decision making, there is a real call for 'applied' research, or research expressly designed to contribute to solving practical problems.

Now keep in mind that while we would all like to save the world's children from hunger, do away with the evils of terrorism, or put a stop to religious persecution, not many of us will be in a position to fully address these types of problem through research processes. Generally speaking, researching real-world problems will see you engaged in problems, or aspects of problems, that while still important and significant, are local, grounded and practical. Researching real-world problems is doing research that responds to real and tangible everyday needs. So whether it be local or national government, non-government organizations, aid agencies, communities, corporations, or in fact any workplace, if there are problems to tackle, then there is a need for research that can aid problem resolution.

So who can benefit from research that tackles real-world problems? The list is endless. For example:

- ☑ **Educators** trying to improve their practice, trying to bring equity to a school system, trying to motivate students, trying to get a handle on bullying …
- ☑ **Nurses**, who know their insights can make way for better practice – if they can only find a way to be heard …
- ☑ **Doctors**, at least the few out there who don't believe they already know it all!
- ☑ **Communities** trying to deal with adolescents with nothing to do but hang around, or trying to protect a local park from corporate development …
- ☑ **People working in local government**, who want to listen to community needs, improve the state of the environment, improve community facilities …
- ☑ **Social workers** trying to get a handle on the problems facing twenty-first century families, the unemployed, and the abused …

5

☑ **Managers** trying to improve what they do and what their company offers, trying to provide safe, healthy, stress-free workplaces, as well as trying to increase profits …

☑ **Aid agencies**, who recognize the value of listening before acting, or those who need to know if their programmes have worked …

☑ **Governments**, who recognize the need for research that can contribute to major public policy debates …

THE POTENTIAL OF RESEARCHING REAL-WORLD PROBLEMS

'We are continually faced with a series of great opportunities disguised as insoluble problems.'

- John W. Gardner

There is a good reason why so many people are interested in conducting research into real-world problems. And that's because the findings, results and conclusions can lead to practical recommendations, genuine change, great opportunities, and real problem solving. As shown in Figure 1.1, research into real-world problems can, and should, open possibilities for change on a number of levels.

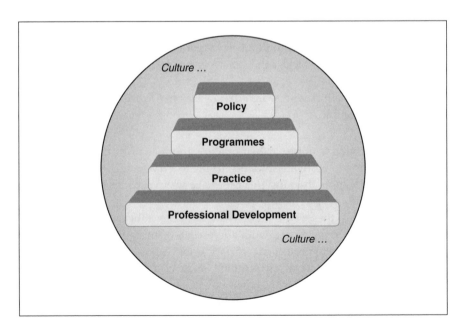

FIGURE 1.1 HIERARCHY OF CHANGE

Figure 1.1 depicts a hierarchy of change with a foundation based on professional development. The thinking here is that the process of conducting research is in itself a learning journey that should have an impact on the researcher; conducting research *is* professional development. The next level up is research that can impact on practice; it is research that can provide data that will allow individuals, organizations, or communities to reflect on, and refine what it is that they do. Moving up another level is programmes. The emphasis here is on a more systemic attempt to change the projects, procedures, plans and strategies used within organizations and communities. And finally, sitting above programmes is policy; here the research goal is to make a contribution to broader guiding principles. It is research that can help set new directions.

Now you'll note that encompassing this hierarchy is a circle labelled 'culture'. The thinking here is that if research is used as a tool for professional development, and can improve practice, programmes and policy, you're likely to see an influence on the culture of an organization or community. In fact, research at this level can help change the ethos of organization so that it is in a position to embrace learning and change.

Professional development

Whether you are a practitioner or an outside researcher, conducting research into real-world problems should always be a path to professional development. Conducting research into real-world problems allows you to:

- *Engage in 'problem-based learning'* – the thinking behind problem-based learning (PBL) is that the best starting point for learning is working through a problem that needs to be solved in a hands-on fashion. The learning here is 'double loop'. Not only do you learn about a problem you are exploring – you also learn how to tackle that problem, hopefully in a manner that will allow you to transfer problem solving skills to a variety of new challenges. The nature of conducting research into real-world problems embeds problem-based learning into the research process.
- *Engage in 'action learning'* – Kolb (1984) stressed the importance of the creation of knowledge through 'transformation of experience'. He suggested that experiential learning is dependent on cycles that include: (1) engagement in real experiences (concrete experimentation); that need to be followed by (2) thoughtful review and consideration (reflexive observation); as well as (3) broader theorizing (abstract conceptualization); and (4) attempts to improve action (active experimentation). Such processes are embedded in various aspects of conducting research. To 'do' research into real-world problems is to engage in cycles of action learning.
- *Enhance communication skills* – gathering credible data is not a task for the shy or faint-hearted. It is a process that is highly dependent on your ability to

7

communicate with others. Whether it is the challenge of gaining access, conducting interviews, or engaging in participant observation – boosting your communication skills is often a side benefit of doing research.

- *Develop research skills* – I know I write research methods textbooks, but I'll still tell you there's only so much you can learn from 'reading' about the conduct of research – the real learning comes from the 'doing'. Without a doubt, it is reflectively conducting research that will teach you how to do it.
- *Produce new knowledge* – you will find out something. You will hopefully get an answer to your research question. You will have produced new knowledge that can make a contribution to problem solving.
- *Engage in, or facilitate, evidenced-based decision making* – it's a really good feeling to know that commonsense, practical decisions are being influenced by data you generate. And, of course, if you are researching within your own organization and are in a position to make decisions yourself, then all the better.
- *Offer a pathway for gaining academic qualifications or getting a raise* – perhaps these goals are not as noble as the learning objectives above – but let's face it, this kind of stuff is often important to us. It is worth considering whether researching real-world problems can be embedded in both academic programmes and/or workplace performance measures.

Practice

The level above professional development is research that can modify practice. And this is exciting, because you get to see the fruits of your research labour. If you are conducting research into your own practice, or practices within a particular organization/ community, one of your research goals will be to gather data that can be instrumental to your ability to either: (a) modify, refine and improve what it is that you do, or (b) make recommendations that can influence the practices of others within a particular setting.

This is often a defining element of research into real-world problems. There is an express goal of facilitating problem solving by providing information for effective decision making related to practice. In working towards this goal, research can be used to:

- *Assess a problem situation* – sometimes called a 'needs assessment', this type of research attempts to provide an overview of a problem situation with a view to determining the need for new practices.
- *Assess/trial/evaluate 'new' practices* – this might involve research that attempts to: (1) explore the strengths/weaknesses and costs/benefits of new ways of 'doing'; (2) trial new practices through an 'action research' framework, something quite common in the education sector; or (3) evaluate the success/failure of new practices.

Programmes

Moving up one level on the hierarchy is research that can impact 'programmes'. Now while practice refers to what individuals 'do', programmes refers to more planned, organized, structured, or defined approaches to the operations, projects and strategies used within an 'organization'. Research at this level can help make convincing arguments for systemic change. For example:

- *Assessing need* – as with 'practice', research into programmes is often aimed at 'needs assessment' in which problem situations are explored. But in this context, it is explored with a view to determining the need for a particular 'change intervention' programme.
- *Assessing potential programmes* – also known as 'feasibility studies', this type of research attempts to explore the strengths/weaknesses and costs/benefits of particular programmes. Studies might look at whether a programme is likely to be accepted by stakeholders; whether there are likely to be problems with implementation; and/or look at the success/cost of such programmes in alternate settings.

- *Programme review* – often referred to as 'evaluative research', studies of this type are conducted to assess the effectiveness of change intervention programmes, and are considered central to rational and informed decision making. The thinking here is that whether it is a new teaching curriculum or a healthy lifestyle campaign, unless the level and effectiveness of change can be assessed, it becomes impossible to know: (1) if the strategy was successful; (2) whether it is cost-effective; (3) whether it should be continued; (4) whether it needs to be modified; or (5) whether it should be expanded.

Policy

Policy can be defined as *'a plan or course of action intended to influence and determine decisions, actions, and other matters'*. In other words, policy has the potential to direct what sits below it, which is precisely why it sits at the top of the hierarchy. Now, the goal here remains the same – making a contribution to problem resolution. But research at this level attempts to do so by producing knowledge that can impact an organization's strategic plans, aims and objectives, and/or mission statement. It is research aimed at producing policy recommendations that can help alleviate problems/problem situations.

Just a few examples of policy that can be influenced and even developed through credible and rigorous research include:

- a school's dress code policy or policy on gender equity
- a workplace's policy to offer in-house child care or increased maternity/paternity leave

- a government's policy on pollutants/emissions or its policy on gun control
- a local council's urban development plan or policy related to encouraging small business
- a hospital's policy on shift work or policy related to decreasing workplace accidents

Now keep in mind that moving from research to policy development is not as straight forward as moving from research to professional development or even from research to individual practice (where you have a high level of control). As you move up the hierarchy of change, your ability to make change happen through research – to have findings lead to action – becomes ever more challenging. Yes, you can argue that there should be a strong correlation between rigorous research expressly conducted for policy development … and the development of policy (that would make sense). But the development of policy is also likely to be influenced by factors other than 'findings'. Power, politics, public will and perception, and of course money, will all play their part.

Culture

Finally, encircling the entire hierarchy is 'culture'. Now research aimed at any level of the hierarchical structure has the potential to influence an organization's culture. Whether it be research undertaken by individuals for professional development or improved practice, or research undertaken by an organization in order to impact programmes and policy, the conduct of research itself can give a sense of empowerment and control in creating futures. In fact, the development of a research culture can be reflective of a move towards a 'learning organiza-tion', or an organization where '… people continually expand their capacity to create the results they truly desire' (Senge 1994, p. 3).

Research can facilitate such a cultural shift in two ways. First, research find-ings themselves may suggest the downside of the current culture and/or the ben-efits of an alternative culture. For example, research findings might suggest that a shift from a top-down to bottom-up ethos, from dictatorial to democratic man-agement, or from profit-driven to people-driven philosophy (and hopefully not those shifts the other way around!) are needed for increased productivity and/or job satisfaction.

Second, the conduct of research itself, particularly if driven by practitioners within an organization, can herald and facilitate a cultural shift towards values that include listening, learning, empowerment and dedication to change – something many feel is a necessity in the twenty-first century. In fact, as we begin to reflect on the legacies of modernization, globalization and industrialization, many are asking if we need to re-examine the cultural ethos that has dictated our current path.

THE CHALLENGE OF RESEARCHING REAL-WORLD PROBLEMS

'The real world is not easy to live in. It is rough; it is slippery.'

- Clarence Day

Undoubtedly, the grounded, practical and applied nature of researching real-world problems is precisely what makes it such a rewarding endeavour with so much potential. On the downside, however, research that aims to offer readily applicable findings must meet the challenges that come from the complex and messy environments in which real-world problems sit.

So if the real-world is 'rough' and 'slippery', as Clarence Day would suggest, you can rest assured that conducting research on real-world problems is not likely to find you with solid and sure footing. You need to be ready for challenges, obstacles and hiccups of all sorts.

Complexity of real-world problems

'I have yet to see any problem, however complicated,
which, when you looked at it in the right way, did
not become still more complicated.'

- Poul Anderson

Problems are amazingly complex things. What might appear straightforward at first glance can have a plethora of complexity hidden right below the surface. As shown in Figure 1.2, even a simple problem will have multiple facets or dimensions that include economic, bio-physical, cultural, social, political and personal elements.

Take schoolground graffiti as an example. Say you want to know why it's so hard for a school to put an end to the practice. Well if you wanted to explore all the relevant literature you'd have to travel down quite a few paths. First, you would need to recognize two distinct perspectives related to this problem: (1) understanding why students want/need to engage in this practice – particularly in the face of a school system trying to curtail it; and (2) why schools see this as a problem and are unable to find a way to curtail the practice. These two perspectives will then lead you into facets of the problem that are: *economic* (anything from the need to understand a possible culture of poverty … to an estimate of the actual expense associated with an effective anti-graffiti campaign); *biophysical* (from what alternatives there are for youth to express themselves visually … to how difficult it might be to secure the school grounds); *cultural*

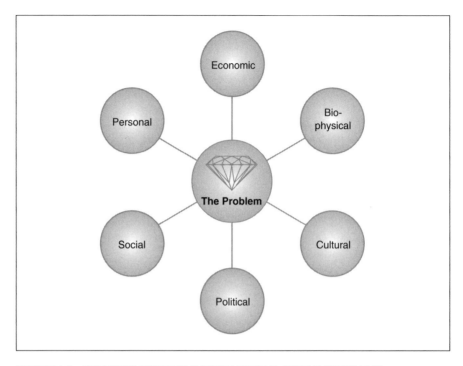

FIGURE 1.2   THE MULTI-FACETED NATURE OF REAL-WORLD PROBLEMS

(understanding youth culture, free expression, and/or a possible associated dis-respect for authority); *social* (understanding issues of peer pressure); *political* (from understanding playground hierarchies … to understanding school system politics that prioritizes what and how problems should be addressed); and even the *personal* (perhaps a student or students hold a vendetta against a particular teacher or even the school).

And these dimensions are not limited to graffiti. In fact, I could have picked just about any problem and outlined its multiple facets; all real-world problems are nested in real-world complexity. So whether the problem you want to address lies in your own professional practice, in a management system, in a polluted waterway, or in a community, as a researcher it is your job to be ready to face, unravel and work with multifaceted complexity.

Conducting research in the 'field'

Now there is nothing like a controlled environment for conducting research. You can test relationships between certain variables, make sure there is nothing that will confound results and in the end make some definitive statements about what's what. But that's not the way real-world problems work. In fact, much of the reason we struggle with such problems is precisely because they are multi-faceted

12

and embedded in messy real-world contexts. Real-world problems, however, do occur in the real world, and that is exactly where they need to be researched.

This raises an array of challenges, for example:

- the need to keep methodological designs flexible
- the need to engage in multiple methods
- the possibility of not being able to account for all variables
- managing your own experiences, insights and biases
- developing empathetic understanding of your full range of stakeholders
- prejudices towards you as a 'researcher'
- the need for highly developed social/communication skills
- being prepared for an array of real-world contingencies without adequate time or money

The payoff, however, is that if you recognize and are able to grapple with multi-dimensionality and messy contexts – and you can still come up with credible findings, conclusions and recommendations – they are much more likely to be realistic, practical, usable and sustainable than any 'tidy' results produced in a closed environment.

Defining a research team

To add to this complexity, and perhaps because of it, researching real-world problems demands reflexive consideration of who is best suited to undertake a particular research project. Now most problem-based research will be driven from an organization, often a workplace – for it is in the course of day-to-day work or within a job description itself that many problems are recognized and dealt with. The question is whether those within the interested organization decide to undertake the research themselves or decide to commission an outside party to do the work.

This means that researching real-world problems can be undertaken and/or managed by: (1) practitioners themselves; (2) 'professional' social or applied science researchers; (3) students – ranging from undergraduate project students to PhD candidates (some of whom may also be practitioners); or (4) a team made up of some combination of the above.

The practitioner

There are plenty of cases where a community member or a workplace practitioner will be the driving force/key researcher for a particular project. A practitioner might personally undertake the conduct of rigorous research in order to:

- carry out a small-scale project that management has determined should be handled in house
- address a pressing need for which there is no external funding

- facilitate best practice in evidenced-based decision making
- evaluate and modify their own practice
- fulfil obligations in their job descriptions
- meet requirements in undertaking a higher degree

The key here will be dedication to credibility through the development of knowledge and skills necessary for the conduct of rigorous research. Now we all know managers who might try to justify some controversial decision by saying something like, 'Well, I've actually done research into this', and proceed to tell you their opinions, or offer a few anecdotes. This is *not* what I am referring to when I talk about practitioner-based research. For me, practitioner-based research is engagement in a rigorous research protocol with a clear goal of obtaining credible data and producing trustworthy results. It doesn't have to be the biggest, most comprehensive study in the world, but it would need to be a study that stands up to the criteria of good research (as highlighted in Chapter 4).

The social/applied science researcher

There is also a role for the 'professional' in researching real-world problems. A workplace might turn to a government or non-government agency for assistance in conducting necessary research. This might involve soliciting the assistance of a(n):

- *government department* – such as a Department of Education or Ministry of Health
- *aid agency* – such as the World Health Organization, OXFAM, or the World Bank
- *university* – many have exceptional research profiles
- *market research company* – who can offer services that can extend beyond who will buy what. *Reader's Digest Australia*, for example, recently used the services of a market research company to conduct a survey in which teenagers gave their parents an overall 'report card'

Another alternative is that a 'professional' researcher may be interested in a particular problem situation and want to drive the research process. The 'professional' will look to work collaboratively with local governments, industry, community, schools, health care system, etc. in order to seek funding and conduct relevant research.

The student

From undergraduate to PhD, students can be instrumental to the conduct of rigorous research into real-world problems. Many upper-level undergraduate research methods subjects, and subjects targeting eventuating professional practice, require the conduct of a small-scale research project. And of course, research on a larger scale is required for Master's and PhD candidates. Now while some Master's and PhD theses will be highly theoretical in orientation, many others will attempt to address real-world problems at a very practical level. This is exciting because not only can such projects enhance personal learning, they can also make a real contribution to the production of knowledge and genuine problem solving. Students researching real-world problems have the opportunity to:

- learn the skills related to the conduct of research
- learn about the realities of working with others
- explore the politics and power of research
- make a real contribution to knowledge, problem solving and situation improvement

A team approach

Of course another possibility, and often a highly attractive one, is any combination of the above. Practitioners, professionals and students alike can each bring something of value to the table. For example, practitioners often have rich local, contextual and experiential knowledge; professionals have expertise and experience; while students are often dedicated, interested and in need of only minimal funding. The key here is to iron out roles and expectations so various agendas can be accommodated with minimal frustration.

One 'team'-based project that comes to mind involved a trial and evaluation of the World Health Organization's *Healthy Workplace Guidelines* in Malaysian industry. Academics from the University of Western Sydney designed the study and advised on data collection and analysis; staff from 3M Australia offered occupational health and safety related training to health and safety officers from the Malaysian Ministry of Health; these Ministry officers offered grounded knowledge, opened industry doors and went on to train industry employees; a University of Western Sydney student recorded the process, collected data, ran the analysis in order to meet university research project requirements; and finally the WHO funded the project.

Working on, for and with others

An additional layer of complexity in researching real-world problems comes from the need to establish a relationship with various stakeholder groups. Researchers need to negotiate whether their research process will see them working 'on', 'for', or 'with' others. While all of these approaches have their place in researching real-world problems, each presents their own opportunities and challenges.

Research 'on' others

Researchers are often seen as scientists whose role is to conduct studies *on* people; to conduct studies that will help illuminate what people do, and why they do it. The goal is the production of knowledge. A prime example of this is the Census where a research study is conducted *on* a particular population, so that the population can be better understood. The researcher tends to take an 'objective' stance and is not heavily intertwined in the life, dilemmas and challenges facing the researched. This approach has a definite place in researching real-world problems and would be highly appropriate when trying to understand something like the extent of a problem.

Research 'for' others

This can mean two different things. In the first instance research 'for' others can refer to research that is undertaken *for* a client – perhaps a workplace or a government department as a consultancy project. In this case, 'for' simply means commissioned research. Now this may sound straightforward, but research of this type often takes the form of evaluation, and as discussed in Chapter 10, there are plenty of cases where those commissioning such research are really after validation rather than a potentially ugly truth.

The second form of research 'for' others refers to research that is conducted *for* the 'good' of the researched. This is often seen in development research or within aid agencies whose agenda is to strive towards social transformation of the 'marginalized' (those without a strong power base or voice) through advocacy and action. And while this may sound like (and is) an admirable goal, it does have its own associated challenges. For one, there is a level of debate around the intertwining of research goals and political agendas – the question being how a researcher will negotiate objectivity. Second, is the risk that researchers will impose their political agenda on the 'marginalized'. It is important to consider whether a research agenda 'arises from', is 'assigned to', or 'imposed on' the researched.

•Research 'with' others

This refers to collaborative research that is conducted by, for and *with* a range of stakeholders. Generally, this type of research involves addressing stakeholder needs, concerns and problems, and finds the key researcher as but one player in a collaborative effort to grapple with real-world problems. Now, as discussed in Chapter 9, this is an approach common in action research strategies where the conduct of research is not seen as the domain of the expert. Participation is based on collaboration between researchers, practitioners and any other interested stakeholders. The distinction between the researcher and the researched is minimized and high value is placed on local knowledge with a goal of working towards empowerment and ownership.

As the icon implies, however, this can be messy. The benefits of conducting research 'with' others can be matched by frustrations related to a lack of control; stakeholders feeling unheard; as well as the difficulties of getting the 'team' working together. The rewards however – meaningful partnerships, sustainable change, ownership and empowerment – can make it well worthwhile.

Researching within your own organization

A final issue quite significant for 'practitioner' researchers (which often includes students with a dual role) is the challenge of negotiating the conduct of research within one's own organization. Now you may think, 'who better to undertake research within an organization than someone with local knowledge, someone who has access, someone who understands the political ins and outs, someone who not only sees problems but tends to be frustrated by them on a day-to day basis, someone that people already know and trust, someone with something to gain for their own professional practice, or something to gain for their own workplace'. And while all of this may be true and together can make an exceedingly compelling argument for practitioner research, as shown in Table 1.1, for each advantage there are disadvantages that practitioners need to carefully consider and thoughtfully negotiate.

PREPARING TO MAKE A START

Okay, in this chapter we've looked at the nature of real-world problems, discussed the role of research in problem solving, and explored some of the potentialities and challenges of conducting this type of research. Hopefully you're sold on the idea and ready to take on the challenge.

The question now is how can you best manage the conduct of research into complex, messy, multi-faceted real-world problems? Well helping you work your way through this, is the task of the following chapters. But in a nutshell, it's all a matter of thoughtful consideration – thinking your way through the process. It's about being well prepared, being ready to think on your feet, knowing how to be strategic and at times even creative. And, of course, being able to check all of this against the criterion of good research.

Just remember there are no easy answers, just you and your ability to manage the research process in a way that best assures credibility. Hard and fast rules don't work. And while this book will guide you through the most effective strategies for dealing with the complexities of researching real-world problems,

TABLE 1.1   OPPORTUNITIES AND DILEMMAS IN PRACTITIONER RESEARCH

The practitioner edge	Opportunities	Dilemmas
Experience	• being able to capitalize on a great depth of experiential, local and insider knowledge	• already having the answers – • being biased/lacking objectivity
Access	• being able to come and go within an organizational setting	• not being seen or respected as a 'researcher'
Trust	• having people be honest and open because they know and trust you	• being unsure if what is said is to you as a confidential friend or to you as a researcher gathering data • losing trust because you are now a 'researcher'
Political nous	• having a good sense of how the organization operates, and how to best manage politics	• getting on the wrong side of the political machine and having to continue to operate within that political environment after the research is done
Dual role	• being in a position to best see research needs and opportunities	• role conflict as managerial responsibilities can be at odds with researcher objectivity and/ or confidentiality
Career opportunities	• making a contribution that will enhance your career	• making a contribution that will undo your career
Improved practice	• evaluating your own practice so that it can be improved.	• finding out that what you are doing and what you believe in is not working and/or not appreciated
Organizational change	• being able to make a real contribution to shifting workplace practice, systems and/or culture	• being responsible for an organization needing to go through the upheaval of changing practices, systems and/or culture

keep in mind that the best researchers are ones who have: (1) built solid foundations; (2) are prepared to delve into problems; and (3) are ready to make meaning with an aim of making a difference.

Laying foundations

Research is something you simply can't go off and do without a basic grounding in theory, techniques, skills and strategies. Chapters 2–6 attempt to lay the foundations for these basics, including:

- developing well-articulated, well-constructed, practical research questions (Chapter 2)
- being able to call on and review relevant literature (Chapter 3)
- being able to work through logical and practical methodological design (Chapter 3)
- writing a winning proposal (Chapter 3)
- conducting research in an ethically responsible manner (Chapter 4)
- being familiar with criteria for credibility (Chapter 4)
- being able to draw an appropriate sample/target group(s) (Chapter 5)
- developing proficiency in data collection and analysis (Chapter 6)

Whether your goal is to conduct research into real-world problems as a student, practitioner, or professional, it is proficiency in these skills that will define credible and rigorous research capable of making a difference.

Delving into problems

Once you have a solid foundation and are familiar with research basics, it's time to match your new knowledge and skills against various research objectives. When researching real-world problems, such objectives will generally involve:

- gaining a better handle on problem situations (Chapter 7)
- trying to find a solution or solutions to a particular problem (Chapter 8)
- engaging in action-based situation improvement through research (Chapter 9)
- evaluating change initiatives (Chapter 10)
- more than one element of the above

What is important to remember is that it is your aims/objectives and your research question that will define your methodological approaches. You have to know what you want to know and what you want to accomplish before you can take on the task of developing a research plan.

Making meaning/making a difference

Finally, the conduct of research into real-world problems is meaningless if nothing comes from your research. You need to be able to move your study from raw data to an end product capable of making an impact. This will involve:

- engaging in meaningful analysis (Chapter 11)
- drawing relevant and compelling conclusions (Chapter 11)
- crafting a credible and engaging storyline (Chapter 12)
- writing up useful 'deliverables' (Chapter 12), and finally
- making sure your research is disseminated and utilized (Chapter 12)

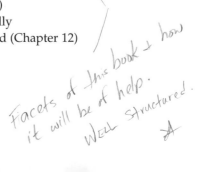

Researching real-world problems is about conducting research that has the potential to make a difference ... to both yourself and to others. I hope you will take up the challenge – and please remember to enjoy the journey!

Chapter Summary

- We may live in a world riddled with problems, but we also live in a world full of problem solvers, in a world dedicated to learning, changing, improving and evolving.

- Research can be the key to informed decision-making related to problem solving. It can be instrumental in gathering data related to: understanding problems; finding solutions; implementing change; and evaluating success.

- Researching real-world problems is about research that is local, grounded, practical and responsive to everyday needs. Local or national government, non-government organizations, aid agencies, communities, corporations and workplaces in general can all benefit from problem-based research.

- Research into real-world problems can open up possibilities for change at the level of: professional development; practice; programmes; policy; and organizational culture.

- Real-world problems, and the contexts in which they sit, tend to be messy, complex, and multi-faceted – posing a number of challenges to the reflective researcher.

- Researchers of real-world problems need to consider: the challenge of conducting research in the field; how to define a research team; whether they are working on, for, or with others; as well as the challenges they will face if conducting research in their own organization.

- As well as an ability to think strategically, preparing to research real-world problems requires: solid foundations; being prepared to delve into problem situations; and being prepared to do what it takes to make a real difference.

Part Two
Laying Foundations

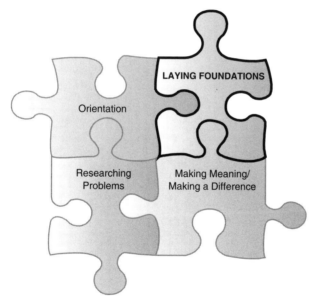

Chapters 2–6 lay the foundation for understanding and engaging in research that tackles real-world problems. Chapter 2 explores the complexity inherent in problem situations and works you through the challenge of moving from tangible problems to 'research-able' questions. Chapter 3 covers some of the essential preparatory work necessary for credible research, and provides context and method for drawing on literature, before working you through the challenges of methodological design and proposal develop-ment. The focus of Chapter 4 is research integrity and looks at issues of credibility in relation to the production of knowledge and ethical issues related to responsibility for the 'researched'. The aim of Chapter 5 is to help you think about the need to define and select your respondents, while the final foundational chapter takes you through the issues and techniques associated with real-world data collection.

Chapter 1 discussed an overview of researching real-world problems. It's scope, effectiveness and usability. It presents the necessary steps for successful researching in real-world problem situations; gave an outline as to how the book is structured and will guide us through this process effectively. I found this chapter to be very helpful and motivational. The most important aspects I found were the stress they placed on the importance of & properly developing the research question that will guide the rest of the research process.

2
From Real Problems to Researchable Questions

'The scientific mind does not so much provide the right answers as ask the right questions.'

- Claude Lévi-Strauss

PROBLEMS AND POSSIBILITIES

A world without problems ... sounds good doesn't it? But if you really think about it, wouldn't a world without problems also be a world with no motivation to transform, progress or evolve; wouldn't it be a world that is, well, stagnant? Okay, you might argue that there would be no need to 'progress' if there were no problems, but that indicates an ambivalent attitude towards change and a framing of the word 'problems' that is less than constructive. For if it is problems that motivate change, perhaps it would be more productive to see problems as opportunities – to frame problems as potentialities. Problems could then be more than just dilemmas, impediments and obstacles – problems could, in fact, be challenges that open up a world of possibility.

Defining problems

So how do we define a problem? Well, defining a problem is something quite different from simply providing a definition of the word. For example, a definition of 'problem' might be:

23

> *Problem:* A situation where there is a gap between what is real and what is ideal or desired.

The definition itself is fairly straightforward. What is more complicated, however, is the challenge of figuring out what qualifies as or constitutes a problem. In the case of the definition above, it means knowing what is 'desired' and what is considered 'ideal'. And that can involve factors such as worldviews, personal and societal norms, ethics, morals, values, politics, law, economics etc. In other words, problems are far from universal.

Take, for example, euthanasia. Is it less than what is 'desired'? Is it less than 'ideal'? Well the answer will certainly rest on perspective. For the Catholic Church, euthanasia would certainly be a moral problem. For a hospital it is likely to be an ethical, political, legal and economic (if there is one thing hospitals hate, it's lawsuits) problem. When it comes to the patient's family, some may find it a moral and/or legal nightmare. But for others, it may be exactly what is 'ideal' and 'desired' within a desperate situation. For these family members, and many patients themselves, euthanasia is a solution rather than a problem.

Situations can also become defined as problems as times and cultures shift and transform. For example, the state of the environment was not a problem until it was defined as such – first by activists and more recently by governments. Domestic violence was not a problem until a cultural shift saw wives as something more than the property of their husbands. And wage differentiation based on race has certainly been deemed a problem in the West, but unfortunately there are still many cultures in which race determines both social and economic status.

So if problems are defined by a gap between what is 'real' and what is 'ideal or desired', and what is ideal or desired is very much dependent on perspective and cultural/historical realities – then deciding what constitutes a problem has the potential to open up tremendous debate. The implication for researchers is that problem identification needs to involve consideration of the various realities and perspectives that inform an issue.

IDENTIFYING PROBLEMS SUITABLE FOR RESEARCH

Now the real-world problems you are likely to identify will come in all shapes and sizes, for example social problems, political problems, economic problems, workplace problems, policy problems, global problems, local problems etc., etc. So the challenge is knowing how to choose, where to start and how to focus your inquiry so that you and your research can make a real impact – make a real contribution to change.

Well it's probably worth keeping in mind that one identifying feature of researching 'real-world' problems is that the task tends to be 'applied' – the conduct of research is undertaken with the express goal of problem solving or facilitating situation improvement. It is more than just an academic exercise or a task designed to satisfy curiosity. So whether your problem is identified through your own knowledge and experience, from broader societal issues, or from listening to the needs of others, it is important to remember that researching real-world problems is an inherently practical affair. Problems suitable for research are problems where you can make a difference.

Drawing on knowledge and experience

Many times it will be your own insights and experiences that point you towards a problem that clearly needs to be researched. Take the workplace for instance. Just about anyone who has ever had a job will tell you that workplaces are rife with problems. For example, what employee doesn't grapple with red-tape, inefficiencies, ineptitude, incompetence, decision makers not in touch with the coal-face, corruption, profit before service, morale and motivation? Your own frustrations are often tied to the frustrations of many – and if they can also be tied to the goals, aims, objectives and vision of the organization, community, or institution in which they sit, then there is a good chance those very frustrations will have 'research' potential.

On the other side of the coin are problems that are not so much attributed to inefficiencies or inadequacies within the workplace itself, but are tied to the client groups with which you might work. Some examples here might be unmotivated students, communities reluctant to recycle waste, or patients who simple cannot/do not follow dietary guidelines. Again, if these frustrations are widely accepted and can be linked to organizational/community goals – then they are likely to have research potential.

Exploring broader issues

Extending beyond your own workplace experiences are problems tied to broader societal/political agendas. For example, timely or contemporary issues such as inadequacies in health care systems, blue–green algae blooms in the local catchment, a sudden increase in high school dropout rates etc., which overlap with your own interests and/or organizational goals, are good issues to explore. At times, growing political interest, sudden media coverage, or even new legal requirements may be enough to motivate a need to conduct research into a particular problem area.

Another sure fire way to locate 'researchable' problems is in literature. The importance of reading for research cannot be overemphasized. When you are conversant with topical literature it becomes quite easy to find researchable problems. You can explore whether an important aspect of a problem has been ignored; whether assumptions underpinning problem investigation need to be re-examined; or whether further questions related to a particular problem have been posed by researchers at the end of their research papers. If you can identify gaps and holes in the literature, you can quite readily generate relevant research topics.

Learning to identify 'needs'

Another approach to identifying suitable research problems, which can open up a whole world of possibilities, is to consciously work towards identifying the needs of others. For example, say your insights suggest that there is a problem – perhaps a sense of dissatisfaction coming from a particular group or from within an organization. It may be worth undertaking a preliminary investigation that can identify the problem or problems from the perspectives of the group. In fact, uncovering these perspectives might end up being a major research question in its own right.

Identifying problems and needs might also come from following media coverage, reading letters to the editor, or listening to stakeholders at various forums including town council meetings, workplace meetings, or any other place where stakeholders may gather to express their concerns.

Now at times, needs identification can be overlooked. There is a real history of researchers 'knowing' there is a problem and 'assuming' that their knowledge is paramount. The researcher is the expert who identifies problems and works towards solutions. But this 'non-reflective' approach to problem identification has left many researchers scratching their heads and wondering why so little sustainable change has come from their research initiatives. Keep in mind that it doesn't matter how legitimate your research findings and recommendations are if they're not meeting the needs of those facing the problems you have identified. Sustainable change is often dependent on making sure that what an expert deems as a problem is actually identified and prioritized as a problem by stakeholders themselves. In short, listening to, and identifying the needs of stakeholders is paramount.

A good strategy here is to undertake a stakeholder analysis. This generally includes:

- Identifying the scope, extent, or number of people/organizations likely to be: (1) adversely affected by a problem situation; (2) causal to a problem situation; and (3) involved in potential problem alleviation. For example, if your problem was a lead smelter operating close to a residential area, stakeholders would include those adversely affected by the smelter, i.e. local residents, local schools, parent groups, smelter employees etc.; those causal to the problem, i.e. representatives from the smelter and/or their parent company; and those who could help in problem alleviation, i.e. the health department, local government authority, the Environmental Protection Authority etc.
- Finding out whether, how and why the problem at hand is seen as an issue or priority issue by the various stakeholder groups identified above.
- Recognizing that even within various stakeholder groups there can be a diversity of attitudes and opinions.

Remembering practicalities

We'll talk about practicalities more fully when we look at the potential methods you might use to investigate your 'problem', but even at the stage of problem identification it is worth keeping practicalities like researchability, funding and political support in mind.

We might know the world is full of problems, but not all of these problems can be solved through research, and fewer still can be solved through short-term, relatively small-scale research projects. This makes being practical exceedingly important. For example, the threat of a major asteroid strike is a real problem for the human race, but it's not a problem likely to be solved through the conduct of a small-scale research study with a limited budget. Or say the problem you have identified is that your manager is a real *#^&! In this case, not only do you have to think about how a research study might or might not inform/help alleviate the problem, but how you might be able to do such research and keep your job at the same time! Now this is not to say that a problem needs to be politically judicious to be researchable. It does, however, highlight the fact that before you decide to research any particular problem, you need to be prepared to carefully consider and sensitively manage political (and financial) realities. In selecting a problem suitable for research you need to think about what you can do, but also what you can't do (see Box 2.1 for a few examples).

Box 2.1   Selecting Problems Suitable for Research

Below is a list of research 'problems' some of my current students/clients are working on and how/why these problems were selected.

1. **A large percentage of non-recyclable materials in household recycle bins** – problem identified and researched by a frustrated council officer in charge of waste management who was undertaking a higher degree.
2. **Decision making in a health promotion centre without any evidence base** – problem identified by the new centre director who was unsure how to prioritize issues.
3. **Violence towards nursing staff in emergency wards** – problem identified by an ex-nurse undertaking an occupational health and safety postgraduate degree after being forced into a career change due to a patient attack.
4. **Bastardization in university residential halls** – problem identified by a student who went through such practices in her first year at university.

(Continued)

Box 2.1   (Continued)

5. **Subcontractors in the construction industry with poor safety records** – problem selected by an occupational health and safety student because of current media coverage related to the topic.
6. **Underutilization of experiential learning in the classroom** – problem identified by an education student through literature she came across in the course of her degree.
7. **Disregard for fire alarms in Hong Kong high rises** – problem identified by fire safety officer undertaking a higher degree who was in charge of an investigation where seven people died because they ignored an alarm.

UNPACKING PROBLEMS

Running alongside the task of problem identification is the need to 'unpack' problem situations. Remember, problems generally have a complex, multi-faceted and sometimes inconsistent nature. So the challenge for any researcher attempting to select a relevant problem is to be able to explore the assumptions embedded within problem definition.

In fact, before any problem is approached through research it is essential that researchers critically explore the assumptions that underpin the nature of the problem at hand. They also need to examine how they as researchers have come to understand a particular problem situation.

As shown in Figure 2.1, and further explored in Box 2.2, this 'unpacking' should involve: exploring the dominant worldview; exploring your own perspectives; and exploring the range of perspectives held by various stakeholders.

Exploring the dominant worldview

Whether it be the broader cultural milieu or the dominant culture that exists within a workplace, we tend to be immersed in settings that are not value-neutral. For example, the Western world, and many of the organizations within it, tends to be dominated by values that emerge from the legacy of Christianity, patriarchy and capitalism. And often situations that come to be defined as problems are the ones that those in power see as bumping up against these dominant worldviews. For example, increases in the percentage of teenagers having sexual intercourse, increases in divorce rates, or falling profits.

Okay, so how does this impact on those wanting to conduct research into real-world problems? Well, there are several ways. First, exploring the dominant

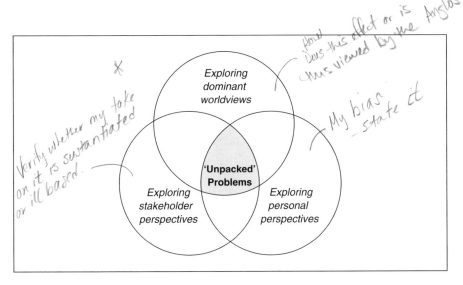

How does this affect or is Anglos ...·
this viewed by the

My bias state it

Verify whether my take
on it is substantiated
or ill based.

FIGURE 2.1   OPENING UP ASSUMPTIONS

worldview will allow you to understand issue prioritization so that you can work effectively within a system. If your research interests fall neatly within the dominant paradigm, getting support and even funding for your research may not be too difficult. Your problem is likely to be a priority to those in power.

On the other hand, if your 'problem' sits outside the dominant framework you may have to do some work to get the support you need. Now keep in mind that anyone (even those without a strong power base) can define a real-world problem – the trick is getting support to enable you to conduct research related to that problem. And this is where understanding the view of the dominant, the view of those with power, is quite important. For example, take the issue of workplace stress. Getting stressed at work is a common phenomenon – and one that is often ignored or simply not prioritized by management. Now for a big corporation the worldview is capitalism and the bottom line is profit, so priority problems will tend to be those that directly effect profit lines. Support for the conduct of research into the problem of workplace stress may therefore rely on arguments that link stress to more than just employee happiness and satisfaction. It is more likely to rely on arguments that highlight a loss of productivity, high turnover and decreased profits. In this scenario, understanding the dominant worldview can help you effectively advocate for research into 'problems' not generally given priority status by those in power.

Finally, being able to 'name' the dominant paradigm can help you identify problems that often face the 'marginalized'. For example, in education, a dominant 'modern' worldview that incorporates a very hierarchical power structure might suggest that problems sit with unmotivated, uninterested, disrespectful students. If, however, you were to recognize that the education system you are exploring has such a paradigm in operation, you may begin to think about the paradigm

29

itself as problematic. The problem may lie with an education system that acts to in fact create students who can be readily classified as unmotivated, uninterested and/or disrespectful. In this case, understanding the dominant paradigm allows you to do more than just work effectively within it. It also allows you to think critically about the paradigm itself and its implications for those subjected to it. The ability to think outside the square and question the system can provide an invaluable contribution for shifting organizational or societal cultures in radical ways.

Exploring your own perspective

> *'Few people are capable of expressing ... opinions which differ from the prejudices of their social environment. Most people are even incapable of forming such opinions.'*
>
> *- Albert Einstein*

Just because you take on a researcher or practitioner-researcher role, you won't suddenly become immune to the cultural forces that shape and surround you. We tend to make sense of the world through the rules we are given to interpret it. But when you are immersed in these rules and surrounded by them, they can, in fact, be very hard to see. Our sense of loyalty, our understandings of family, our belief in justice and equity, for example, are embedded within us and are reinforced on a daily basis. They become part of how we understand and make sense of the world ... and how we might go about researching it. It is, therefore, crucial to remember that being able to critically unpack a problem relies on a level of self-reflection.

In order to be a reflective researcher you need to:

- Consider your own worldviews, beliefs, biases, prejudices and subjectivities as they relate to a particular problem situation. The ability to 'name' your own positioning is a prerequisite for being able to unpack any problem situation. In fact, stating your political/personal positioning in relation to your research topic is now a common, and in some genres, expected part of a research thesis.
- Accept that others may not think or process the world as you do. There are a million different ways to view the world. It's important to remember that your particular understanding is not a universal understanding.
- Be sensitive to issues of race, class, culture and gender – these fundamental constructs can be associated with wide divergence in how situations can come to be framed as 'problems'.

Exploring the range of perspectives held by various stakeholders

Problems are generally complex, and as highlighted in Box 2.2, unpacking problem situations demands that consideration be given to all the varied perspectives that can come from those with vested interests. Now there are two ⓵ points to consider when looking at stakeholder perspectives. First is that there are likely to be a range of stakeholders involved in, or impacted by, any particular problem situation. Second is that there will not always be a common perspective ⓶ within a particular stakeholder group. Keep in mind that full understanding will rely on hearing an array of voices. If you only listen to those talking the loudest, you will surely fall short of rich understanding.

conclusion

Box 2.2 *Weighing Up the Problem – Prezlee's Story*

Being a new mother I was interested in knowing why pregnant women must suffer the humiliation of being weighed by a nurse during prenatal visits rather than being able to weigh themselves. It seemed simple enough and important enough – disempowerment is certainly a critical issue in the medical field. But then my supervisor asked me to think about the following questions:

Why is this a problem? I could answer this one and proceeded to talk about the whole disempowerment of women/patients issue.

Is it a problem for you? Easy question – definitely, and not just for me, but also for my friends that had gone through a similar experience.

For all pregnant women? Uh oh – when I thought about this I realized I really had no idea if this was a problem to women from different cultures or a different class structure … I guessed it was, but I really had no idea – my first assumption uncovered.

For doctors, nurses, administration? Again, when I then sat down to think about the issue from the perspective of doctors, nurses and administration I realized that from their perspective it may actually be a practice that affords them benefits such as consistency, control and empowerment. Hmmm … I'd have to explore that.

(Continued)

> **Box 2.2   (Continued)**

What dominant paradigms are in operation here? I enjoyed mulling over this one. Power structures of the medical profession, patriarchy, class and gender discrimination – I thought my question was a simple one – I didn't realize the issue could be so rich.

What prejudices, biases and preconceived notions do you have? I could think of four: (1) that being weighed in is humiliating; (2) that the medical profession is disempowering to patients; (3) that this needs to shift; and (4) that I sometimes assume that everyone else thinks just like me.

How will the answers to these questions influence your work? I realized that if I hadn't thought these issues through I would have probably found exactly what I was looking for because I would have only been ready to hear what I already knew, probably from pretty like-minded people. After thinking through my answers I realized I'd have to go back to the drawing board and really explore what it is I know about this issue, what I assume, and what complexities I will need to work through.

In the end I did end up exploring this particular issue – but after running through the questions above – I certainly went into my study with a much richer understanding of my 'simple' problem.

FROM PROBLEMS TO RESEARCH QUESTIONS

Okay – so you've had a good think about various problems you might want to explore and you've chosen a practical problem by drawing on your insights and experiences, assessing needs and perhaps even delving into a bit of literature. You've also taken the time to reflexively consider the nature of this problem, its relation to various paradigms and your own biases and subjectivities. You've even attempted to appreciate the problem from the viewpoint of various stakeholders. It must be time to start researching.

Well not quite. There is just one step to go, and that is moving from a problem suitable to research to a **research question**. Now you may ask, 'Is this really necessary', and the answer is an unequivocal 'YES'. You might be surprised at just how many options there are in moving from a problem to a question, and I am a firm believer in the importance of a well-developed research question. It is an absolutely essential starting point for the research journey.

The nature and importance of research questions

There are a lot of people who feel ready to jump into a research project before they have taken the time to really think through and develop a research question. Research questions are, however, fundamental and the ability to articulate ideas into well-formed research questions is an essential skill.

So why is it that research questions are so crucial? Well, when you get right down to it, to conduct research is to embark on a decision making journey. The process, in fact, demands that you constantly engage in decision making that is logical, consistent and coherent. And what do you think the benchmark for logical, consistent and coherent decision making is? It's that the choices you make will take you one step closer to being able to credibly answer your ... research question. So without clear articulation of your question – you're really travelling blind.

Put simply, research questions:

- *Define an investigation* – a well-articulated research question can provide both you and your eventual readers information about: your topic; your context; your aims and objectives; the nature of your question; potential variables; and relationships that might exist between these variables.
- *Set boundaries* – along your research journey you are likely to find yourself facing plenty of detours and diversions. A well-defined question can remind you that your research project needs to have boundaries.
- *Provide direction* – it's worth remembering that if you don't know what you want to know, you will not be in a position to know how to find it out. A well-defined, well-articulated research question will provide direction and point to: the theory you need to explore; the literature you need to review; the data you need to gather; and the methods you need to call on.
- *Act as a frame of reference for assessing your work* – not only does your question provide continuity and set the agenda for your entire study, it also acts as a benchmark for assessing your decision-making processes. As stated, the criteria for all decision-making related to the conduct of your research will be whether or not choices lead you closer to credible answers to your research question.

Developing the question

Hopefully you are now convinced that research questions are indeed pivotal to the research process. But how exactly do you go about articulating one? Well, if you have thought it all through and feel comfortable with the problem situation you want to explore, but you are not quite sure how to best articulate your research question, I'd suggest working through the following five-step process:

1. Using only short one- or two-word responses, write down the answers to the following questions:

   - What is your topic? i.e. chronic back pain, recycling, independent learning …
   - What is the context for your research? i.e. a school, local government authority, a hospital, community …
   - What do you want to achieve? i.e. to discover, to describe, to change, to explore, to explain, to develop, to understand …
   - What is the nature of your question? i.e. a what, who, where, how, when, or why question.
   - Are there any potential relationships you want to explore? i.e. impacts, increases, decreases, relationships, correlations, causes etc.

2. Starting with the nature of the question, that is, who, what, where, how, when, begin to piece together the answers generated in step 1 until you feel comfortable with the eventual question or questions. For example, say your problem was a large percentage of non-recyclable materials in household recycle bins (as discussed in Box 2.1). The answers from step 1 might lead to a number of questions:

   - **Topic:** recycling; **Context:** domestic/community; **Goal:** to explore why there is a lack of efficiency; **Nature of your question:** who and why; **Relationship:** correlation between demographic characteristics and inefficient recycling
     Question: Is there a relationship between household recycling behaviours and demographic characteristics?
   - **Topic:** recycling; **Context:** domestic/households; **Goal:** to understand how individuals go about the task of recycling; **Nature of your question:** how; **Relationship:** N/A
     Question: How do individuals engage in decision making processes related to household domestic waste management?
   - **Topic:** recycling; **Context:** domestic/community; **Goal:** to describe the nature of recycling inefficiencies so that an effective community awareness campaign can be developed; **Nature of your question:** what; **Relationship:** N/A
     Question: What are the most common non-recyclable items found in household recycle bins?

3. If you have developed more than one question (remember any one problem can lead to a multitude of research questions), decide whether you need to select one or more questions and make that selection.

4. Narrow and clarify until your question is as concise and well articulated as possible. Ambiguity can often arise when questions are broad and unwieldy, so being precise makes the research task easier to accomplish. Remember, the

first articulation of any research question is unlikely to be as clear, helpful and unambiguous as the third, fourth or even fifth attempt.

5. Assess the question(s) in relation to the question checklist that follows.

The real-world research question checklist

Once you come up with a research question, you need to assess if it's going to be researchable at a practical level. Run through the following checklist. If you find yourself feeling uncomfortable with the answers, it may indicate a need to rethink your question.

☑ **Is the question right for you?**   There's a bit of a double-edged sword here. On one side you need to consider whether your question has the potential to hold your interest for the likely duration of the study. You don't want to take something on that you don't have the motivation to see through. On the other side, however, you need to consider whether interest or perhaps passion over a particular issue will threaten the credibility of your study. Are you biased? And can you control your biases so that your study results will stand up to scrutiny?

☑ **Does the question have significance for an organization, an institution, a group, a field, etc.?**   You need to consider whether relevant stakeholders will regard your findings as significant. Remember, the role of research is to do one or more of the following: advance knowledge; aid individuals; improve professional practice; and/or impact programmes and policy. Research questions need to be significant – not only to you, but to a wider group of stakeholders as well. If the response from parties who should be interested is, 'so what/who cares' – you need to go back to the drawing board.

☑ **Can it lead to tangible situation improvement?**   A distinguishing feature of researching real-world problems is that the problems you will attempt to research are, in fact, real – and there is a genuine motivation to fix or alleviate problems and improve situations. A key criterion for your research question is thus assessing whether your findings are likely to stay in the realm of theory and do little more than sit on a shelf, or whether your results will actually be useful for enacting change.

☑ **Is the question well articulated?**   A research question not only indicates the theory and literature you need to explore and review, it also points to the data you will need to gather, and the methods you will need to adopt. This makes clear articulation of research questions particularly important. The question needs to be as unambiguous and clearly defined as possible.

Take the question, 'Is health care a problem in the US?' As a question for general debate, it's probably fine. As a research question, however, it needs a fair bit of clarification. How are you defining health care? What boundaries are you putting on the term? How are you defining the problem? Social, moral, economic, legal, all of the above? And who are you speaking for? A problem for whom? The more clarity in the question, the more work the question can do, making the direction of the study that much more defined.

☑ **Is the question researchable?** Perhaps the main criterion of any good research question is that you will be able to undertake the research necessary to answer the question. And there are a number of constraints to doing this.

First, you have to assess whether the question can be answered through a research process. For example, the question, 'Would the national education system work better if only women were allowed to teach?' This can lead to speculation, but unless you fire all male teachers and see what happens, it'll be hard to come up with any definitive answers to this particular question.

Now even if your question is 'researchable' in theory, you also need to consider if you will be constrained by time, funding, expertise and ethical clearance. Making sure your question is feasible and that it can lead to a completed project is worth doing early. Nothing is worse than realizing your project is not 'doable' after investing a large amount of time and energy.

☑ **Does the question have a level of political support?** Research into real-world problems almost always occurs within a political context. It might be a government body, a business, a community etc., but common to all of these settings is that political agendas will often direct which projects get off the ground. Therefore, when it comes to finalizing your question, it makes a tremendous amount of sense to assess that question in relation to the current political landscape. Funding, dedicated workload and access can all be dependent on your ability to be political.

Changing focus

So you now have the perfect research question; it meets all the criteria and you feel you're ready to go. Let's set it in stone. Well maybe not – research questions can, and often do, change, shift and evolve during the early stages of a project; and not only is this fine, it is actually appropriate as your engagement in the research process evolves both your knowledge and thinking. Yes, developing a clear question is essential for direction setting, but it is important to remember that the research journey is rarely linear. It is a process that generates as many questions as it answers, and is bound to take you in unexpected directions.

As you get started on your research, you may come across any number of factors that can lead you to: query your aims and objectives; see you modify your question; add questions; or even find new questions. The challenge is assessing whether these factors are sending you off the track, or whether they represent developments and refinements that are positive for your work.

A note on hypotheses

Before concluding this chapter, I want to briefly discuss the role of, and need for, a research hypothesis. Now a hypothesis is basically a logical conjecture (hunch or educated guess) about the nature of relationships between two or more variables expressed in the form of a testable statement.

The role of a hypothesis is to take your research question a step further by offering a clear and concise statement of what you think you will find in relation to your variables, and what you are going to test. It is a tentative proposition that is subject to verification through subsequent investigation.

For example, let's consider the question 'Is there a relationship between household recycling behaviours and demographic characteristics?' Your hunch is that age has a large impact on recycling behaviour – basically, you suspect that young people put anything in the recycle bin. Here you have all the factors needed for a hypothesis: logical conjecture (your hunch); variables (recycling behaviours and age); and a relationship that can be tested (recycling behaviours *depend* on age). It is therefore a perfect question for a hypothesis – maybe something like 'children and teenagers are more likely than adults to put inappropriate materials in recycle bins'.

Basically, if you have a clearly defined research question – and you've got variables to explore – and you have a hunch about the relationship between those variables that can be tested, then a hypothesis is quite easy to formulate.

Now not all research questions will lend themselves to hypothesis development. For example, take the question 'How do individuals engage in decision making processes related to household domestic waste management?' Now remember that a hypothesis is designed to express 'relationships between variables'. This question, however, does not aim to look at variables and their relationships. The goal of this question is to uncover and describe a process, so a hypothesis would not be appropriate.

Generally, a hypothesis will *not* be appropriate if:

- *You do not have a hunch or educated guess about a particular situation* – your goal may be to build broad understandings.
- *You do not have a set of defined variables* – your goal might be to simply identify relevant variables.
- *Your question aims to explore the 'experience' of some phenomena* – for example, what is it like to start school with English as a second language.
- *Your question centres on developing rich understandings of a group* – for example, what it means to be a cancer survivor.
- *Your aim is to engage in, and research, the process of collaborative change* – in 'action research', methodology is both collaborative and emergent, making predetermined hypotheses impractical.

In short, whether a hypothesis is appropriate for your question depends on the nature of your inquiry. If your question boils down to a 'relationship between variables', then a hypothesis can clarify your study to an extent even beyond a well-defined research question. If your question, however, does not explore such a relationship, then force fitting a hypothesis simply won't work.

Chapter Summary

- Defining the word 'problem' is different from understanding what constitutes or qualifies as a problem. Problems are not universal and are dependent on worldviews, perspectives, history and culture.

- Identifying problems suitable for research involves looking for problems that can be addressed through the research process. Insights can come from your own knowledge and experience, the exploration of broader issues, and learning to identify the needs of others.

- Problems are generally complex and multi-faceted – and therefore need to be explored so that embedded assumptions can be uncovered. This process involves exploring: dominant worldviews; personal subjectivities; and stakeholder perspectives.

- Developing a well-articulated research question is an important part of the process because it defines the investigation; sets boundaries; provides direction; and acts as a frame of reference for assessing your work.

- The process of question development involves: working through your topic, context, goals, nature of the inquiry, and potential relationships; articulating those components into a relevant question(s); and narrowing and clarifying until the question is as concise and unambiguous as possible.

- In order to assess your question you will need to explore whether your question: is right for you; will be of broad significance; can lead to tangible situation improvement; is well articulated; is researchable; and will have political support.

- Redefining your questions is a normal part of the research process. Forming the right 'questions' should be seen as an iterative process that is informed by reading and doing at all stages.

- Hypotheses are designed to express relationships between variables. If this is the nature of your question, a hypothesis can add to your research. If your question is more descriptive or explorative, generating a hypothesis may not be appropriate.

3
Preparing to Research Real-World Problems

'Spectacular achievement is always preceded by spectacular preparation.'

- Robert H. Schuller

BEFORE YOU DIVE IN

Once armed with a 'researchable' question, the next stage in the research journey is to work on and develop your 'game plan'. For my money, there are three distinct stages to the development of this plan. The first is reading. Reading for research is essential. Knowledge builds, and it is virtually impossible for researchers to work towards the production of new knowledge, if they don't have a good handle on the current state of play.

The second stage is to develop your methodological design. This is the 'how' section of your research plan; how you will move from questions to answers, how you will collect your data, and how you will analyse that data. It will have elements that are as broad as questions related to paradigm, and as specific as questions dealing with the nuts and bolts of who, where, when, how and what.

The final stage in developing your game plan is the formal write-up of the plan itself; also known as the research proposal. Now when it comes to researching real-world problems very few projects get off the ground without some sort of approval. It may be as simple as verbal approval from your lecturer or employer. But it might also require a more formal approval process gained through an ethics committee, a corporate executive board, or a funding body. And of course you may need approval from more than one of the above. In all of these situations, clear articulation of your plan will be necessary in order for you to *sell* your project. Specifically, you will need to articulate: (1) what you are trying to find out; (2) why finding it out is important/significant; and (3) how you plan to find it out. And the best way to start this process is by reading.

READING FOR RESEARCH

There really is no way around it; reading is an essential part of the research process. Why? Well because you can't really engage in research from a platform of ignorance. When you are learning and your goal is to take on board knowledge that is already out there – well, then it doesn't really matter if you know a little or a lot. The goal is self-education, which needs to, and should, start from wherever you are.

Conducting research is a bit different. When you are conducting research, you are engaging in a process of knowledge production. You are producing knowledge that you hope others will learn from, act on and improve situations with. That demands responsibility for knowing what you are talking about. Sure, a lot of knowledge can come from experience – and I strongly advocate drawing on your experience. But even rich experience is likely to be seen as anecdotal if it is not set within a broader context. Reading is what can give you that broader context.

The purpose of reading

Reading acts to both ground and expand your thinking. It can help generate ideas, it can be significant in the process of question formation, and it is instrumental in the process of research design. It is also crucial in supporting the writing process. A clear rationale supported by literature is essential, while a well-constructed literature review is often a prerequisite in research proposals and research accounts.

Reading will help you:

- *Focus your ideas and expand relevant background knowledge* – nobody knows everything about a particular topic and reading can certainly help you get up to speed.
- *Develop appropriate questions* – popular media covering current debates, controversy and disputes around a particular issue can help generate questions of societal significance, while engagement with more 'scientific' literature can point to knowledge 'gaps'.
- *Argue the relevance of your work* – a well-articulated rationale is part and parcel of any research proposal and writing one will require you to draw on literature that can argue the societal and scientific significance of your study.

- *Inform your thinking/approach with theory* – almost every discipline area, for example, nursing, education, management etc., as well as broader areas of sociology and philosophy, rest on rich theory that can add both depth and credibility to your study.
- *Design suitable methods* – reading can support the design of methods in a number of ways. Reading can: (1) support learning related to relevant methodologies and methods; (2) allow you to critically evaluate, and possibly adopt, methods considered 'standard' for exploring your particular research question; (3) help you in assessing the need for alternative methodological approaches; and (4) support you in the design of a study that might overcome methodological shortcomings prevalent in the literature.
- *Construct and write a literature review* – a thorough and critical review of past research studies conducted on your topic and/or similar topics is often a criterion of fundable/rigorous research.

Types of literature

The array of literature you might find yourself delving into may be a fair bit broader than you first imagine. Because reading for research is something that informs all aspects of the research journey, almost any type of reading is fair game. For example, you are likely to call on:

- *Discipline-based reference materials* – if you are relatively new to a particular discipline or paradigm, subject-specific dictionaries and encyclopaedias can help you navigate your way through the discipline's central terms, constructs and theories.
- *Books* – this might include introductory and advanced texts, anthologies, research reports, popular non-fiction and even fiction works that can provide background and context, or inform theory and method.
- *Journal articles* – these take you beyond background readings to readings providing rigorous research accounts. This type of literature is therefore instrumental when you are getting serious about conducting research.
- *Grey literature* – this refers to both published and unpublished materials that do not have an International Standard Book Number (ISBN) or an International Standard Serial Number (ISSN), including conference papers, unpublished research theses, newspaper articles and pamphlets/brochures.
- *Official publications statistics and archives* – these materials can be a valuable source of background and contextual information, and often help shape a study's rationale.
- *Writing aids* – this includes bibliographic reference works, dictionaries, encyclopaedias and thesauruses, almanacs, yearbooks, books of quotes, etc. Such resources can offer significant support during the writing-up process, and can be used to: (1) improve the linguistic style of your work; (2) add points of interest to the text; (3) check facts; and (4) reference those facts.

Sourcing your readings

Recognizing the need for and purposes of reading doesn't put the literature in your hands. You still need to find and access it. Now there are two distinct strategies that can help you in your quest to find relevant literature. The first is to call on experts who can give you the advice you need to make a start. The second is to hone your search skills and hit the library and Internet.

Calling on 'experts'

If there is one resource you don't want to overlook in your hunt for relevant readings it's your local/university librarian. Information technology is changing at a rate of knots, so students, practitioners and professional researchers alike need to call on experts who can orient them to the latest computer/Internet searching facilities. It's also worth knowing that many university librarians are designated to a particular academic area, for example, social science, nursing, education, environment, etc. These 'specialists' can introduce you to relevant databases, journals (both hardcopy and electronic), bibliographies, abstracts, reviews etc., specific to your area.

'Academics' can also be quite helpful in your search for relevant literature. If you have access, talk to supervisors, professors and lecturers. They often know the literature and are able to point you in the right direction; or can at least direct you to someone better acquainted with your topic, who can give you the advice you need to make a start.

Finally, you can call on experts in the field. There is a good possibility that another researcher has recently sourced and reviewed your area of literature – or an area quite close. Have a look at relevant journal articles, as well as Master's and PhD theses. These works generally require comprehensive literature reviews and thorough bibliographies that can give you a huge head start when it comes to sourcing your readings. And don't forget you can also turn to practitioners; those who actually work in relevant fields often know the literature.

Honing your search skills

On the up side, literature now abounds. Library search facilities often allow you to explore way beyond the confines of their local holdings. And, of course, an amazing amount of research literature is now accessible on the Internet using commonly available search engines. In fact, the popular search engine *Google* has recently launched *Google Scholar* (scholar.google.com), which allows you to search specifically for abstracts, peer-reviewed articles, books, theses and technical reports across a variety of disciplines.

Now the downside of this incredible availability is an increasing need to develop skills for wading through it all. If you are regularly on the Internet, you have an advantage because the skills you need to negotiate the Web are the same as those you need to find literature. Basically, you need to be able to run a search engine using key words. It is, therefore, essential to be able to identify your topic, subtopics, variables, theories, theorists, methods, key concepts, etc. in the form of key words. You can then search for works by both single and combined key words searches.

Say, for example, you were interested in the relationship between *high-density housing* and *health*. You would start your literature hunt by running a search using these key words. Now this is likely to lead you to a mass of relevant literature, which can then be culled by adding key variables you find particularly relevant or interesting. For example, say, *socio-economic status*. Using this process you can add additional key words to narrow your search, remove keywords to capture more literature – or swap key words around to see what you come up with.

Figure 3.1 highlights the relevance of the generated literature based on key concepts and their interrelationships. Now some areas of intersection may not

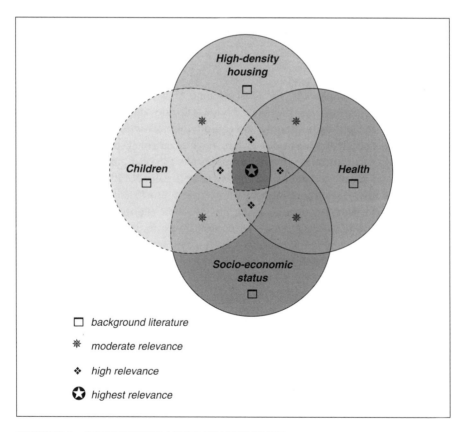

FIGURE 3.1   INTERSECTING AREAS OF LITERATURE

good concept
— how to?
Next steps!

yield much literature, but if you keep playing around with ideas, concepts and variables, you are bound to build a solid literature base.

Managing the literature

Now a mound of literature is only so helpful if you're not systematic and it ends up sitting in a pile in the corner of your office or study. Crucial to using literature is your ability to manage it, and this involves being able to: (1) quickly and efficiently assess relevance; (2) systematically keep track of sources; and (3) make relevant notes.

Assessing relevance

The ability to quickly and economically wade through literature in order to assess relevance and 'get the gist' is important to efficient researching. If you are reading a journal article, have a look at the abstract or executive summary. This should give you a good sense of relevance. In a book, peruse the table of contents, the back cover blurb and the introduction. Also have a look at both chapter and overall conclusions. Within a few minutes you should be able to assess whether a work is likely to be of value to your own research process.

Being systematic

Nothing is worse than looking for a lost reference that you really need. It could be a quote with a missing page number, or a fact with no citation, or a perfect point that needs to go right there – if only you could remember where you read it. If you can incorporate each of your resources into a management system you will be saving yourself a lot of future heartache. Systematically file your papers, keep rigorous references and use a consistent style. Yes it can be a pain, but if you are organized and diligent now – it will certainly pay off when it's time to call on your resources. You might also want to consider using bibliographic file management software such as *Procite, Endnote* or *Reference Manager*. These programs can automatically format references in any number of styles, such as Harvard/author–date, Vancouver, etc., once basic bibliographic details are entered.

Keeping notes

Again, it may sound like a pain, but I strongly recommend developing a systematic approach to note taking that allows for a methodical and organized review of materials from first read. Keep in mind that the last thing you probably want to do is read and then reread your materials because you forgot stuff or it gets jumbled in your mind.

Keeping notes or 'annotating' your references can help remind you of the relevance, accuracy and quality of your sources. Now this doesn't mean you need to take huge amounts of formal notes. Annotations are generally for your eyes only and are jotted down in order to minimize the time it takes to incorporate these works into your own. Things you might want to note while reading include:

- *Author and audience* – literature is full of propaganda, uninformed opinion and less than credible research. Ask yourself, who is doing the writing? What are their qualifications? Are they professionals, politicians, researchers, unknown? And who is the work written for? Is it for an academic audience, general public, constituents, clients? This process can help you assess a work's credibility.
- *Summary* – the aim here is to note key points that will help you research and write. Write what you think you will want to know later on, and try not to fall into the trap of trusting your memory. Now keep in mind that you can write annotations in any manner/style you want; you don't have to be formal. Doodles, mind maps, quotes, page numbers, etc. are all fair game.
- *Critical comment* – while summary is important, it is just as important to capture your critical reflections. Now this doesn't mean you have to be 100% negative. In academic reviewing, the word 'critical' means informed and considered evaluation. Ask yourself: Is this new? Is this old? Is this cutting edge? Is this just a rehash? Are there fundamental flaws in the methodology? Are author biases coming through? Do you believe the results are credible? In other words, what did you *really* think of this particular work.
- *Notes on relevance* – this is where you try to make the connection between what others have done and what you want to do. Ask yourself how this work sits in relation to your own. Is there anything in the work that makes a light bulb go off in your head? Is there some flaw in the thinking/methods that makes you want to explore this area/topic/question from a different angle? Is there a quote, passage, or section that really gets to the heart of what you are trying to do or say?

If you can get into the habit of treating your readings systematically, you will be in a position of strength when it comes time to call on those reading throughout the research process.

Conducting and writing a 'literature review'

While not necessary in all real-world research write-ups, a formal 'literature review' is often required in funding proposals and formal research reports. And yes, the task can be daunting. Conducting and writing a good literature review isn't easy. You need to negotiate multiple purposes, work towards logical structure with appropriate content, and make convincing arguments.

The purpose
You'd think that the purpose of a literature review was to simply review the literature – but it's actually much more. A well-written literature review will:

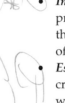

- **Inform** *readers of developments in the field* – the literature review should provide your readers with an up-to-date account and discussion of relevant theories, methods and research studies that make up a particular topic's body of literature.
- **Establish** *researcher credibility* – the literature review allows you to establish credibility through: (1) rigorous and critical evaluation of relevant research works; (2) a demonstrated understanding of key issues; and (3) the ability to outline the relationship of your own work to that of the rest of the field.
- **Argue** *the need for, and relevance of, the present study* – the literature review needs to make an argument for your own research agenda; it needs to set your study within the context of past research.

The writing process

Now a literature review is actually an argumentative piece of writing that needs to go well beyond a 'he said'/'she said' report. Remember, the goal here is to *inform, establish* and *argue*. And to do this well, you'll need to:

- *Read a few good, relevant reviews* – you need to have a sense of what a good literature review is, before you are in a position to construct your own.
- *Decide on coverage* – this can involve exhaustive coverage that cites all relevant literature; exhaustive coverage with only selective citation; representative coverage that discusses works that typify particular areas within the literature; coverage of seminal/pivotal works; or a combination of the above.
- *Write critical annotations as you go* – if you can sort and organize your annotations by themes, issues of concern, common shortcomings, etc. you may find that patterns begin to emerge. This can go a long way towards the development of your own arguments.
- *Develop a structure* – your literature review might be organized by topical themes, the tasks that you need the literature review to accomplish, or the arguments you wish to make.
- *Write purposefully* – the literature review is driven by the researcher and needs to have and make a point. If your audience doesn't know why you are telling them what you are telling them, you need to reconsider your approach.
- *Use the literature to back up your arguments* – rather than review, report, or even borrow the arguments of others, use the literature to help generate, and then support, your *own* arguments.
- *Adopt an appropriate style and tone* – the trick here is to avoid being over-critical, but to also avoid being too deferential. Keep in mind that when you are writing a literature review you are doing so as a fellow researcher who is engaging, learning, debating, arguing and contributing.
- *Be prepared to redraft* – whether you are a student or professional researcher, you're not likely to get away without a redraft or two (or three or four).

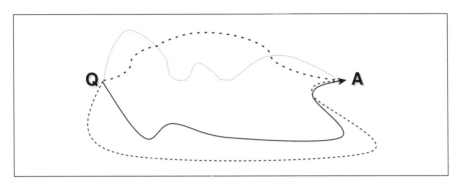

FIGURE 3.2   FROM QUESTIONS TO ANSWERS

DESIGNING METHOD

It may sound incredibly obvious, but the goal in designing method is to have your approach either (1) answer your well-articulated research question or (2) test your skilfully constructed hypothesis. Now clearly this implies that to design method you need to have either a well-articulated question or a skilfully constructed hypothesis, and this is true (see Chapter 2). If you don't know where you want to go, you simply can't determine a path for getting there.

So let's talk about paths for a minute. Is there only one path that can get you from questions to answers or are there several options? And if there are several options, how do you go about choosing the path you should travel along?

Well, rarely is there only one path to get from A to B or from questions to answers. As indicated in Figure 3.2, there are almost always possibilities. Paths can be varied and diverse, but in all likelihood there will be more than one way to generate the data that will lead to credible answers.

The question then becomes how can you find yourself travelling along the most productive path; how can you make decisions that will ensure you are approaching your study in a manner that will best lead to credible data and trustworthy results?

Well to figure that out, you really need to know and understand the criteria relevant to working through the gamut of possibilities. For my money there are two such criteria. The first is that your methodological design addresses your question(s). The second is that all elements of your design are practical or 'doable'. This means that you have, or can develop, the skills and interests needed to implement your design, and that you will not be undone by a lack of ethics approval, stakeholder support, time, resources, or access.

Addressing the question

When you know what it is you want to know, it's generally not too hard to figure out how to get there. As discussed in Chapter 2, a well-articulated research question defines an investigation, sets boundaries, provides direction and acts as a frame of reference for assessing your work. In this way your question acts as a blueprint for decision making related to method.

Now this does not mean your question must be set in stone from its first articulation. Research is generally an ongoing and iterative process of development and redevelopment that may see questions shift at various stages throughout the research process. What needs to be stressed, however, is that in the end, there needs to be a goodness of fit between your final questions and your methodological design. One, the other, or both may evolve, but in the end, your questions and your design need to have the tightest of relationships.

Working towards aims and objectives

The aims and objectives related to your research question will be a key determining factor in your exploration of potential methodologies. Now when researching real-world problems, you are generally trying to do one or more of the following: (1) understand a problem; (2) find workable solutions; (3) work towards that solution; or (4) evaluate success and/or failure. And as discussed below, each of these distinct goals tend to be aligned with particular methodological approaches.

- *Understanding a problem* – attempting to develop better understanding of a problem situation might involve looking outwards towards broad societal attitudes and opinions, or inwards using deeper exploration into the intricacies and complexities of your problem situation. Take, for example, the issue of workplace stress. You might want to know, 'How common is stress in the workplace?' If this were your question, outward exploration, say a population study using a survey approach, might be called for. If, however, your interest was in understanding how a particular staff group reacts to stress, or what it feels like to live with workplace stress, you might look at more inwardly focused strategies that allow you to delve deeper into complexity, for example ethnography or phenomenology. (The strategies mentioned above are covered fully in Chapter 7.)
- *Finding workable solutions* – the quest to find workable solutions might involve: assessing needs and visioning futures; locating potential programmes, interventions, and/or services; or exploring the feasibility of particular change initiatives. For example, sticking with the issue of workplace stress, your goal might be to understand what can be done to reduce such stress. Specific questions might be, 'Is workplace stress a priority issue for employees?', 'What vision do employees have for a different workplace culture?', 'What programmes have been introduced in other settings to reduce stress?', or 'Will programme X be suitable/cost effective for my workplace?' Now these types of question are sometimes referred to as 'front end analysis' and are common

48

approaches in applied/evaluative research. So if this is where your aims/objectives are pointing, you'd need to explore this area of literature. (Strategies for finding solutions are covered more fully in Chapter 8.)

- *Working towards solutions* – when I talk about working towards solutions, I'm referring to research goals that go beyond the production of knowledge. I'm referring to research that has the goal of change directly embedded in its research agenda. Now this might refer to improving practice, shifting systems, or even working towards some level of fundamental or radical change. For example, let's say your goal was to collaborate with staff on a co-learning project that developed and implemented a stress reduction strategy. Now whether you want to work on changing employee behaviours, workplace practices or the broader corporate culture, your desire to produce knowledge while actioning change is likely to lead you towards the literature related to 'action research'. (Action research strategies are covered fully in Chapter 9.)

- *Evaluating change* – the goal here is to answer the question, 'Has a change initiative/programme been successful?' Now your interest in evaluation might be related to outcomes, that is, Did programme X meet its objectives? But it might also be related to a process that is, How and how well is programme X being implemented? So, for example, if you wanted to evaluate a recently introduced stress reduction programme you might ask, 'Has programme X reduced stress?' This question would lead you to literature related to 'outcome' or 'summative' evaluation. If however, you wanted to ask, 'What are the strengths, weaknesses, opportunities, threats, etc. related to the implementation of this programme?', you would need to explore 'process' or 'formative' evaluation literature. (Evaluation research is discussed more fully in Chapter 10.)

From question to methods

Once your broader methodological approaches are in line with your aims and objectives, you will need to go a step further and think about the actual methods that will be best suited for collecting and analysing your data.

Now there is a real tendency for researchers, and that includes student, practitioner, and professional researchers alike, to be quite wedded to particular methods. They might have it in their minds that they will do a survey or a series of interviews – even before they've really engaged in a critical examination of what their question logically demands. But keep in mind that the goal in developing method is working towards what is most appropriate for answering your question. It is important that you don't fall prey to the belief that one way of doing things is inherently better than another, or to think that it's okay to stay within your comfort zone. Methods need to fall from questions.

Now if you followed the guidelines for question development covered in Chapter 2, it should be quite easy to see how and why questions point to methods. The process of question development should leave you with clear articulation of not only your topic and context, but also your goals, the nature of your question and who might hold the answer to that question. A well-articulated question should lead you to: who you need to talk to; what you need to ask; and as an extension of this, what data collection methods/tools you might use.

For example, say you were interested in the impact of working nightshifts on nursing practice. If you attempted to design your study from here – there would be all kinds of possibilities. You could look at stress manifest in the workplace, turnover rates, level/occurrence of 'mistakes', job satisfaction levels – of nurses, patients, doctors, etc., etc., etc. And because there are so many possibilities, you don't have enough definition to take you down any particular methods path.

But say you were able to narrow your question to, 'Is there a relationship between nurses working nightshift and a tendency to burn out of the profession?' Because this is more clearly defined, it can more readily point to method. Right away you know who you are talking about, that is, nurses who work nightshift – so you have your population. You also know you have to look at the construct of 'burnout'. Now you might be able to get out some data from employment records – but you probably need to get some information straight from nurses themselves. So that gives you a couple of choices: you can survey, you can interview, or you can do a bit of both. And this decision will likely depend on your goals, that is, whether you want to assess the extent of a problem and be able to generalize from your sample, in which case a survey approach is likely to work; or whether you are interested in more in-depth exploration and engagement, in which case you would probably want to go with more in-depth interviews.

In any case, clarity and precision in your question can readily lead to a range of method possibilities that can be explored and considered on the basis of both their logic and practicality.

Assessing practicality

Once you have worked through research approaches that will meet your objectives and fall neatly from your question(s), there will still be a need to assess the practicality of your approach. It is worth keeping in mind that the best possible design is worthless if you are going to come up against major barriers to implementation.

By running through the following questions, you can quickly assess the practicality of your methodological plan.

☑ **Do you have/can you develop necessary expertise?** Interviewing, observing, theorizing, surveying, statistical analysis – various methods of data collection and analysis will require certain skills. And while you can develop new skills, time/interest can be an issue. Remember that competence is not a luxury – it is required. Your skills or lack thereof will affect the quality of the data you collect and the credibility of the findings you generate.

☑ **Is your method ethical?/Is it likely to get required ethics approval?**
A clear criterion of any research design is that it is ethical; and ethicality is likely to be audited by an ethics committee. If a study calls for interaction with people, it will often require formal workplace and/or university ethics committee approval. Chapter 4 talks about ethics in some detail, but to summarize, an ethical study takes responsibility for integrity in the production of knowledge and ensures that the mental, emotional and physical welfare of respondents is protected.

☑ **Do you have required access to data?** A major challenge for researchers is gaining access to data. Whether you plan to explore documents, conduct interviews or surveys, or engage in observation, the best-laid plans are worthless if you can't find a way to access people, places and/or records.

☑ **Is your timeframe realistic?** If you have not given yourself long enough to do what your design demands, you are likely to: miss deadlines; compromise your study by changing your methods mid-stream; do a shoddy job with your original methods; compromise time that should be dedicated to other aspects of your job/life; or finally, not complete your study at all.

☑ **Do you have required financial/organizational support?** Whether you need to cover the cost of materials, postage, transcription etc., or the cost of bringing in a professional researcher to help with data collection or analysis, you will need finances. It is important to develop a realistic budget for your study. Research into any problem, no matter how worthy, will not be practicable, or in fact, possible if you cannot cover costs. Also make sure that, if appropriate, you have organizational support for time to be dedicated to your project. Not being able to find time can be as debilitating to your study as not being able to find money.

Getting down to details

Once you feel comfortable with your general research plan – that is, you think your approach will meet your aims and objectives and will answer your research question in a way that is quite practical, it is time to really get down to the nuts and bolts of that plan.

Okay, so what constitutes nuts and bolts? Well as shown in Table 3.1, getting right down to the nitty gritty is about being able to answer fundamental questions related to the who, where, when, how and what of your approach. If you can answer these questions, you are well on your way to articulating a clearly defined plan.

Can you over-design?

Before leaving the nuts and bolts of method, I want to briefly touch on the issue of over-design. Now I am a strong believer in having a plan and thinking your

TABLE 3.1   GETTING DOWN TO DETAILS

Who

Who do you want to be able to speak about?	➤ *This is your 'population', or the realm of applicability for your results. For example, are your findings applicable to employees of only one hospital, all hospitals in Chicago, all hospitals in the US?*
Who do you plan to speak to/observe?	➤ *This is your sample. As discussed in Chapter 5, it is quite rare to be able to speak to every single person you wish to speak about, so the key is ensuring that your sample is either intrinsically interesting/ valuable or is representative of a broader population*

Where

What is the physical domain of your sample?	➤ *This relates to working out how far afield you need to go in order to carry out your methods. Will you need to travel to different geographic areas? Are there various sites you need to visit?*
Are settings relevant to the credibility of your methods?	➤ *This involves considering how place can impact method. For example, if you wanted to conduct job satisfaction interviews with teachers, you would need to consider whether an informal chat at a pub on a Friday night will generate data distinct from that gathered at a staff meeting*

When

How do your methods fit into your timeframe?	➤ *It can take longer than you think to collect, analyse and draw conclusions from data. It is important to make sure your methods fit into your overall timeframe*
Is timing relevant to the credibility of your methods?	➤ *This involves considering how timing can impact method. For example, a community survey conducted between the hours of 9 and 5 is likely to lead to a large under-representation of workers, and an over-representation of stay-at-home mothers and retirees*

How

How will I collect my data?	➤ *As discussed in Chapter 6, this involves deciding on the methods and tools you will use to collect, gather and/or generate your data*

TABLE 3.1 (CONTINUED)

How will I conduct my methods?	➤	*This involves even further consideration of nuts and bolts. For example, considering if you will tape record your interviews or take notes; or whether your observations will involve you joining an organization, or just sitting in on a number of meetings*
What		
What will you look for/what will you ask?	➤	*Depending on your methods, this might involve developing questionnaires, drafting interview questions, creating observation checklists, and/or developing frameworks for document analysis. The best advice here is to get support. These tools are difficult to get right, and it may take a few trials or pilots to develop them to a point where you are comfortable with the data they generate*

way through the best possible approach for conducting your study. And most of the time this will mean being able to define and articulate the details that make up your approach. There are, however, several situations where you'll need to leave some give or flexibility in your plan.

Okay, to start with, life is unpredictable, and research really isn't any different. You can have a plan – but that won't stop circumstances from arising to which you will need to be responsive. Whether it's surveys that aren't returned, a workplace that suddenly won't give you access, or a key informant that drops out of the picture, hurdles will arise, and if you want to get over them you'll need to be flexible.

Another scenario that demands flexibility is when your plan involves developing research protocols based on what emerges from initial data. This is common in 'grounded theory' where initial data collection protocols are defined, but subsequent data collection and analysis are highly emergent. In this type of research your plan actually 'evolves as you go'.

Finally, if you are working together with stakeholders on a research project, it is important that all stakeholders feel comfortable with, and even have a chance to contribute to, methodological protocols. Action research, for example (discussed in Chapter 9), is a highly participative and collaborative type of approach in which defined research designs are outside the full control of the lead researcher. In fact, the action research process is emergent and often cyclical, and is based on collaborative input from the stakeholder/researcher team. Flexibility is a part of design.

DEVELOPING A PROPOSAL

Say you have worked towards a well-informed and well-defined research plan. Chances are you will now need to write it up as a proposal. Now many see the development of a proposal as an opportunity to clarify thinking, bed down ideas and articulate thoughts in a way that will provide a study outline and a blueprint for future action. And yes, it is all these things. BUT – and this is important – a proposal is not something you write for yourself. It is, without a doubt, a sales pitch. Your proposal is your opportunity, and sometimes your only opportunity, to sell your project and get your study off the ground.

The role of the proposal

Pretend for a moment that you believe you have a really great study ready to go. With just a bit of funding you will be able to get your project off the ground and maybe make a real difference. The only problem is your workplace cannot fund every project that gets proposed. In fact, this year they have five lots of $20,000 up for grabs, but they have received 18 proposals. Without a doubt it is a competition. So the question is, what can you do to walk away with the cash? Well I think you need to convince the powers that be of three things:

1. *That your problem and your question are worth exploring* – and, even tougher, worth funding. You need to argue the significance of the problem you are addressing and why research can make a difference to that problem. This is the job of your proposal's introduction and rationale.
2. *That you are the right woman/man for the job* – now this might be done through a resumé or CV, but within the proposal itself it is generally done by showing critical engagement with the literature. If you are arguing that you should receive funds that will allow you to conduct a study aimed to produce new knowledge, you need to show that you are conversant with the body of knowledge/literature as it currently exists. In other words, you need to show that you are a player – and this is the job of your proposal's literature review.
3. *That the methodology you are proposing is logically and ethically sound* – does it make sense, will it answer your question, is it practical, is it ethical? The methods section of your proposal needs to convince readers that your approach is an efficient, effective and ethical way to get credible answers to your questions.

Now keep in mind that the weight given to these three elements will vary based on the type of committee you are addressing and the type of approval you are seeking. For example, a proposal written to get you into a PhD programme really needs to sell you as a potential researcher. A proposal written for an ethics committee needs to focus on the relationship between methods and participants, while a workplace proposal would have a strong emphasis on practicalities.

Elements of the proposal

In my experience, when a person or a committee has the power to make major decisions about someone else's work/future, they like to wield that power, and they often like to wield it in very pedantic ways. When it comes to assessing research proposals, this translates to committees wanting what they want, the way they want it, and when they want it. For the person writing the proposal this means:

- constructing your proposal according to, or as close to, the recommended section/headings as possible
- being meticulous about spelling and grammar
- keeping to word limits
- adhering to deadlines

Also remember to be concise and succinct, direct and straightforward. Clarity is key. Try not to ramble or show off intellect by using flowery language. And one more thing – remember to write in the future tense. A proposal is about what you *will* do, not what you are doing now, or have done in the past.

Now as far as content, varying expectations of each committee make it hard to offer a definitive proposal proforma. But generally, you can expect to include some combination of what is highlighted in Box 3.1.

Box 3.1   Elements of a Research Proposal

Most proposals will need to include some combination of the following:

Title
Go for clear, concise and unambiguous. Your title should indicate the specific content and context of the problem you wish to explore in as succinct a way as possible.

Summary/abstract
Proposals often require a project summary – usually with a very tight word count. The trick here is to briefly state the what, why and how of your project in a way that sells it in just a few sentences – and trust me, this can take quite a few drafts to get right.

(Continued)

Box 3.1 *(Continued)*

Aims/objectives

Most proposals have one overarching *aim* that captures what you hope to achieve through your project. A set of *objectives*, which are more specific goals, supports that aim. Aims and objectives are often articulated in bullet points and are generally 'to' statements, for example, to develop ...; to identify ...; to explore ...; to measure ...; to explain ...; to describe ...; to compare ...; to determine ...; etc. In management literature you are likely to come across 'SMART' objectives – SMART being an acronym for **S**pecific, **M**easurable, **A**chievable, **R**elevant/results-focused/realistic and **T**ime-bound. The goal is to keep objectives from being airy-fairy or waffly; clearly articulating what you want to achieve aids your ability to work towards that achievement – a message that certainly holds up when researching real-world problems.

Research question/hypothesis

As discussed in Chapter 2, a well-articulated research question (or hypothesis) should define your investigation, set boundaries, provide direction and act as a frame of reference for assessing your work. Any committee reviewing your proposal will turn to your question in order to get an overall sense of your project. Take the time to make sure your question/hypothesis is as well-defined and clearly articulated as possible – and this may involve defining key terms.

Introduction/background/rationale

The main job of this section is to introduce your topic and convince your readers that the problem you want to address is significant and worth exploring and even funding. It should give some context to the problem and lead your readers to the conclusion, that yes – research into this area is absolutely essential if we really want to work towards situation improvement or problem resolution.

Literature review

As discussed earlier in this chapter, a formal 'literature review' is a specific piece of argumentative writing that engages with relevant scientific and academic research in order to create a space for your project. The role of the literature review is to inform readers of developments in the field while establishing your own credibility as a 'player' capable of adding to this body of knowledge.

Theoretical perspectives

This section is more likely to be required for academic proposals than workplace-based proposals and asks you to situate your study in a conceptual or

Box 3.1   (Continued)

theoretical framework. The idea here is to articulate the theoretical perspective(s) that underpin and inform your ideas, and in particular, to discuss how 'theory' relates to and/or directs your study.

Methods

Some form of 'methods' will be required in all proposals. The goal here is to articulate your plan with enough clarity and detail to convince your readers that your approach is practical and will lead to credible answers to the questions posed. Under the heading of methods you would generally articulate:

- *the approach/methodology* – for example if you are doing ethnography, action research or maybe survey research
- *how you will find respondents* – this includes articulation of population and sample/ sampling procedures
- *data collection method(s)* – for example surveying, interviewing, document analysis etc;
- *methods of analysis* – whether you will be doing statistical or thematic analysis and perhaps variants thereof.

Limitations/delimitations

This is generally a section required in 'traditional' or 'scientific' research. *Limitations* refer to conditions that may impact on results, for example small sample size, or access to records. *Delimitations* refer to a study's boundaries, that is, children of a certain age only, or schools from one particular region. Now remember that your overarching goal here is to convince readers that your findings will be credible in spite of any limitations or delimitations. So the trick is to be open about your study's parameters without sounding defensive or apologetic. It might also be worth articulating any strategies you will be using to ensure credibility despite limitations.

Ethical considerations

Whenever you are working with human participants there will be ethical issues you need to consider (see Chapter 4). Now if this were an application for an ethics committee you would need to focus much of your proposal on ethical issues. But even if this were a proposal for approval or funding – your readers would still need to be convinced that you've considered issues related to integrity in the production of knowledge and responsibility for the emotional, physical and intellectual well-being of your study participants.

(Continued)

Box 3.1   (Continued)

Timeline

This is simply superimposing a timeline on your methods, and is often done in a tabular or chart form. The committee reading your proposal will be looking to see that your plan is realistic and can conform to any overarching timeframes or deadlines.

Budget/funding

This is a full account of costs and who will bear them. While not always a required section for ethics proposals or proposals for academic student research, it will certainly be a requirement for a funding body. Now it is definitely worth being realistic – it is easy to underestimate costs. Wages, software, hardware, equipment, travel, transcription, administrative support etc. can add up quite quickly and running short of money mid project is not a good option. But also keep in mind that if you are tendering for a commissioned project, it is a good idea to get a ballpark figure of their budget. This will put you in a position to design your methods accordingly and hopefully make you competitive.

References

This can refer to two things. The first is citing references, the same as you would in any other type of academic/professional writing. Believe it or not, it's often missed. Second, is that some committees want a list of say 10 or 15 primary references that will inform your work. This information can help a committee assess your knowledge, your credibility and also give a better indication of the direction your study may take.

FURTHER READING

There are quite a few readings that can help you navigate your way through the complexities of working with literature, designing methods and developing research proposals. You may find the following sources a good place to start:

Reading for research

Hart, C. (2000) *Doing a Literature Review*. London: Sage.
Hart, C. (2001) *Doing a Literature Search*. London: Sage.
Galvan, J. L. (1999) *Writing Literature Reviews: A Guide for Students of the Social and Behavioral Sciences*. Glendale, CA: Pyrczak Publications.

Methodological design

Creswell, J. W. (2002) *Research Design: Qualitative, Quantitative and Mixed Methods Approaches*. London: Sage.

Tashakkori, A. and Teddlie, C. (eds) (2002) *Handbook of Mixed Methods Social and Behavioral Research*. London: Sage.

Research proposals

Locke, L. F., Spirduso, W. W. and Silverman, S. J. (1999) *Proposals That Work: A Guide for Planning Dissertations and Grant Proposals*. London: Sage.

Ogden, T. E., Goldberg, I. A. (eds) (2002) *Research Proposals: A Guide to Success*. New York: Academic Press.

Chapter Summary

- Once armed with a 'researchable' question, you will need to develop your 'game plan'. This plan involves engaging with literature, designing methods and developing a research proposal.

- Reading is an essential part of the research process that generates ideas, helps form significant questions and is instrumental in the process of research design. It can also support you in writing up your research.

- The range of literature you can call on is diverse. Reference materials, books, journals, grey literature, official publications, archives and writing aids are all fair game.

- When sourcing your readings you should call on librarians and supervisors, as well as other researchers. Their expertise, in conjunction with the development of your own search skills, should aid you in navigating your way through reading.

- Managing the literature requires skills that allow you to quickly assess relevance, systematically organize references and keep diligent and relevant notes.

- Literature reviews should engage with relevant scientific and academic literature in order to create a place for new research. A well-written literature review should inform readers, establish researcher credibility and argue a study's relevance.

- There are two main criteria in designing method: (1) your design addresses your question(s) – your methods should work towards meeting your aims and objective while offering a clear path for getting answers; and (2) your methods are feasible and practical.

- Getting down to the nuts and bolts of design involves being able to answer questions of who, where, when, what and how. There will be times, however, when you will want to have flexibility, particularly when working collaboratively with stakeholders or when using a grounded theory approach.

- A research proposal offers an opportunity to clarify your thinking, bed down ideas and articulate your thoughts in a way that will provide you with an outline of your study and a blueprint for future action. But it is also your opportunity to 'sell' your project and get your study off the ground.

- A good proposal will convince readers of three things: (1) that your problem/question is worth exploring; (2) that you are the right person for the job; and (3) that the methods you are proposing are logically and ethically sound.

- Proposals differ in requirements, but most will ask you to articulate some combination of the following: title; summary/abstract; aims/objectives; research question/hypothesis; introduction/background/rationale; literature review; theoretical perspectives; methods; limitations/delimitations; ethical considerations; timelines; budget/funding; and references.

4

Striving for Integrity in the Research Process

Chapter Preview
The Need for Integrity
Integrity in the Production of Knowledge
Integrity and the 'Researched'
Criteria for Researching with Integrity

'All our science, measured against reality, is primitive and childlike - and yet it is the most precious thing we have.'

- Albert Einstein

THE NEED FOR INTEGRITY

Science is 'primitive and childlike', yet it is 'precious'. These are Einstein's words. So what did he mean by this and what implication does it have for researchers? Well, science is primitive and childlike simply because the quest to capture reality is a challenge we have not, and probably will never, fully meet. But it is precious because it is so central to our ability to learn, to grow, to shift, to change – to make a difference. And this means that research needs to be handled with the utmost care. At every stage, the goal needs to be responsibility and integrity. The challenge demands nothing less.

So how is integrity defined in the research world, and what strategies can you call on to make sure your own research studies meet this criterion? Well, I think there are two broad arenas in the research game where you need to consciously work towards integrity. The first is in your quest to produce knowledge – your responsibility here is to make sure you have captured 'truth'; reached conclusions not tainted by error and unrecognized bias; and have conducted your research with professional integrity. The second is in working with others – your responsibility here is an ethical one that ensures the rights and well-being of those involved with your study are protected at all times.

61

INTEGRITY IN THE PRODUCTION OF KNOWLEDGE

If the goal of conducting research is to produce new knowledge, knowledge that others will come to trust and rely on, and maybe even enact change on the basis of, then certainly this production of knowledge needs to be approached with both integrity and rigour.

But this is easier said than done. Most research into real-world problems involves working with others – and research that involves people provides a host of challenges to research integrity. In fact, you might say, people are the worst. Bacteria, cells, DNA etc. generally behave in the laboratory – you know what to expect, and the little bacteria are not attempting to consciously or sub-consciously throw you. But people are tough. They have hidden agendas, falli-ble memories and a need to present themselves in certain ways. They can be helpful, defensive and/or deferential – and there will be plenty of times when you won't know when they're being what.

And then there is the researcher. Also a fallible, biased or subjective human entity, who is faced with the challenge of producing 'unbiased', trustworthy results. Now when you combine a subjective researcher with an unpredictable 'researched' it makes the production of credible knowledge no easy feat.

So how do you begin to work towards integrity in the production of knowl-edge? Well, as I flush out in the next section, for me it starts with breaking the job down into manageable tasks, namely:

- recognizing and balancing subjectivities
- building trust
- approaching methods with consistency
- making relevant arguments
- providing accurate research accounts

Recognizing and balancing subjectivities

The question here is not *whether* researchers are subjective entities, but rather do they *recognize* themselves as subjective, and can they manage their personal biases? It is imperative that researchers attempt to: (1) recognize their biases and worldview; (2) consider how their worldview may affect the researched and the research process; and (3) attempt to balance subjectivities in a manner that ensures the integrity, validity and authenticity of any potential knowledge produced (see Box 4.1 at the end of this section).

Now for traditional scientists, for example those working in a laboratory, this means putting aside any preconceived notions and aiming for pure objectivity. Strict methodological protocols and a 'researched' that is outside the self gener-ally make this a manageable task. For social science researchers, however, the challenge is somewhat more difficult. It is society itself that is being researched, and as products of a society, social science researchers need to recognize how their own worldview makes them value-bound, and how their values can influence the research process.

Yes, it would be nice to think that researcher attitudes and even attributes such as gender, age, ethnicity, religion, education, social class etc. were not factors in conducting research, but they are. You have a gender, you come from a particular place, you have the characteristics of a certain race or races, you have some level of education and you have been socialized in a particular way. And if you as a researcher don't take this into account and work towards 'neutrality', you can readily fall into the trap of judging the reality of others in relation to your own reality. In fact, researchers who do not act to consciously manage their own positioning, run the risk of conducting 'self-centric' analysis; that is, being insensitive to issues of race, class or gender, and hearing only the dominant voice.

Conducting 'self'-centric analysis

Without reflective consideration of your own researcher reality, bias can colour your interpretations. You have to actively guard against the tendency to understand and judge the things you see according to the rules and guidelines that *you* use to make sense of the world. Others have different rules – and the meanings they associate with particular utterances and events will vary accordingly. I'll give you an example. Suppose you're a well-educated, straight-laced, middle-class woman who has just started teaching in an inner city high school. You have become quite interested in attitudes towards drug use, and pick up student conversations about getting high, smoking dope, and even doing Ecstasy. Now from your perspective, these students are on the edge of reason, humanity and decency – 'What has the world come to!' In your world, only those scraping the bottom of the barrel do 'that kind of thing'. But you have to remember that you are not researching your world – you are in the world of high school, and the challenge facing you is avoiding the temptation to assign the values of your personal world to your research world. For you see in this high school, these might be 'normal' kids – doing 'normal' things.

Being insensitive to issues of race, class or gender

Insensitivity to issues of race, class, gender etc. refers to the practice of ignoring these constructs as important factors or variables in a study, and can be a by-product of 'self-centric' analysis. Researchers need to recognize and appreciate the reality of the researched; otherwise they run the risk of ignoring unique and significant attributes. For example, a study of student motivation in a multi-cultural setting would not be very meaningful without ethnicity as one significant variable. Yes, career ambitions, study enjoyment, perceived relevance etc. can be important predictors of motivation, but all of these factors can be motivated by family and culture. For example, in many Anglo-Asian households student success and failure is seen as parental success and failure, and this can be a huge student weight and/or motivator.

Insensitivity to issues of race, class and gender can also lead to dichotomization, or the tendency to put groups at two separate ends of the spectrum without recognition of overlapping characteristics. We do this when we talk in absolute terms about 'men' and 'women' or 'blacks' and 'whites'. Research that dichotomizes is often research that has fallen prey to stereotypes.

Finally, insensitivity to race, class and gender can lead to double standards where the same behaviours, situations or characteristics are analysed using different criteria depending on whether respondents are black or white, male or female, rich or poor, etc. For example, let's say you wanted to explore reasons for marital infidelity. If you were to use different sets of responses for males and females in which your preconceived notions about men being 'easily bored' and women being 'quite needy' came through, you would have a double standard. Remember that in the conduct of research, there is an essential need to guard against the assumptions and biases inherent within our society.

Hearing only the dominant voice

It's very easy to listen to those who are speaking the loudest or to those who are speaking your 'language'. But when you do this – you are likely to end up missing an important undercurrent; a whole other voice. I have struggled with this in my own teaching. When I give a workshop, I try very hard to relate to my students – to communicate with them rather than lecture at them. So I need to engage in 'dialogue' and get a two-way conversation going. And I think I do this fairly well. In every class a core group of students makes this easy for me.

But who is in this core group? Well, it really can be a mixed bag, but I can tell you who it isn't. It's not generally the international students; they tend to stay in the background. Now there are a number of reasons for this. For one, many come from an educational system where they are not invited to participate. Others struggle with English as a second language. But another factor could be me and my reality. The examples I use, the personal anecdotes I share, my 'in your face' American style, can all conspire so that those with demographic characteristics similar to mine are the ones who speak up the most. So it is the Asian and Indian students in my class who can go unheard (as they are likely to do throughout their Western university careers).

As a teacher, my challenge is to find a way to engage all of my class and to make sure I'm reaching every student – and that they're reaching me. The challenge for the researcher is similar. If you do not consciously work on strategies for appreciating diversity and hearing the marginalized, you run the risk of gathering data and reaching conclusions that ignore those in society who often go unheard. Attempting to empower traditionally marginalized voices is essential in responsible research. Indigenous peoples, minorities, children, women, gays and lesbians are often not heard, yet their voices are essential to any full understanding.

Box 4.1   *Managing Researcher Subjectivities*

Managing subjectivities is more than something you *should* do. It is, in fact, a task which is *crucial* to the production of credible data and trustworthy results. Researchers need to:

Appreciate their own reality and worldview
- Articulate your subjectivities. Your ability to manage subjectivities is dependent on being able to recognize and articulate them. In fact, the first chapter of many PhD theses now includes a section on researcher positioning.

Appreciate alternative 'realities'
- Actively explore the personal and societal assumptions that underpin the understandings of the researcher and the researched … and accept that these might be quite distinct.
- Suspend initial judgements. We live in a society where it is common to judge what we do not understand. Yet as researchers, not understanding is precisely why it is important not to judge.
- Check your interpretation of events, situations and phenomena with 'insiders'. This is particularly relevant in cross-cultural research. Finding out how someone from within a cultural reality understands a situation can help illuminate your own potential biases.

Get the full story
- Attempt to empower silenced voices – those we seek out and those willing to participate are often those with the strongest voices. Your research design should seek representation from all those you wish your research to speak for or about.
- Seek out and incorporate alternative and pluralistic points of view. In a bid to crystallize interpretations, the richness and complexity that can come from outside viewpoints can be lost.

Building trust

Also crucial to the production of credible knowledge is your ability to get your respondents to talk to you with honesty and openness. Now there could be any number of complex reasons why respondents might be reluctant to fully expose themselves in a research process. But there is one thing I know for sure … if respondents feel intimidated or judged in any way, they will not open up. As a researcher, building trust is absolutely dependent on: (1) understanding how research participants are likely to react to you; and (2) being able to suspend and withhold judgement.

Researcher attributes

Do you know who in our society generally contributes to the 'scientific' production of knowledge; in other words, who society's researchers tend to be? Well, it is generally those with power, position, privilege and education. Those being 'researched', however, don't necessarily come from that same background, and this can set up a real power divide that can damage trust.

Building trust is reliant on recognizing the power and privilege associated with your own attributes and working to minimize any real or perceived power differential between you and the 'researched'. If you have difficulty doing this, the 'researched' is likely to feel alienated, intimidated and/or uninterested by the research process.

Some of the researcher attributes that need to be considered when attempting to build trust include:

- *Gender* – the rapport and trust you will build with respondents, the slant on stories you will hear, and the memories you will draw out, can be very dependent on gender. For example, some women might only feel comfortable talking about the loss of a child with another woman. Or imagine conducting an interview on promiscuity; the answers you might elicit could be highly dependent on your own gender. Now there are no hard and fast rules here. What is important is to consciously think through the issue of gender and whether it is likely to be a factor in building trust.
- *Age* – trust is often dependent on your ability to relate to your respondents and their ability to relate to you, and age can certainly be a factor here. For example, there are very few parents in the world who can ask their teenagers 'What did you do this weekend?' and get the full story – especially if the weekend was any good! Like it or not, age can be a critical factor in credible data collection. And again there are no hard and fast rules, just a mandate that you consider how age might influence researcher–researched relationships.
- *Ethnicity* – the ethnic and cultural background of the researcher can certainly influence the research process. It's sad to say we still have much inequity,

suspicion and mistrust running across ethnic and racial lines. But that's a reality – and it's a reality that can affect your ability to gain trust. Say, for example, you wanted to research attitudes towards education in a Hispanic community. While a 'white' outsider might struggle to gain trust, a Hispanic insider might have an easier time opening up honest and open lines of communication.

- *Socio-economic status/education* – societal position can also have great bearing on the research process, with researchers often coming from a position of privilege. As a researcher, you need to think about breaking down barriers, and convincing the 'researched' that you are not sitting in judgement. Being aware of your own socio-economic status and educational background, as well as that of the researched, puts you in a position to manage any potential power-related issue that might influence your study.

- *Position of power in a particular setting* – this is an issue that can be particularly relevant when you're researching within your own workplace or in another organization where you have a formal role. You need to consider how you might go about building researcher–researched trust when you might be someone's boss or someone's employee in your day-to-day occupational capacity. Will they trust you? If you are the boss – can you convince your employees/respondents that you will not use data in a capacity other than for research? If you are an employee – do you think you can get management to give you more than patronizing organizational rhetoric? If you are a co-worker – will your colleagues trust that there will be confidentiality? There is always an additional dimension in building trust when you are known in a setting and are likely to be perceived as wearing more than one hat. Clarifying roles and expectations will be crucial.

Now it may seem as though these issues are more likely to be a factor in research that involves close interaction with the researched – and this is true. But it is also worth thinking about how a researcher's attributes can come through even in something like a survey instrument. In a survey, there are unlimited opportunities to leave respondents feeling alienated. An example might be a survey that quizzes knowledge rather than asks opinions. Not many will be willing to take a quiz, particularly if they believe they've been set up to fail.

A classic example here are some IQ tests of the 1960s that were clearly based on 'Middle American' assumptions. Back then, it seems that IQ was based in part on knowing how to 'properly' set a table – not likely to be general knowledge for a poor child from the inner city, nor for a child from an Asian background (where do those chopsticks go?). Again, there are no easy answers here. In the end, it is up to individual researchers to consider how 'they' impact the research process and to manage that process in a way that can best yield trustworthy and credible results.

Listening without judgement

I was recently reminded how hard it can be to build trust when you are struggling to withhold judgement. I often give workshops in Hong Kong and one of my students, whom I like and respect, flew from there to Australia (where I now work and live) for a visit. Over lunch, he and his wife told me that their youngest son, who is 10 and has just gone off to boarding school in the UK, has been crying on the phone every day saying that he hates it, is being picked on, and really, really wants to go home. Now my youngest child is 10, and I was raised, and still live, in a cultural reality where I could not even contemplate sending my 10-year-old that far away from home. But in no way do I question that this family's decision was made out of love and a desire to give their child the best. It's just that it's so far from my own reality and the way I have been socialized.

I really had to make a conscious effort to suspend judgement and, as a researcher, this is something you really need to do. People can sniff out judgement from a mile off, and if you don't make an effort to suspend or withhold it, you won't stand a chance at building trust and getting to the heart of an issue. Be conscious of your verbal and nonverbal cues here – what you say, how you say it, your facial expressions and your body language can all work to build trust or alienate the other.

Approaching methods with consistency

Once you have worked through some of the issues related to the management of subjectivities and the building of trust, the quest for integrity in the production of knowledge turns to questions of method. It is important to remember that regardless of approach, researching is not a haphazard activity. Rather, it is an activity that needs to be approached with discipline, rigour and a level of standardization. If the goal is to have your research stand up to scrutiny and be taken as credible, it is important that readers are confident that your methods have been implemented in ways that best assure consistency.

Often consistency in methods is referred to as 'reliability' or the extent to which a measure, procedure, or instrument provides the same result on repeated trials. A good example here is bathroom scales. If you were to jump on your scales ten times in a row and got the same results each time, the scales would be reliable. The scale could be wrong – it might always be ten pounds heavy or ten pounds light (personally, I prefer the light variety), but it would be reliable. A more complicated example might be trying to measure job satisfaction with a questionnaire. The questionnaire would only be reliable if results were not dependent on things like who administered the questionnaire, what kind of day the respondent was having, or whether or not it was a weekend.

The flipside of this is that people are complex and multi-faceted. At any given time, for any given reason, they may only reveal part of themselves. Say, for example, you wanted to ask about stress – this is something that can, and often does, vary from day to day. So developing methodological tools that are 'reliable' might not be straightforward. But nevertheless, the process of data collection needs to be more than haphazard. In fact, it should be 'dependable'. Methods need to be designed and developed in ways that are consistent, logical, systematic, well-documented and designed to account for research subjectivities.

Making relevant and appropriate arguments

Assume you now have some great data. You're pretty sure you've been able to manage your biases in ways that really got your respondents to open up, and you've done this using data collection tools and analysis strategies capable of holding up to a good level of scrutiny. The next step is to put forward some credible arguments. Now this will involve a few challenges we've already discussed, i.e. keeping a check on subjectivities and exploring multiple interpretations. But as discussed below, it will also involve weighing up your findings in light of your study's limitations, and being confident that you are speaking for an appropriate group of people.

Being true to your study's limitations

Very few researchers get to conduct their studies in a way they consider ideal: there is rarely enough time or money; the cooperation of others might be less than ideal; and there could be a whole list of things you would have done differently with the benefit of hindsight. So what do you do?

Well, making appropriate arguments is about being able to attest to the credibility of your data and the trustworthiness of your results – in spite of any limitations. Yes, it can be tempting to downplay difficulties and write up your research as though everything went smoothly in a study that was optimally designed. But if you are challenged here, your ethics and credibility can come into question. As outlined in Box 4.2, a much better approach is to take it in three steps. The first step is to honestly outline the study's limitations or shortcomings. The second step is to outline the strategies that you have employed to gather credible data and generate trustworthy results because of, or in spite of, any limitations. The third step follows from the second and is a 'therefore' type of statement that offers justification or rationalization for the data and findings of your study.

Box 4.2   Being True to your Study's Limitations

The following student excerpt is a good example of the three-step approach to outlining your study's limitations:

(Continued)

Box 4.2   (Continued)

While the original data collection protocol was to survey a random sample of the population, preliminary investigation showed that the extent of this population is unknown. A directory of men who have experienced domestic abuse simply does not exist. It also became clear that many men who had experienced this type of abuse did not want to be approached **[Step 1]**. It was therefore decided to ask for volunteers through the use of flyers in counsellors' offices, and combine that with snowball sampling that asked the volunteers to pass on the request to anyone else they might know of who has experienced a similar situation **[Step 2]**. While there is no guarantee that the results from this sample will be representative of the greater population, this study, through the use of willing and open volunteers, does offer valuable insights to the phenomenon, and sheds much light on an under-explored area of domestic violence **[Step 3]**.

Speaking for an appropriate group of people

Also crucial to a good argument is making sure you are speaking for an appropriate group of people. I'm talking here about your findings' applicability or the extent to which the findings of your study can extend beyond a particular sample or setting. Now the credibility of a research project relies in part on the broad applicability of its findings. While conclusions relevant to only a particular sample or only within a certain research setting can provide important knowledge for key stakeholders, it does limit the broader generation of new knowledge.

So, you're after wide applicability but that applicability must be appropriate. Any sample you use should be representative of a wider population and large enough for you to be confident that your findings do reflect larger trends. Now meeting these criteria mean that your findings are 'generalizable'. The key (as discussed in Chapter 5) is ensuring both adequate and broad representation, and this is generally not too difficult in medium-to-large scale survey research.

But what if your research project is centred on a particular case, or is designed to collect more in-depth qualitative data that will limit your sample size? Under these circumstances, you may not be able to argue generalizability. Yet broader applicability may still be a goal. If this is the case, your goal will be 'transferability' or highlighting 'lessons learned' that are likely to be applicable in alternative settings or populations. For example, the results of an in-depth case study in any one school will not be representative of all schools – but there will definitely be lessons learned that can illuminate relevant issues and provide rich learning within other school contexts. The key here is providing a detailed description of the research setting and methods so that applicability can be determined by those reading the research account.

Providing accurate research accounts

Finally, integrity in the production of knowledge is reliant on researchers providing open and accurate descriptions of the research process. As well as allowing other researchers to attempt to replicate or reproduce findings, open and accurate accounts help establish a study's credibility by making them auditable (others can see exactly how findings were generated).

This actually provides a check on integrity. It's difficult to blatantly fabricate data; falsify results; omit cases; fiddle with numbers; plagiarize; and even misrepresent authorship, if your methods are out there for all to see.

INTEGRITY AND THE 'RESEARCHED'

Researchers, and that includes student and practitioner researchers alike, must be able to call on some level of training or experience when undertaking a research study. As a researcher, you are responsible for knowing what you're doing. The reasons for this are two-fold. First, it is central that you are in a position that allows you to meet criteria associated with integrity in the production of knowledge. Second, and perhaps even more important, as a researcher, you have an explicit and fundamental responsibility towards the 'researched'. The dignity and well-being of respondents, both mentally and physically, is absolutely central to research integrity. Understanding how this responsibility is best negotiated at a legal, moral and ethical level is a prerequisite for any potential researcher.

Legal obligations

In a nutshell, researchers are not above the law. Some might like to be – but clearly, they are not. The laws of society stand in the world of research. If it is illegal for the general public, then it is illegal for researchers and research participants. Now for most researchers, the criterion of non-engagement in illegal activities is not too difficult to appreciate or meet. Most recognize the logic here. But a more common legal dilemma is faced by researchers who: (a) wish to study illegal activities; or (b) come across illegal activities in the course of their investigations. For example, I've had students with interests in everything from cock-fighting, to abuse of patients by hospital staff, to corporal punishment in private schools. And a dilemma that faces these student researchers is knowing whether they have an obligation to report any illegal activities they may come to know of in the course of their study. This could also happen in an interview situation. For example, say you were interviewing parents about stress and you came to know of a case of child abuse. Do you maintain confidentiality, or are you obligated to report the abuse?

Well the law here is quite ambiguous and can vary by both country and case. You may or may not be obligated to report illegal activities, but in most

71

countries, the courts can subpoena your data and files. Legal precedents suggest that researcher assurances of confidentiality do not hold up in court. As a researcher, you are not afforded the same rights as a lawyer, doctor, or priest.

Moral obligations

When we talk about morals, we're talking about rights and wrongs, societal norms and values. In research, this boils down to responsibility for the dignity and welfare of both individuals and cultural groups. Put simply, research should not be offensive, degrading, humiliating, or dangerous. In fact, it should not be psychologically or physically damaging in any way.

Some moral considerations in the conduct of research include:

- *Conscientiousness* – this refers to a need to keep the interests of respondents or participants at the forefront in any decision making processes related to the conduct of research. It is important to remember that researchers hold a certain position of power, and being conscious of this power is essential in ensuring the well-being of those involved in your research project.
- *Equity* – equitable research is concerned with the practice of asking only some segments of the population to participate in research, while other segments are immune from such requests. For example, prisoners, students, children, minorities, etc. may have characteristics that make them targets for research studies. It is important that particular groups of individuals are not treated as, or made to feel like, 'guinea pigs'.
- *Honesty* – gone are the days when researchers could 'dupe' respondents and lie to them about what was going to happen, or why a research study was being done in the first place. There is an expectation that researchers are open and honest and that details of the research process are made transparent.

Ethical obligations

Ethics tend to be based on moral obligations, but put a professional spin on what is fair, just, right or wrong. Ethics refers to principles or rules of behavior that act to dictate what is actually acceptable or allowed within a profession. Most universities and large bureaucratic institutions, such as hospitals or some government departments, require you to obtain ethics approval from relevant committee(s) in order to undertake a study. This will require you to carefully examine all aspects of your study for ethical implications.

Now there are quite a few researchers who believe that getting ethics approval is simply a bureaucratic process of hurdle jumping designed to take up limited and precious time. But there are actually some good reasons to take the process seriously. An ethics committee is there to: (1) ensure integrity in knowledge production; (2) promote responsibility towards participants; and, quite paramount,

(3) protect both the researcher and the granting institution from any potential legal ramifications that might arise from unethical research.

Ethical guidelines for the conduct of research will vary by professional code, discipline area and institution, but generally cover the following areas.

- *Ensuring respondents have given informed consent* – a participant can only give 'informed consent' to be involved in a research study if they have full understanding of their requested involvement – including time commitment, type of activity, topics that will be covered and all physical and emotional risks potentially involved. Informed consent implies that participants are: *competent* – they have reasonable intellectual capacity and psychological maturity; *autonomous* – they are making self-directed and self-determined choices; *involved voluntarily* – they are not unaware, forced, pressured, or duped; *aware of the right to discontinue* – participants are under no obligation (or pressure) to continue involvement; *not deceived* – the nature of the study, any affiliations or professional standing, and the intended use of the study should be honest and open; *not coerced* – positions of power should not be used to get individuals to participate; *not induced* – while it may be acceptable to compensate individuals for their time and effort, an inducement should not compromise a potential participant's judgement.

- *Ensuring no harm comes to respondents* – this includes emotional or psychological harm as well as physical harm. Now physical harm is relatively easy to recognize, but risks of psychological harm can be hard to identify and difficult to predict. Whether it be resentment, anxiety, embarrassment, or reliving unpleasant memories, psychological 'harm' can be unplanned and unintentional, yet commonplace. Keep in mind that as well as being ethically and morally unacceptable, risks of harm can give rise to legal issues. We're talking about lawsuits here. So even if your conscience or your professional ethics can justify your decisions, the potential for legal action may be enough to make you reassess your approach.

- *Ensuring confidentiality, and if appropriate, anonymity* – *confidentiality* involves protecting the identity of those providing research data; all identifying data remains solely with the researcher. Keep in mind that pseudonyms may not be enough to hide identity. If others can figure out who you are speaking about, or who is doing the speaking, you need to further mask identity or seek approval for disclosure. *Anonymity* goes a step beyond confidentiality and refers to protection against identification even from the researcher. Information, data and responses collected anonymously should not be identifiable with any particular respondent. Now as well as masking identity, protection of confidentiality and anonymity should involve: secure storage of raw data; restricting access to the data; the need for permission for subsequent use of the data; and eventual destruction of raw data.

73

CRITERIA FOR RESEARCHING WITH INTEGRITY

The research game is certainly not easy. There are a lot of things that need to be considered in the quest for integrity. In fact, it is such a complex process – fraught with the potential for error, inaccuracy, misinterpretation and even 'harm' to those involved in the process – that many of the concepts I have talked about in this chapter have been distilled into 'criteria for' or 'indicators of' good research.

Being familiar with these criteria or indicators should be prerequisite knowledge for anyone attempting to engage in research. Knowledge of appropriate criteria allows you to assess the integrity of not only your own work, but also the work of others. But unfortunately, knowing what criteria and indicators are relevant and appropriate for a particular research project is not without ambiguity. 'Appropriate' indicators are hotly debated and tend to be offered according to the paradigmatic understandings held by those doing the offering.

I've taken a somewhat different approach here. Rather than be prescriptive and offer a defined set of criteria, I have developed a checklist that is structured around the key issues discussed in this chapter (see Box 4.3). The actual indicators related to each issue can be called upon dependent on the research context.

Box 4.3   *Key Issues and Associated Indicators for 'Good' Research*

---

1. Have subjectivities been acknowledged and managed?
There are three strategies and associated indicators that reflect the management of subjectivities. These are:

- **Objectivity** – conclusions are based on observable phenomena; findings are not influenced by emotions, personal prejudices, or subjectivities.
- **Neutrality** – subjectivities are explicitly recognized and negotiated in a manner that attempts to avoid biasing results/conclusions.
- **Subjectivity with transparency** – acceptance and disclosure of bias or subjective positioning and how it might impact the research process including conclusions drawn.

2. Are methods approached with consistency?
The two indicators that are most often used to asses consistency are:

- **Reliability** – concerned with internal consistency, or whether data/results collected, measured, or generated are the same under repeated trials.
- **Dependability** – accepts that reliability in studies of the social may not be possible, but attests that methods are systematic, well-documented and designed to account/control for subjectivities and bias.

Box 4.3   (Continued)

3. Has 'true essence' been captured?

Capturing true essence depends on many factors, including your ability to *build trust* and take your *study's limitations* into consideration. The following two indicators are often called upon to assess 'truth':

- **Validity** – concerned with truth value; that is, whether conclusions are 'correct'. Also considers whether methods, approaches and techniques actually relate to what is being explored.
- **Authenticity** – concerned with truth value, but recognizes that multiple truths may exist. Concerned with describing the deep structure of experience/phenomenon in a manner that is 'true' to the experience.

4. Have you spoken for an appropriate group of people?

Another way to approach this is to ask if your findings are applicable outside your immediate frame of reference. The goal of broad, yet appropriate, applicability is generally assessed by two distinct indicators:

- **Generalizability** – whether findings and/or conclusions from a sample, setting, or group are *directly applicable* to a larger population, a different setting, or to another group.
- **Transferability** – whether findings and/or conclusions from a sample, setting, or group lead to *lessons learned* that may be germane to a larger population, a different setting, or to another group.

5. Is the research process open and accountable? Can it be verified?

When you are dealing with a process that has the potential for bias, error, inaccuracy and misinterpretation, it's important to be able to call on indicators related to accountability. Two indicators that attempt to address this issue are:

- **Reproducibility** – concerned with whether results/conclusions would be supported if the same methodology was used in a different study with the same/similar context.
- **Auditability** – accepts the idiosyncratic nature of research contexts, and the associated difficulty in aiming for reproducibility. Auditability therefore seeks full explication of methods to allow others to see how and why the researchers arrived at their conclusions.

6. Will the project be considered useful by relevant stakeholders?

This is particularly relevant in applied research where the goal is situation improvement or problem alleviation. While 'truth' is still a goal, the main game

(Continued)

Box 4.3   (Continued)

---

is whether or not the research project has been able to make a contribution that is more than theoretical.

- **Usefulness** – concerned with the practical and relevant contribution a research process can have for stakeholders.

7. Have research participants been treated with integrity?

The goal here is to ensure that participants are treated with respect and dignity at all times. Treating research participants with integrity means that all three of the following indicators are met:

- **Legality** – concerned that the research process is not in breach of the law, including any obligation to report illegal activities that researchers may come to know of in the course of their research.
- **Morality** – centres on the societal norms that should act to protect research participants. These norms include conscientious decision making, equity and honesty through full disclosure.
- **Ethicality** – refers to a professional 'code of practice' designed to protect the researched from an unethical process, and in turn protect the researcher from legal liabilities. Key ethical considerations include informed consent, causing no harm and a right to privacy.

Chapter Summary

- Throughout the research process, responsibility and integrity should be paramount considerations. This includes responsibility and integrity in the production of knowledge, and responsibility and integrity in dealing with research participants.

- When researching real-world problems, integrity in the production of knowledge can be complicated by the human element. Idiosyncrasies of both researcher and researched alike make striving for integrity a challenge.

- Recognizing and balancing subjectivities is central to integrity in knowledge production. If this is not done, researchers risk conducting 'self-centric' analysis; being insensitive to issues of race, class, or gender; and hearing only the dominant voice.

- Building trust is also crucial to knowledge production. Trust can be impacted by researcher attributes, for example gender, age, ethnicity, socio-economic status, education, and the power that a researcher holds in a particular setting; as well as a researcher's ability to listen without showing or passing judgement.

- Integrity in knowledge production without consistency in methods is difficult to achieve. It is important that methods are designed and developed in a consistent, logical, systematic and well-documented manner that can account for researcher subjectivities.

- The ability to make relevant and appropriate arguments is crucial. Researchers need to make arguments that acknowledge and take limitations into account. It is also imperative that an appropriate group of people is being spoken for or about.

- Integrity in knowledge production also relies on providing accurate accounts of the research process.

- Integrity and the 'researched' refers to researcher responsibility for the dignity and welfare of research participants.

- Legal obligations include the design of studies not in breach of the law. Researchers must also consider their obligation to report illegal activities.

- Moral obligations relate to societal norms that protect research participants. These include conscientious decision making, equity and honesty through full disclosure.

- Ethical obligations refer to professional 'codes of practice' designed to protect the researched from an unethical process, and in turn protect the researcher from legal liabilities. Key issues include informed consent, causing no harm and a right to privacy.

- A checklist for exploring integrity can help researchers critically review relevant literature and design sound methodologies. Issues related to integrity include: researcher subjectivities; consistency in methods; capturing truth; speaking for an appropriate group of people; the need for accountability; stakeholder usefulness; and integrity in dealing with research participants.

5

The Quest for 'Respondents'

Chapter Preview
Who Holds the Answer?
Cases: Delving into Detail
Key Informants: Working with Experts and Insiders
Samples: Selecting Elements of a Population

'I might not know who holds the answer - but I do know you can't ask just anyone, and you certainly can't ask everyone.'

- L. B. O'Leary

WHO HOLDS THE ANSWER?

I gave up asking my father questions a long, long time ago. He was one of those dads who said, 'Well, you're going to have to find that out for yourself' (a straight answer just once in a while would've been nice!). But he did give me advice about finding answers. He was the one who said 'You can't ask just anyone, and you certainly can't ask everyone'. So I learned quite young that getting the right answers depends an awful lot on the effort you put in to figuring out who to ask.

Now although my dad is a self-professed expert on many, many things, he's no expert on research. But when it comes to gathering data in a research context, his advice is spot on. Figuring out who might hold the answer to your questions, and how you will open up opportunities to gather information from those in the know, is absolutely fundamental to collecting credible data. Finding answers is reliant on finding those who hold the answers.

So let's think about this for a minute. In most models of social science research, what we are after is answers that are held by some population. We want to know what the 'masses' do, think, or feel. And this could certainly be the case when researching real-world problems. Your answers may rest with a broad segment of society. But what if you think your answers are held by the 'few' rather than the 'many'? What if you think your answers are held by experts and insiders, or within the experiences of a particular individual? What if you believe your answers are held within the practices of a setting such as a school or workplace? ✳ Well, when researching real-world problems you may need to look at several strategies for finding those with the answers. Delving into the experiences of an individual or a setting (by defining an appropriate case) and working with those in the know (by selecting key informants) can be as crucial to answering a research question as is seeking broad societal representation (sampling a population).

There are, however, some challenges. Whether you decide to work with cases, key informants, or samples, finding 'respondents' who are appropriate, representative, open, honest, knowledgeable, have good memories, are not afraid to expose themselves and do not need to present themselves in any particular way, might be more difficult than you expect. At times you will need to be systematic. For example, you may decide to use a defined sampling strategy in order to locate a representative sample that can be generalized to a broader population. At other times you will need to be strategic. For example, you may decide to turn to where you know you have an 'in' and can call on pre-existing relationships. And at all times, you will need to be aware of the complexities of working with others in a bid to fulfil your own research agenda. Whether you decide to work with cases, informants, or samples, there are plenty of issues you will need to work through.

CASES: DELVING INTO DETAIL

In the social and even applied sciences, we tend to have a bias towards 'representative samples'. Because we can make arguments about generalizability (see Chapter 4), we tend to think that this is where we need to go in order to gather credible data. But my goal in the conduct of rigorous research (and a goal I strongly advocate) is to determine the best possible means for credible data collection. And researching real-world problems often means delving into detail, digging into context and really trying to get a handle on the rich experiences of an individual, community group or organization. Answers to your research question(s) may lie in the rich history of an event, or in the day-to-day practices of a workplace. In other words, when researching real-world problems, legitimate, valid and worthwhile answers may be held by or within a particular 'case'.

> *Case:* A bounded system, or a particular instance or entity that can be defined by identifiable boundaries.

> *Case study:* A method of studying elements of the social through comprehensive description and analysis of a single situation or case. For example, a detailed study of an individual, setting, group, episode, or event.

Opportunities in working with cases

Applied research into real-world problems, undertaken through the window of cases, is more common than you might realize. Practitioners working in the field or within an organization often limit their methodological design to a particular context in a bid to maximize both relevance and practicality. Case studies concentrate research efforts on a particular 'case', and often on one site. This can minimize travel, facilitate access and reduce costs. On a more strategic level, case studies attempt to build holistic understandings through prolonged engagement and the development of rapport and trust within a clearly defined and highly relevant context. The goal is richness and depth in understanding that goes beyond what is generally possible in, for example, large-scale survey research.

While case studies might not always be 'representative' or 'generalizable', they can add a tremendous amount to a body of knowledge. Cases can:

- *Have an intrinsic value* – cases might be extremely relevant, politically 'hot', unique, interesting, or even misunderstood, for example, exploring a cult undergoing high media scrutiny.
- *Be used to debunk a theory* – one case can show that what is commonly accepted might, in fact, be wrong, for example, societal assumptions related to violence in prison can be called into question through in-depth case exploration that attempts to understand the phenomenon from a prisoner's perspective.
- *Bring new variables to light* – exploratory case studies can often bring new understandings to the fore, for example, in-depth exploration of a particular hospital emergency room might uncover new stressors yet to be identified in the literature.
- *Provide supportive evidence for a theory* – case studies can be used to triangulate other data collection methods or to provide support for a theory, for example, a particular organization might be explored as a lived example of a twenty-first century learning organization.
- *Be used collectively to form the basis of a theory* – a number of cases may be used to inductively generate new understandings, for example, finding empowerment as a common theme in the ability to recover from the stress of divorce, might be the basis of new insights.

Case selection

If you have determined that your research question can be illuminated by delving into cases, you will need to turn your attention to the process of case selection. Now there are two distinct processes involved in case selection. The first is to define your case, or to set the boundaries that will give meaning and characterization to the class of 'elements' you wish to explore. The second involves selecting an individual case or series of cases that meet your definition and sit within your case boundaries.

Defining your case

To define a case, you need to set clear and distinctive characteristics. Perhaps the broadest and easiest distinction here is to decide if your cases will be made up of individuals, institutions, events, cultural groups, etc. Will you be looking at people, places, or things? Once this is determined, more specific criteria can be applied. For example, if your cases will be made up of individuals, you might turn to characteristics such as employment status, gender, or race to narrow the case description. If you are looking at institutions, you might look at function (factory, hospital, school, etc.), location, or size. Cultural groups (groups bound together by social traditions and common patterns of beliefs and behaviours) can be further defined by things like geography, social networks, or shared hardships. Finally, for events, defining characteristics will be the nature of the event as well as things like timeframe, geography, size etc.

As shown in Figure 5.1, possibilities are wide open. The only criteria are that your boundaries are clear, and you are able to argue the importance of case exploration within those boundaries.

 *INDIVIDUALS*	Defined by characteristics such as … • Gender, race, class • Education • Experiences • Employment • Geography i.e. inner city high school students or hospital patients with depression	*INSTITUTIONS*	Defined by characteristics such as … • Function • Public/private • Size • Location i.e. households in a rural area, local government offices, or large factories in Asia
CULTURAL GROUPS	Defined by characteristics such as … • Race, class, gender • Language • Experiences • Employment • Social networks • Geography i.e. students living in a boarding school or members of a cult	*EVENTS*	Defined by characteristics such as … • Nature • Size • Timeline/timeframe • Location i.e. anti-war protests in the US or soccer riots in the UK

FIGURE 5.1   DEFINING A CASE

Case selection

Once your class of cases has been defined, your boundaries are clear and you know precisely what it is that you are trying to delve into, you will need to select the right case (or cases) from the range of possibilities. Now depending on your goals, you may decide to delve into only one case, or you may want to compare and contrast two or more cases. You might also decide to analyse a number of cases so that you are in a position to argue representativeness.

After determining the appropriate number of cases to be explored, the selection of any particular case or cases is generally done through a strategic process. Researchers often handpick cases with a particular purpose in mind. Factors that will influence case selection include:

- *Pragmatics* – there is nothing wrong with being practical. Pragmatics can involve *commitments* such as being commissioned or sponsored to study a particular case, or *timely opportunities*, where you take advantage of current events and work at being in the right place at the right time, for example, studying a community recovering from a flood event, or exploring a recent sports-related riot. Pragmatics can also involve *accessibility* where you take advantage of access that might normally be hard to get, for example exploring a case that has connections to your own workplace, or delving into a case involving an individual with whom you have an existing relationship based on mutual trust and respect.
- *Purposiveness* – researchers will often select cases they hope will enable them to make particular arguments. For example, if the purpose is to argue representativeness, you may select a case considered 'typical'. 'Extreme' or 'atypical' instances may be chosen in order to debunk a theory or highlight deviations from the norm; while wide variance in cases might be used to build new understandings and generate theory. The section on non-random sampling at the end of this chapter provides strategies that can be used in purposive case selection.
- *Intrinsic interest* – researchers might also select a particular case because it's interesting in its own right. It might be relevant, unique, unfamiliar, misunderstood, misrepresented, marginalized, unheard, politically hot, or the focus of current media attention. In this situation, the challenge is to argue the inherent worth and value of a particular case.

It's worth keeping in mind that a prerequisite to all case selection should be access. It is absolutely essential that researchers who wish to delve into cases will be able to reach required people and data. When working with individuals, your ability to generate rich data will depend on building high levels of trust and rapport. In an organizational setting, you may need to gain high level access to relevant records and documents or be allowed broad access to an array of individuals associated with a case. No matter what the situation, the holistic understanding and rich detail demanded in cases studies will require you to have access to what is going on 'inside'.

Selecting respondents within cases

I know we've already talked about case selection, but since researching real-world problems often involves working with cases defined as organizations, workplaces, community/cultural groups and even events, it's worth talking about how you might select and work with individuals *within* a particular case. Now if your 'case' *is* an individual – you need go no further. But if your case is an organization, group or event you may need to consider further strategies for sourcing 'respondents'. The next two sections of this chapter talk about selecting key informants and sampling populations, and both of these strategies can sit under a case study approach. As you read over the rest of this chapter, keep in mind that key inform- ants can be central to both gaining access and insider knowledge; while sampling within your case can be an effective strategy for ensuring broad representation.

KEY INFORMANTS: WORKING WITH EXPERTS AND INSIDERS

Working with key informants means you are attempting to gather some insider or expert knowledge that goes beyond the private experiences, beliefs and knowl- edge base of the individual you are talking to. Your goal is to find out what this individual believes 'others' think, or how 'others' behave, or what this individual thinks the realities of a particular situation might be. Working with key inform- ants means you believe the answers to your research questions lie with select individuals who have specialized knowledge and know what's really going on.

But who really knows what's going on? Well, in my workplace, it's certainly not me; I try very hard to stay out of the loop. In fact, if your case study involved my little academic world, I'd recommend you try talking to my Head of School, or the Dean – but then again they may end up giving you the party line; when you work at that level, you are sometimes forced to call on rhetoric. Wait! I have an idea; you should try talking to Joycee from administration. She's an institu- tion unto herself, and if anyone knows what's going on – it's her. While she does- n't have official 'power' she does have knowledge – which, of course, is a form of power in its own right.

Now this tends to be the case in almost any institution, organization, or com- munity group you might want to explore. There tend to be people 'in the know'. Whether through a position of power or some less official means, some people have a knack for knowing what's really going on. So when you're researching real-world problems, set in real-world contexts, it is not unusual for 'experts' or 'insiders' to be precisely the right people to help you answer your research questions.

> *Key informants:* Individuals whose role or experiences
> result in them having relevant information or knowledge
> they are willing to share with a researcher.

Opportunities in working with key informants

There is nothing like having an inside track, or having an expert at your fingertips. In fact, the insights you can gather from one key informant can be instrumental not only to the data you collect, but how you process that data, and how you might make sense of your own experiences as well as the experiences of others. Key informants can give you access to a world you might have otherwise tried to understand while being locked on the outside.

Now this doesn't mean that all your data should come from key informants. Informants may end up being just one resource you call on in a bid to build understandings. In fact, there are a number of distinct ways key informants can be used in the research process. Key informants can:

- *Be instrumental to preliminary phases of an investigation* – key informants can be called upon by researchers to build their own contextual knowledge. They might also be used to help generate relevant interview questions; or be called on to aid in the construction or review of a survey instrument.
- *Be used to triangulate or confirm the accuracy of gathered/generated data* – data from interviews with key informants can be used to confirm the authenticity of other data sources such as data gathered by survey, observation or document review. Key informants might also be called upon in a less formal way to overview data to confirm credibility, or to explore researcher interpretations for misunderstandings, misinterpretations, or unrecognized bias.
- *Be used to generate primary data* – in-depth interviews with key informants can also be a primary source of qualitative data in its own right.

Informant selection

I think the most important consideration in the selection of key informants is your ability to gather open and honest information from them. Key informants must be accessible and willing to share information. If they have the knowledge you are after, but are not willing to share it, they will not be of any use to your study.

Informant types

It is also important to recognize that key informants do not need to be foremost experts. In fact, there are a number of characteristics that might make someone a useful informant. Depending on your research question and context, any or all of the following might have something to offer:

☑ **Experts** – the well respected, who sit at the top of their field

☑ **Insiders** – those who sit on the inside of an organization, culture, or community who are willing to share the realities of that environment

☑ **The highly experienced** – perhaps not deemed an expert – but someone with a rich depth of experience related to what you are exploring

☑ **A leader** – this might be at a formal or informal level

☑ **The observant** – individuals in an organization or community who have a reputation for knowing who's who and what's what

☑ **The gossip** – similar to the observant but enjoy passing on their observations (and sometimes rumours) – it will pay to make sure your information here is accurate

☑ **Those with secondary experience** – for example, if exploring the problem of youth suicide, in addition to youth, you might look to certain counsellors, teachers, or parents to provide relevant insights

☑ **Stool pigeons** – individuals who want to be classic police type 'informants' – you'll need to be wary of both overt and hidden agendas!

☑ **The ex** – this might include someone who is disenfranchised, alienated, recovered, converted, retrenched, fired, or retired

Working through appropriate selection

There are four distinct challenges you need to face before you can work with key informants. The first is to identify the type of informant you are after, and then identify individuals who have the characteristics associated with that type. The advice here is to ask around. You can also try a snowball technique in which you generate a list of respondents through a referral process (see Figure 5.3). One person in the know is likely to lead you to a host of others.

The second challenge is to confirm the status of those identified. Do they really have the expertise, experiences or insider knowledge that will inform your study in a credible way? The advice here is to seek confirmation by looking for things like a long record of involvement, direct personal experiences and detailed comments from potential informants that show internal consistency. You are after more than just broad generalizations.

The third challenge is to look for and recognize informant subjectivities. Remember, all respondents will have a particular worldview and some will have a real agenda operating. Some may want to be listened to, some may have an axe to grind, some may like the sound of their own voice, some think they know a lot more than they do (Gee, it sounds like I'm describing my family at Thanksgiving dinner…), and some think that their particular take on an experience is how the world should or does respond to the same experience. Bear in mind that you need to develop and build a strong relationship with your key informants. Not only do they need to feel comfortable so they can open up to

TABLE 5.1 OPPORTUNITIES AND ETHICAL DILEMMAS
IN WORKING WITH KEY INFORMANTS

Opportunities	Ethical dilemmas
Building relationships of trust to enhance flow of information	• Having informants become too emotionally invested • Developing friendships that are one-way • Making promises you cannot or do not intend to keep
Gaining the ability to avoid or skirt around official channels and protocols	• Putting informants in an unethical position • Acting unethically in regard to the organization you might be exploring
Being able to get your hands on confidential information	• Asking for, expecting, or accepting illegal/unethical conduct from your informants • Acting unethically, and possibly illegally, in regard to the organization you are exploring
Being able to really dig into the emotional aspects of a topic	• Asking your informant to make a large emotional investment • Having your informant relate private and personal details of others • Asking your informants to relive their own unpleasant memories

you, you also need to end up in a position that allows you to know how to best treat the data they provide.

The final challenge is related to ethics. Now if you look at the list of informant types – and think about the motivations I outline above, it should be pretty obvious that ethics and integrity need to come into play when selecting and working with key informants. In addition to the challenge of managing bias (both yours and theirs), you will need to think about the power position you are in as a researcher. You have to remember that key informants can be put, and can put themselves, in very vulnerable positions. It is your responsibility to respect their needs at all times.

Table 5.1 highlights some of the ethical issues you will need to negotiate when selecting and working with key informants.

SAMPLES: SELECTING ELEMENTS OF A POPULATION

As stated at the beginning of this chapter, in most models of social science research, when we are looking for answers, what we are after is answers that are held by a population. We want to know what the 'masses' do, think, or feel. The idea is to get a snapshot or picture of what people really do and what they really think. Rather than delving into cases, or attempting to gather expert or insider knowledge, the goal here is capturing the reality of a 'population'.

Population: **The total membership of a defined class of people, objects, or events.**

Now the ultimate in population research is to be able to ask everyone – in other words, to be able to gather data from every element within a population. But with the exception of in-depth research into very small, defined and accessible populations, or the conduct of a funded 'census', which is basically a survey of every element within a population, the goal of asking everyone just isn't practical. Your study will probably involve a population that you cannot reach in its entirety; it will either be too large, or it will have elements that you simply cannot access.

Yet our inability to access every element of a population does little to suppress our desire to understand and represent it. This means we will have to sample. The idea here is to speak to the 'few' in order to capture the thoughts, knowledge, attitudes, feeling, and/or beliefs of the 'many'.

Sampling: **The process of selecting elements of a population for inclusion in a research study. Many samples attempt to be representative, that is, the sample distribution and characteristics allow findings to be generalized back to the population.**

Opportunities in working with a 'sample'

So why would you choose to work with a sample? Well samples can make the research process manageable. They allow you to explore groups of people, organizations and events that you simply could not access in their totality. Whether your population is too large, too widely dispersed, too difficult to locate, or too hard to access, sampling can provide you with a window for exploring an unwieldy population.

Sampling can also be used to represent a population with some level of 'confidence'. Certain sampling strategies actually allow you to calculate the statistical probability that your findings are representative of a greater population. Sampling is therefore key to making research affordable, and if done with integrity, also credible.

Sample selection

Sampling is therefore a process that is always strategic, sometimes mathematical, and generally quite tricky. The goal is to select a sample that is: (1) broad enough to allow you to speak about a parent population; (2) large enough to allow you to conduct desired analysis; and (3) small enough to be manageable.

Meeting these goals will require you to think through a number of sampling issues, including the need to define your population; determine appropriate sample size; and select a suitable sampling strategy.

Defining your population

It is absolutely crucial you have a very clear and well-defined population in mind before you do any sampling. You don't want to fall into the trap of asking just anyone, and figuring out who you were trying to target after the fact. This means you'll need to go into your study knowing the total class of 'elements' you want to be able to speak about.

For example, say you want to present findings that will be representative of 13–18-year olds in the United States. Your population here is made up of *individuals* (the most common type of population in social/applied science research) with a particular set of defining characteristics, in this case both *age* (13–18) and *geography* (in the United States). Keep in mind that in a study of individuals you might have used other defining characteristics, such as, gender, marital status, race etc.

Now just like with cases, populations are not always made up of individuals. Depending on the nature of the research question, the 'elements' of your population might be households, workplaces, or even events. For example, your population might be hospital emergency rooms across Europe. In this case, it is a particular type of *organizational setting* that makes up the population. Defining characteristics include both *geography* (across Europe) and *type of setting* (hospital emergency room). Other possibilities for defining 'organizations' might include number of employees, years of operation, public or private etc. An example of a population made up of events might be professional soccer games held in Sydney in 2005. Defining characteristics here are *type of activity* (professional soccer matches), *geography* (Sydney) and *time period* (2005).

Determining sample size

Once your population in clearly defined, you will need to figure out how many elements of that population should be in your sample. I tend to get asked, 'How many do I need?' And it's a tough question because the answer really is 'It depends'. There are no hard and fast rules. Sample size is highly dependent on the shape and form of the data you wish to collect, and the goals of your analysis. For example, the in-depth nature of collecting qualitative data will generally limit your sample size; you simply can't collect that type of data from thousands. But fortunately you don't have to. Qualitative data analysis strategies aren't generally dependent on large numbers. On the other hand, the statistical analysis of quantitative data will require a minimum number. Statistics and the ability to work with probabilities rest on adequate and appropriate sample size.

The following guidelines might help you work through the intricacies of determining appropriate sample size:

WORKING WITH QUALITATIVE DATA   While not necessarily a prerequisite for qualitative data collection, the goal of generating a representative sample can pose a real dilemma for researchers, since the nature of collecting qualitative data generally limits sample size. There are two strategies you can call on here. The first is to 'handpick' a small sample using criteria chosen to assure representativeness. For example, selecting your sample based on a clearly defined population profile, for example individuals with the average age, income and education of the population you are studying. Rather than relying on numbers, you will need to logically argue that your sample captures all the various elements/characteristics of your population.

The second strategy is to select a sample large enough to allow for minimal statistical analysis (see next section). This will give you the option of quantitatively summarizing some of your findings in order to make more mathematical generalizations about your population. While we tend to dichotomize qualitative and quantitative research, the best studies are not afraid to cross this constructed boundary.

WORKING WITH QUANTITATIVE DATA   When working with quantified data, the basic rule of thumb is to attempt to get as large a sample as possible. The larger the sample, the more likely it is to be representative, hence generalizable. But most researchers working in real-world settings struggle at the other end, and need to know minimum requirements. Now, as highlighted in Table 5.2 below, the most basic statistical analysis requires a minimum of about 30 respondents; anything smaller and it can be difficult to show statistical significance – particularly if findings are widely distributed (have a large standard deviation – see Chapter 11).

As you move to more sophisticated analysis, the use of any 'subdivisions' within your sample will require approximately 25 cases in each category. For example, you may have a sample of 100, but if you want to compare men aged 18–35 with women of the same age, you will need to be sure you have at least 25 in each of these categories. Similarly, if you want to conduct multivariate analysis (the analysis of simultaneous relationships among several variables) you will need at least 10 cases for each variable you wish to explore.

Another way to approach sample size is to use the following formula:

$$n = [(K \times S)/E]^2$$

where K is desired confidence level, S is sample standard deviation and E is the required level of precision

TABLE 5.2 REQUIRED SAMPLE SIZE

Population \ Confidence levels	95% C.L. ±5% C.I.	99% C.L. ±5% C.I.	99% C.L. ±1% C.I.
30	28	29	Insufficient
100	80	87	99
500	217	286	485
1,000	278	400	943
5,000	357	588	3,845
10,000	370	624	6,247
50,000	381	657	12,486
100,000	383	661	14,267
1,000,000	384	665	16,369

Personally, I don't believe in working formula unless I have to, so I tend to use a 'sample size calculator' where the only things you need to know are: the population size; the confidence interval – what range you will accept above and below the mean, say ± 5%; and the confidence level – how sure you want to be that your findings are more than coincidental, generally 95% or 99% (see Chapter 11).

Table 5.2 was generated using a calculator from www.surveysystem. com/sscalc.htm, and gives you some idea of the required sample size for more commonly used confidence levels. Note that as the population increases, shifts in sample size do not increase as dramatically. What does require a significantly increased sample size, however, is a desire for higher levels of confidence.

ADDITIONAL ISSUES   There are two other issues you will need to keep in mind when determining sample size. The first involves the challenge of working with both qualitative and quantitative data. Unless you have unlimited time and money, there will usually be some trade-off between the collection of rich in-depth qualitative data and the level of statistical analysis that might be possible. The second issue involves remembering practicalities. While a very large sample might seem ideal, it can be an expensive option. Realistic planning from the start can protect you from setting unachievable goals.

Employing a sampling strategy

Once you have defined your population and determined appropriate sample size, you will need to adopt a strategy for gathering your sample. There are two main ways to go about this. The first is to use a strategy for random selection. The second is to use a strategy that aims to strategically select your sample in a non-random fashion. The best method will depend on a number of factors, including the nature of your question, the make-up of your population, the type of data you wish to collect and your intended modes of analysis.

RANDOM SAMPLES   Random samples rely on random selection, or the process by which each element in a population has an equal chance of selection, for example, names drawn out of a hat, or computer-generated random numbers. The process attempts to control for researcher bias and allows for statistical estimations of representativeness. The process, however, demands that (1) all elements of a population are known and accessible and that (2) all elements are equally likely to agree to be part of a sample.

If this is not the case, two types of error can occur. The first is *coverage error*, or the situation in which the list you draw your sample from is incomplete. For example, while every name in the hat has an equal chance of being drawn, all the names need to be in the hat first. Surveys reliant on e-mail addresses can have this problem. Unless everyone in a particular population has email, coverage is likely to be incomplete.

The second type of error is *non-response bias*, or the situation in which those who accept an invitation to be in a sample are somehow intrinsically different from those who decline. For example, in conducting a customer satisfaction survey, it might be that those who agree to participate have an axe to grind. If this is the case, your eventuating sample will not be representative of your population.

It is therefore important to consider whether the lists you draw your sample from (the sampling frame) are complete. If this is not possible, you'll need to think about how you can give a voice to any sector of the population that might miss inclusion. You will also need to explore issues of non-response, and come up with strategies that will ensure broad representation. Figure 5.2 highlights the random sampling strategies you are likely to call on in conducting research into real-world problems.

NON-RANDOM SAMPLES   Non-random samples are just that – they are samples that are not drawn in a random fashion and are sometimes called 'purposive' or 'theoretical' samples. In order to generate a sample that is meaningful, and possibly representative, non-random sampling demands conscientious decision making. Now non-random samples are considered by some to be inferior because they cannot be statistically assessed for representativeness – they are sometimes seen as second best or last resort. There is a growing belief, however, that there is no longer a need to 'apologize' for these types of samples. Researchers using non-random samples can generate meaningful samples, and even credibly represent populations, if (1) selection is done with the goal of representativeness in mind and (2) strategies are used to ensure that samples match population characteristics.

Certainly, non-random selection offers researchers flexibility when working with populations that are hard to define and/or access (for example homeless women or sports people who have used steroids). There is, however, an added burden of responsibility in ensuring that eventuating samples are not biased. Specifically, researchers who are after representativeness need to be aware of *unwitting bias* and *erroneous assumptions*.

91

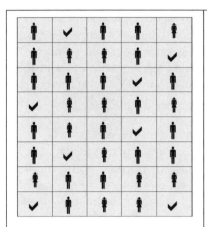

Simple random sampling

- Involves identifying all elements of a population, listing those elements, and randomly selecting from the list
- All elements have an equal chance of inclusion
- Considered 'fair', and allows for generalization
- Rarely used in practice because the process of identifying, listing and randomly selecting elements is often unfeasible
- Resulting samples may not capture enough elements of particular subgroups you are interested in studying

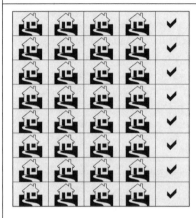

Systematic sampling

- Involves selecting every nth case within a defined population. For example, going to every 10th house or selecting every 20th person on a list
- Easier to do than devising methods for random selection
- Offers a close approximation of random sampling as long as elements are not in a particular order, for example, you would not have a random approximation if you were to go to every 10th house, which just happened to always be a stand-alone home on the corner in a neighbourhood with lots of duplexes

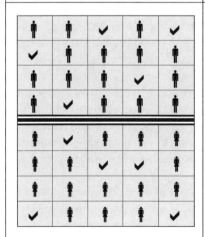

Stratified sampling

- Involves dividing your population into various subgroups and taking a random sample within each one
- Ensures that your sample represents key subgroups of the population, for example males and females
- Representation of the subgroups can be proportionate or disproportionate, for example, if you wanted to sample 100 nurses with a population of 80% females and 20% males, a proportionate stratified sample would be made up of 80 females and 20 males. In a disproportionate stratified sample you would use a ratio different to the population, for example 50 males and 50 females
- Stratification can be used in conjunction with systematic as well as random sampling

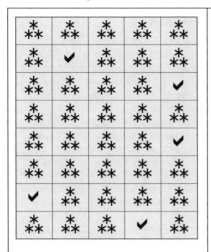

Cluster sampling

- Involves surveying whole clusters of the population
- Clusters can include schools, hospitals, regions, etc.
- Clusters are sampled so that individuals within them can be surveyed/interviewed. The thinking here is that the best way to find high school students is through high schools; the best way to find hospital patients is through hospitals
- Often conducted in multiple stages, for example, if your population is hospital patients in Australia you would use a random sampling strategy to select regions across Australia, then use a sampling strategy to select a number of hospitals within these regions … before employing another sampling strategy to select your final patients from these selected hospitals
- Full population lists are not required, and eventuating samples can be geographically contained

FIGURE 5.2   RANDOM SAMPLING

Unwitting bias refers to the tendency to unwittingly act in ways that confirm what you might already suspect; something that can be quite easy to do when you are handpicking your sample. For example, you may want to conduct a focus group that can help evaluate an initiative you have started in your workplace; unless you make a conscious decision to do otherwise, it's just too easy to stack the deck in your favour.

Erroneous assumptions is somewhat different and refers to sample selection that is premised on incorrect assumptions, for example, assuming that you can go to the local McDonald's to select a representative sample of teenagers in a small town without realizing that a certain sector of that town's teenage population wouldn't be caught dead there.

You might also make erroneous assumptions about the characteristics of 'elements' within your sample. Say, for example, you want to study teenage 'angst' and you select what you believe are extreme cases of angst. If your assumptions are incorrect and what you see as extreme is actually quite average, the generalizations you make will not be valid.

Now, in order to control for such biases, it is well worth brainstorming your own ideas, assumptions and expectations as they relate to both your research questions and your sample. This will put you in a strong position to work towards the development of an appropriate sampling strategy. Figure 5.3 highlights the non-random sampling strategies that you are likely to call on when

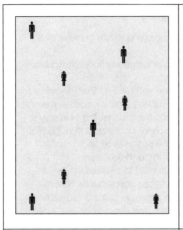

Handpicked sampling

- Involves the selection of a sample with a particular purpose in mind
- Representativeness will depend on the researcher's ability to select cases that meet particular criteria, including typicality, wide variance, 'expertise', etc.
- Other options include the selection of critical, extreme, deviant, or politically important cases. While not likely to be representative, the selection of such cases allows researchers to study intrinsically interesting cases, or enhance learning by exploring the limits or boundaries of a situation or phenomenon

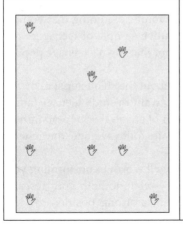

Snowball sampling

- Involves building a sample through referrals
- Once an initial respondent is identified you ask them to identify others who meet the study criteria. Each of those individuals is then asked for further recommendations
- Often used when working with populations that are not easily identified or accessed, for example, a population of homeless persons can be hard to identify, but by using referrals a sample can build quite quickly
- Snowballing does not guarantee representativeness. An option here is to develop a population profile from the literature, and assess representativeness by comparing your sample to your profile

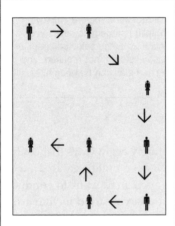

Volunteer sampling

- Involves selecting a sample by asking for volunteers. For example, putting an ad in the newspaper or going to local organizations such as schools, or community groups
- While convenient, it is not likely to be representative. The characteristics of those who volunteer are likely to be quite distinct from those who don't
- Arguments for representativeness will rely on strategies used to minimize the difference between volunteers and the rest of the population

A note on 'convenience' sampling

In the course of your reading, you may have come across something referred to as 'convenience' sampling; that is, selecting a sample in a manner convenient to the researcher. In fact, non-random sampling is sometimes referred to in this way. But please keep in mind that convenience sampling has no place in credible research

There needs to be more to a sampling strategy than just convenience – yes limited time and resources may make convenience *one* factor in sample selection, but I do not believe convenience should be the main criterion or descriptor of a sampling strategy. Regardless of type, all sampling strategies need work towards the ultimate goal of research credibility

FIGURE 5.3   NON-RANDOM SAMPLING

researching real-world problems. Keep in mind that while they can be used to build a representative sample, these strategies can also be called upon in studies that do not rely on representativeness, for example, when the goal is to build knowledge by working with cases and/or key informants.

FURTHER READING

There is plenty of literature out there that can help you in your quest to work with both cases and samples, and I have included a few recent sources here to get you started. Selecting and working with key informants, however, is not so expressly dealt with in the literature. For more information on *selecting* key informants you will need to turn to literature on 'non-random' sampling. For the most relevant sources on *working with* key informants, I'd suggest you turn to literature on in-depth interviewing, which I have included at the end of Chapter 6.

Cases/case studies
Hammersley, M., Foster, R. and Gomm, R. (2000) *Case Study Method: Key Issues, Key Texts*. London: Sage.
Tavers, M. (2001) *Qualitative Research through Case Studies*. London: Sage.
Yin, R. K. (2002) *Case Study Research: Design and Methods*. Thousand Oaks: Sage.

Samples/sampling
Levy, P. S. and Lemeshow, S. (1999) *Sampling of Populations: Methods and Applications*. New York: Wiley-Interscience.
Rao, P. S. R. S., Rao, Poduri S. R. S. and Miller, W. (2000) *Sampling Methodologies with Applications*. New York: Lewis Publishers, Inc.
Thompson, S. K. (2002) *Sampling*. New York: John Wiley & Sons.

Chapter Summary

- Knowing who might hold the answer to your questions and how you will open up opportunities to gather information from them is fundamental to collecting credible data.

- Studying elements of the social through comprehensive description and analysis of a single situation or case is called a case study. While not necessarily representative, cases can add to new knowledge through their ability to debunk theory, generate theory and support existing theory.

- Case selection involves defining your case and selecting an individual case or series of cases that meet your definition and sit within your case boundaries.

- The selection of any particular case can be made on the basis of pragmatics (such as commitments, opportunities and access); purposefulness (to facilitate the ability to make relevant arguments); and/or intrinsic interest.

- Key informants can be a valuable source of information when researching real-world problems. They can be used in preliminary phases of an investigation; to triangulate and confirm data; or as a primary source of data in its own right.

- Informant selection can involve individuals in any variety of roles, including experts, the experienced, leaders, the observant, gossips, those with secondary experience, insiders, stool pigeons and 'ex'es.

- Four challenges you will need to meet in selecting and working with key informants include: (1) identifying potential informants; (2) confirming the status of those identified; (3) negotiating potential informant agendas; and (4) remembering ethical responsibilities.

- Answers to our questions are often held by populations, but we don't often get to speak to everyone we wish to speak about – so understanding populations often involves selecting and working with samples.

- The process of sample selection involves defining your population, determining sample size and employing an appropriate sampling strategy.

- In random samples, every element of a population has an equal chance of selection. Strategies include simple random sampling, systematic sampling, stratified random sampling and cluster sampling.

- In non-random samples, respondents can be handpicked; they can be found through snowball techniques; or they may volunteer. To select a sample on the basis of convenience alone can threaten a study's credibility.

6
Selecting Appropriate Data Collection Methods

'It is a capital mistake to theorize before one has data.'

- Sir Arthur Conan Doyle as Sherlock Holmes

DATA COLLECTION: WORKING THROUGH THE OPTIONS

Data: **Factual information, especially information organized for analysis, reasoning or decision making.**

I think Sherlock Holmes was right; the key to the whole research thing is 'data'. Your ability to answer a research question is highly reliant on getting your hands on, and make sense of, data. Now for researchers working with real-world problems there are a range of possibilities for data collection, and this chapter will work you through the fundamentals. Being familiar with the basic process of data collection and having a critical understanding of the pros and cons of various collection strategies, puts you in a strong position to direct further readings (offered at the end of the chapter) and confidently and appropriately design and implement your study.

Options and possibilities

Trying to get your hands on data, and even deciding on appropriate methods of data collection, is something we actually do in the real world more often than you might think. Take, for example, the following scenario. You suspect your partner is cheating on you (bastard! – oh sorry, I'm being a bit sexist … wench!). But you're not 100% sure, so you need confirmation. You run through your options. As you see it, you can:

1. Get on the phone and ask every single one of your friends if they think it could possibly be true. Now you might get a wide range of opinions here – but some of your friends might not want to go there.
2. Ask directly – grill both him and his friends. While this might get you to the source, the challenge will be trying to get an honest answer out of the lying son of a #*^% …. And as for his friends, do you really think they're going to go behind his back?
3. Spy on him or hire a private investigator. Now you might actually feel a bit guilty about this, particularly if you're wrong. And he finds out what you've been up to, you'll be the one in the doghouse. On the other hand, he certainly can't lie if caught in the act.
4. Rifle through (I'll change gender for a moment just to make it fair) her personal belongings to see if the cheating hussy left any evidence behind. Not a bad strategy – and one you won't be able to stop yourself from doing anyway.
5. Set him up and see if he takes the bait. You're in control here – but it's risky, you could be asking for trouble.

Well, you see, these options (along with their associated opportunities and challenges), actually represent the five methods of data collection we're going to work through in this chapter. The first option, 'get on the telephone', equates to a survey. The second option, 'ask directly', relates to interviewing – both a respondent (him) and key informants (his friends). The third option, 'to spy', is a form of observation, while the fourth, 'rifle through belongings', is a method of unobtrusive data collection. Finally, the fifth option, 'the set-up', is actually a type of experimental design.

So, in our little scenario, which approach or approaches should you go for? Well, this is the dilemma. Each option has its advantages and disadvantages and each will bring something a bit different to the table. So you need to weigh it up. You need to consider: (1) which option will give you the most accurate information; (2) which will give you the most satisfaction; (3) which you find morally, ethically and legally acceptable; and (4) which are most practical. In short, the answer is, it depends; and it depends on any number of factors.

And this is precisely the case in any data collection scenario. One method of collection is not inherently better than any other; each has pros and cons that must be weighed up in view of a rich and complex context, for this is precisely where real-world problems sit. In fact, the circumstances of the problem you are researching are likely to dictate that you look to more than just one method to get a full picture of a problem situation.

The data collection process

No matter what method or methods of data collection you decide to use in your research study, it is important to recognize that, unlike in the scenario above, the collection of research data needs to be rigorous. In fact, it is the systematic and rigorous nature of your approach that will help define your data as more than anecdotal evidence, and act to give credibility to your eventual findings. Data collection is a complicated process that needs to be tackled in a thoughtful and methodical manner.

Now this chapter does cover five distinct data collection strategies – but in terms of process, the methods actually have quite a bit in common. As covered in Box 6.1, each requires: thorough and thoughtful planning; meticulous and well-considered development; effective and sufficient piloting; reflective and weighed modification; deliberate implementation and execution; and appropriate management and analysis.

Box 6.1   Data Collection Basics

Step 1:   Planning – consideration of 'who', 'where', 'when', 'how' and 'what'
A crucial part of the process. The success of your approach will hinge upon the forethought you've put into the planning process. You will need to consider:

- **Population and sample/respondent/participants** – this is who (or what) you plan to speak about (population) – and gather data from (sample). It can include people, documents, communities, artefacts, etc.
- **Access** – you'll need to think about how you will locate and access facilities, people, places, documents, etc. You'll also need to consider any language or cultural barriers that might keep you from fully accessing your sample.
- **Your role** – the challenge here is presentation of self. Will you be an objective scientist, change agent, confidante?
- **Your biases** – this involves recognizing and controlling for your own subjectivities in ways that can best ensure the credibility of any data you may collect.

Box 6.1   *(Continued)*

- **Ethics/ethics approval** – this involves considering any ethical dilemmas inherent in your project, and asks if you've sought and received appropriate ethics approval.
- **Method** – involves thoughtfully considering potential methods of data collection and analysis. Also involves conducting an inventory of the skills/resources needed to carry out your project.
- **Data** – this means knowing exactly what it is you are looking for or trying to find. You will also need to consider if the shape and form of the data you will collect will be compatible with intended modes of analysis.
- **Details** – this refers to thinking through all the details, including tools, timing, location, recording methods, etc.
- **Contingencies** – you need to be ready for the unexpected, the unplanned and the unfortunate. This means having a back-up plan ready to go.

Step 2: Developing – preparing the 'tools'
The tools you will need to develop will depend on method. They may involve interview schedules, observation checklists, questionnaires, experimental checklist etc. In developing tools, you will need to:

- **Explore existing possibilities** – have you sought out existing tools? Remember you don't need to reinvent the wheel. If a relevant tool exists, such as a somewhat applicable questionnaire, you can adopt, adapt and modify.
- **Prepare data collection tools** – this might involve generating questions for questionnaires and interviews, or creating checklists for observation. You will need to generate themes, work through questions/categories, engage in critical review, and offer logical and systematic presentation.
- **Prepare any data recording tools** – if note taking, consider/develop a form that can aid this process. If audio or video taping, be sure to acquire and become familiar with the equipment.

Step 3: Piloting – conducting a 'trial'
Giving thoughtful consideration to planning and development is essential – but not sufficient. The only way to really know if something is going to work is to give it a try.

- **Have a run-through** – if interviewing or surveying, try piloting your process with a few respondents whose background is similar to those in your 'sample'.

(Continued)

> ## Box 6.1 (Continued)
>
> If observing, a trial run will allow you to see if there are any problems in a real-world context. The same is true in working with documents or artefacts. A pilot will allow you to assess the effectiveness of your proposed method.
>
> - **Reflect** – regardless of method, reflect on the piloting process and note any difficulties you encounter. Depending on method, this might include problems with access, response rates, cultural 'ignorance', bias, comfort zones, recording/note taking, objectivity, conversational flow, ambiguities, credibility etc. Also review your data and note any difficulties you might encounter in making sense of your record.
> - **Seek feedback** – attempt to gather feedback from your pilot group. For surveys and interviews this will involve asking about question clarity, structure, introductory information, instructions/prompts, time taken, or anything else you want to know or your group wants to discuss. In the case of observation, you can attempt to confirm your record by checking with an insider, asking another observer to compare notes, or triangulating your observational data with other data types.
>
> ### Step 4: Modifying – refining your approach
>
> Remember, collecting data is not a skill you are born with. Review and refine until you are comfortable with the process and data collected.
>
> - Make modifications – this will be based on the feedback from your pilot group, as well as the quality of the data generated.
> - Back to the start? – if the need for modification is substantial, you may need to revisit your planning, development and piloting process. This may even involve a return to the ethics committee.
>
> ### Step 5: Implementing – the actual process of data collection
>
> As you can see, this is step five. So you should've gone through four steps before getting here. Only now are you ready to go and collect some data. Now there are many researchers who want to jump in at this point without fully engaging with the steps above. But trust me, short-cutting the process is a sure-fire way to get into trouble.
>
> - **Administration** – depending on methods, this might involve mailing/distributing surveys, setting up appointments, arranging site access, organizing experimental logistics, or gathering data/artefacts.
> - **Data collection** – this can be done by a number of approaches, including surveys, interviews, observation, unobtrusive methods and experimentation. Each of these approaches is taken up in detail later in this chapter.

Box 6.1   *(Continued)*

Step 6: Managing and analysing – keeping track and making sense
I will cover this more fully in Chapter 11, but suffice it to say that unless your data is effectively managed and thoughtfully analysed, all the hard work above will be wasted.

- **Organize/collate your data as soon as possible** – when the time comes to work with your data, nothing is worse than a partially forgotten conversation or illegible notes. Be systematic and organized – use a database if appropriate.
- **Statistical and/or thematic analysis** – it's time to see what your data yields. Methods of analysis will vary according to data type. But all analysis should work towards addressing your research questions in insightful ways.

REACHING OUT TO THE MASSES: SURVEYING

'The real now talks constantly. News reports, information, statistics, and surveys are everywhere.'

- Michel de Certeau

You're probably all too familiar with surveys and surveying. I hate to admit it, but when I was an undergraduate at Rutgers University, I actually worked for a market research company. Yes, I was one of those highly annoying people who called at dinner time and asked if you'd mind 'answering just a few short questions that should only a take a couple of moments of your time'. As the French author Michel de Certeau said, 'surveys are everywhere'. Market research, political polling, customer service feedback, evaluations, opinion polls, social science research – when we want to know what the masses are thinking we tend to survey.

> *Surveying:* The process of collecting data by asking a range of individuals the same questions related to their characteristics, attributes, how they live, or their opinions.

Survey pros and cons

There really are no easy answers when it comes to selecting methods of data collection. There will always be tradeoffs between opportunities and challenges, and this is certainly true when thinking about conducting a survey. While surveys can offer much to the production of knowledge, their reputation for being a relatively simple, straightforward and inexpensive approach is not really deserved – they can actually be a somewhat thorny and exasperating process, particularly if done well.

Now on the plus side, surveys can:

- ☑ reach a large number of respondents
- ☑ represent an even larger population
- ☑ allow for comparisons
- ☑ generate standardized, quantifiable, empirical data
- ☑ generate qualitative data through the use of open-ended questions
- ☑ be confidential and even anonymous

They do, however, have their downside. Constructing and administering a survey that has the potential to generate credible and generalizable data is a truly difficult task. It is not something you can do off the top of your head. Challenges associated with surveying include:

- ☒ capturing the quantifiable data you require
- ☒ gathering in-depth data
- ☒ getting a representative sample to respond
- ☒ getting anyone at all to respond!
- ☒ needing proficiency in statistical analysis
- ☒ only getting answers to the questions you've thought to ask
- ☒ going back to your respondents if more data is required

Survey options

You may think that all surveys are the same, but there are actually quite a number of possibilities. You will need to work through a few key issues before you can determine which will best suit you and your research agenda. Table 6.1 covers fundamental survey types by the issues you will need to consider.

Survey construction and administration

As a research supervisor, I have certainly found survey construction to be the activity most underestimated in terms of difficulty. And that's not just by students – professional researchers can also have a hard time getting this right. Yet it is essential because the data that even a poor survey generates can be reported as truth and used in all kinds of decision making processes.

The best advice I can give is to take it in steps and get lots of feedback from your peers and other researchers. You'll also need to have a trial run. Piloting

TABLE 6.1   SURVEY TYPES

Will your survey simply describe or attempt to explain?	
Descriptive surveys: the goal is to get a snapshot – or to describe your 'respondents' by gathering: *demographic information* i.e. age, socio-economic status and gender; *personal information* i.e. political opinion or use of illegal drugs; and *attitudinal information* i.e. attitudes towards multinational corporations, greenhouse gases, or health care costs	➢ *A classic example here is political polling, which attempts to describe voter intentions*
Explanatory surveys: the goal is to gather descriptive data, but also establish cause and effect. In other words, to figure out why things might be the way they are	➢ *A recent Australian survey collected data describing attitudes to the Iraq conflict – as well as data used to establish what might shape and form those attitudes, e.g. personal experience, familial attitudes, and political leanings*
Do you plan to sample or ask everyone in your population?	
Census: a survey that does not rely on a sample. In other words, a survey that covers every single person in a defined population	➢ *The US census is a classic example. A smaller-scale census might be all the students in a particular school*
Cross-sectional surveys: surveys that use a sample or cross-section of respondents to represent a target population. The goal to be able to 'generalize' findings	➢ *Most surveys fall under this category, e.g. a community survey that targets only 1 in 10 households – but aims to represent the entire community*
Will you survey over a period of time – and if so, do you want to explore changing times or changing people?	
Trend surveys: a trend survey asks the same cross-section (similar groups of respondents) the same questions at two or more points in time. The goal here is to see if *classifications* of individuals change over time	➢ *An example here is a three-phase survey conducted over a 20-year period (1986, 1996, 2006) that asks newlyweds their attitudes towards marriage. The goal is to assess if attitudes of newlyweds in the new millennium are the same as attitudes of newlyweds in the 1980s and 1990s*

(Continued)

TABLE 6.1 (CONTINUED)

Panel study: a panel study involves asking the same (not similar) sample of respondents the same questions at two or more points in time. The goal here is to see if *individuals themselves* change over time	➤ *Using the example above, if you had surveyed newlyweds in 1986, you would survey these same individuals in 1996 – 10 years after their marriage – and again in 2006 in order to assess attitudinal shifts as individuals get older*
How do you plan to administer your survey?	
Face to face surveys: *Pros:* good response rate, allows rapport and trust to be established, can motivate respondents, allows for clarification, prompting, probing, and the reading of nonverbal cues *Cons:* can be lengthy and expensive, can limit geographical range, does not assure anonymity or confidentiality, and requires surveyor training	➤ *One example here is the 'mall' or 'supermarket' survey where you are stopped by someone with a clipboard ready to ask you a series of questions*
Telephone surveys: *Pros:* relatively inexpensive, allows wide geographic coverage, offers some assurance of anonymity and confidentiality and allows for some clarification, prompting, probing *Cons:* response rate can be low – it's easy to catch people at a bad time, respondents can hang up on you if they have had enough, and you are limited to surveying only those with a telephone	➤ *In market research the telephone tends to be the mode of choice*
Self-administered surveys: *Pros:* can offer confidentiality/anonymity, allows wide geographic coverage, and gives respondents the opportunity to answer in their own time *Cons:* response rates can be very low, does not allow for clarification, and can end up being costly	➤ *This can include both snail mail and email. Email can save you thousands in printing and postage costs, but you are limited to surveying within 'online' populations. Additionally, the proliferation of 'spam' mail means that unless your respondents know you, your survey may not even get looked at*

might be important in all data collection methods – but in surveying, I'd say it is absolutely crucial. It is almost impossible to get a questionnaire just right the first time around.

As discussed more fully below, developing a questionnaire will entail: (1) formulating your questions; (2) deciding on response categories; (3) providing background information and clear instructions; (4) making determinations about organization and length: (5) working on aesthetically pleasing layout and design; and finally (6) administrating the survey. Which, of course, all needs to be done in conjunction with several stages of seeking feedback, piloting and redevelopment.

Formulating questions

What is it that you want to know? Who are your respondents and what do you think they can tell you about what you want to know? What do you think is the best way to go about asking them? In order to formulate your questions, you need to be able to answer all of the above. Only then will you be able to search for relevant questions or attempt an initial drafting of original questions. Now there is certainly more than one way to ask the same question. In fact, the possibilities are almost endless. And the dilemma here is that subtle (or not so subtle) differences can affect the data you generate. So what do you do?

Well survey construction is a very well researched topic. In fact, there are volumes written about it, and at the end of this chapter I provide a few key references to which you can refer. Within this text, however, Box 6.2 offers a distillation of the most fundamental 'rules' related to question wording that you can apply. The aim here is to help you avoid the pitfalls of leading, offending or confusing your respondents.

Box 6.2   Questions to Avoid

Good questions should be unambiguous, inoffensive and unbiased. But this is actually easier said than done. It's not difficult to fall into the trap of constructing question that are:

Poorly worded

- **Complex terms and language** – big words can offend and confuse. If they're not necessary, don't use them. This is my favourite example: '*Polysyllabic linguistic terminology can act to obscure connotations,*' vs. '*Big words can be confusing.*'
- **Ambiguous questions** – frames of reference can be highly divergent, so writing an ambiguous question is easy to do. Take, for example, the question '*Do you use drugs?*' 'Drugs' is actually an ambiguous term. Some respondents will only consider illegal drugs, while others may include prescription drugs. Others might use a frame of reference that includes alcohol and/or cigarettes.

(Continued)

Box 6.2   (Continued)

- **Double negatives** – like many people, I have a hard time with double negatives. Take the following Yes/No question, *'Do you disapprove of the Government's new policy on Aged Care?'* To state that you do approve, you'd have to choose 'No', which can be quite confusing.
- **Double-barrelled questions** – this is when you ask for only one response to a question with more than one issue. For example, *'Do you consider the President to be an honest and effective leader?'* Respondents may think yes, effective – but definitely not honest.

Biased/leading/or loaded

- **'Ring true' statements** – these are statements that are easy to agree with simply because they tend to 'ring true'. Some good examples here are agree/disagree statements,' like *'You really can't rely on people these days,'* or *'Times may be tough, but there are generally people around you can count on.'* Both of these somewhat opposite statements are likely to get high percentage of 'agrees' because they tend to sound reasonable.
- **Hard to disagree with statements** – these are statements where your respondents are likely to think 'Yes that's true, BUT …' They are not, however, given a chance to elaborate and are forced to either agree or disagree. For example, *'It is good for young children if their mothers can stay at home through the week.'*
- **Leading questions** – leading respondents in a particular direction can be done unintentionally, or can be done intentionally for political purposes. Consider how the wording of these agree/disagree statements might affect responses. *'Protecting defenceless endangered species from inhumane slaughter is something the government should take seriously,'* vs. *'The protection of biodiversity should be a government priority.'*

Problematic for the respondent

- **Recall dependent questions** – these are questions that rely on memory. For example, *'How many relationships have you had?'* Without boundaries such as level of significance or timeframe, this question can be easy to answer 'incorrectly'.
- **Offensive questions** – if respondents take offence to a question or a series of questions, not only are they likely to skip them, they may just throw out the entire survey. Offensive questions can range from *'What do you think you did that caused you to gain so much weight?'* to *'How much money do you earn?'*

Box 6.2   (Continued)

- **Questions with assumed knowledge** – try not to assume that your respondents know about, or are familiar with, the same things as you. Take for example the agree/disagree statement '*Marxist theory has no place in 21st century politics*.' You shouldn't be surprised to find out that a common response here is, 'What kind of academic crap is this!' – followed by a quick trip to the trashcan.
- **Questions with unwarranted assumptions** – respondents are likely to be at a loss when it comes to answering a question that contains an assumption they do not agree with. For example the question '*What was the most enjoyable part of your hospital stay?*' assumes that the respondent enjoyed something about their hospitalization.
- **Questions with socially desirable responses** – this is more likely to be an issue in face to face surveying. For example, a respondent may be uncomfortable disagreeing with the statement '*Do you think women serving in the armed forces should have the same rights and responsibilities as their male colleagues?*'

Now working within these guidelines is a start, but is unlikely to be enough. Once you have drafted your questions run them past an experienced researcher or two. They are likely to pick up things you have missed. You can also trial your questions with your peers. They will certainly be able to tell you if you managed to confuse, offend, or lead them in any way. Finally, once you've made modifications based on feedback received, you will need to run a pilot study. The idea here is to distribute your survey to a small group of individuals whose characteristics match that of your sample and then thoroughly debrief with them. Remember – in the end it is not what you think, or even what your supervisor or peers think that counts. The only opinion that really matters will be that of your eventual respondents.

Response categories

As if getting your questions as precise and non-problematic as possible wasn't enough, a good survey, and good survey data, is equally dependent on the response categories you decide to use. And there are a lot of things to consider here. For one thing, response categories will influence the data you collect. For example, if you add an 'I'm not sure' option to a controversial Yes/No question, it will affect your findings. Secondly, different types of response categories generate data with different types of measurement scale; and data with different measurement scales demand quite distinct statistical treatment. In fact, understanding the difference between nominal, ordinal, interval and ratio data (as discussed in Chapter 11) will definitely facilitate the process of survey construction, particularly determining response categories. But until you actually have some data to play with, understanding the relationship between data types and survey construction is quite abstract.

This makes conducting your first survey a real challenge. So again, I'll turn to the need for a good pilot study. Not only will a pilot study allow you to assess your questions and response categories from the perspective of your respondents, it will also allow you to generate a mini data set that you can enter into a database, and work with statistically. This really is the best way to see how your data collection protocols, including response category determination, will impact on your analysis.

So what are the options when it comes to response categories? Well, as highlighted in Box 6.3, there are quite a few:

Box 6.3   Response Categories

Responses to survey questions can be either open or closed:

Open responses
Respondents are asked to provide answers using their own words. They can offer any information/express any opinion they wish, although the amount of space provided for an answer will generally limit the response. The data provided can be rich and candid, but can also be difficult to code and analyse.

Closed responses
Respondents are asked to choose from a range of predetermined responses. The data here is generally easy to code and statistically analyse. Closed response categories come in many forms, each with their associated issues.

- #### Yes/No – Agree/Disagree:

Do you help your child with homework?	Yes/No
Do you think children in first grade should be given homework?	Agree/Disagree

While it can be easy to work with 'binomial' data (or data with only two potential responses), you need to consider whether respondents will be comfortable with only two choices. For example, in the first question, a respondent might be thinking 'Does only two or three times a year count?', or for the second question, 'It depends on how much you're talking about.' A potential strategy is to offer a Don't know/No opinion option – but this allows for a lot of 'fence sitting'.

110

Box 6.3   (Continued)

- **Fill in the blank:**

   How much do you weigh?   _____

Even a simple question like this (assuming your respondents know the answer and are willing to tell you) can lead to messy data. Will respondents write 90 kgs, 198 lbs, or 14 stone? Of course you can convert these answers to one system, but that isn't going to be possible if they just put 90.

- **Choosing from a list:**

   Who do you enjoy working with the most?

   Doctors   *Patients*   *Nurses*   *Administration*

There is an assumption here that there will not be any 'ties'; you need to consider what you will do if more than one option is circled. You also need to make sure all options are covered (are exhaustive) and don't overlap (are mutually exclusive). A potential strategy is to offer an 'Other' or 'Other:_____' option.

- **Ordering options:**

   Please rank the following according to how you think Government spending should be prioritized:

   Health care   Education   Environment   Defence   Family allowance   Pensions

These questions tend to be quite difficult for respondents, particularly if lists are long. It's worth remembering that if respondents get frustrated trying to answer, they are likely to leave the question blank, leave it half finished, or just write anything at all.

- **Likert-type scaling:**

   It is acceptable for teenagers
   to use obscenities

1	2	3	4	5
Strongly disagree	Disagree	Unsure	Agree	Strongly agree

Likert scales offer a range of responses, generally ranging from something like 'Strongly disagree' to 'Strongly agree'. In Likert scaling, you need to consider: the number of points you will use; whether you will force a side by using an even number of responses; and whether you think your respondents are likely to 'get on a roll' and keep circling a particular number.

Information and instructions

A survey instrument is not complete without some level of background informa-tion. This information is included: (1) to give credibility to the study; and (2) to make your respondents feel like they're a part of something. In your background information it's a good idea to include: the sponsoring organization/university; the survey's purpose; assurances of anonymity/confidentiality; return information, including deadlines and return address; and a 'thank you' for time/assistance. This information can be included at the start of the survey, or as a cover letter.

Also crucial are your instructions. What might be self-evident to you may not be so obvious to your respondents. Instructions should introduce each section of the survey; give clear and specific instructions for each question type; provide examples; and be easy to distinguish from actual survey questions. In fact, I'd suggest using a distinct font – try changing the style, size, boldness, italics, underlining etc. It may take a couple of drafts to get your instructions as clear and helpful as possible. Be sure you seek advice and feedback from other researchers, peers and your pilot group.

Organization and length

Once you are comfortable with all the various elements of your survey, you will need to put it together in a logical format that is neither too long nor too short. Too short – and you won't get all the data you need. Too long – and your survey might be tossed away, returned incomplete, or filled in at random. People might not mind spending a few minutes answering your questions, but ask for much more and they may not be bothered to help you out. Now appropriate length is another aspect of your survey you can assess in your pilot run. Be sure to ask your trial respondents what they thought of the overall length and the time it took to complete the survey.

In terms of logical organization, there are a few schools of thought. Some sug-gest that you start with demographics in order to 'warm up' your respondents. Others, however, suggest that you start with your topical questions and finish off with questions related to demographic information. What's right for your survey will depend a lot on the nature of both your questions and your respon-dents. In fact, you may want to pilot two different versions of your questionnaire if you are unsure how it should be laid out.

There is one consistent piece of advice, however, and that is to avoid starting your survey with questions that might be considered threatening, awkward, insulting, difficult etc. It's really important to ease your respondents into your survey and save sensitive questions for near the end.

Layout and design

All done! Well almost. You've written clear and unambiguous questions with appropriate, well thought out response categories that are accompanied by clear instruction and organized into a sensitive, logical and manageable form. And you've done this by going through multiple iterations taking into account as much feedback as possible. There's only one thing left – aesthetics.

Aesthetics is important. Your survey needs to look professional – no poor quality photocopying, faint printing, messy and uninteresting layout etc. Respondents are more likely to complete a survey that is professionally presented. It is also worth keeping in mind that the potential for mistakes increases dramatically if surveys are cluttered, cramped, or messy. So the effort here is well worth while.

Administration

Now you're done! You just need to get that survey out there and get people to answer it. To execute your survey you will need to:

1. Distribute your questionnaires, by mail, email, telephone, door to door, or face to face.
2. Collect your completed questionnaires.
3. Send out reminder letters if response rates are low.
4. Put a low response rate plan into action if not enough data has been gathered by your deadline.
5. Record and manage responses so they are ready for analysis.

THE QUESTION AND ANSWER PROCESS: INTERVIEWING

'I like to listen. I have learned a great deal from listening carefully. Most people never listen.'

- Ernest Hemingway

Interviewing: the 'Art of Asking' or the 'Art of Listening'? Well both are crucial to the interview process – but while we tend to spend plenty of time discussing the questioning side, I don't think we spend nearly enough time on the listening end of things. According to Hemingway, 'Most people never listen'. And unfortunately, there are too many researchers and interviewers out there who would rather talk than listen. Remember, your job is to talk only enough to facilitate someone else's ability to answer. It is your interviewee's voice that you are seeking, and it is their voice that needs to be drawn out.

Interviewing: **A method of data collection that involves researchers seeking open-ended answers related to a number of questions, topic areas, or themes.**

Interview pros and cons

What could be better than getting out there and actually talking to real people ... asking them what they really think ... finding out first-hand how they genuinely feel? Well, when you conduct an interview you're able to put yourself in a position to see, hear and get a sense of your respondents. Sounds good, doesn't it? And yes – interviewing has the potential to do all of the above. But like any other data collection method, its opportunities are balanced by a series of challenges. As they say ... there's no such thing as a free lunch.

The interview process can:

☑ allow you to develop rapport and trust
☑ provide you with rich, in-depth qualitative data
☑ allow for nonverbal as well as verbal data
☑ be flexible enough to allow you to explore tangents
☑ be structured enough to generate standardized, quantifiable data

Now while many of these 'pros' are the result of the human element in interviewing – so too are the 'cons'. The closer you become to your respondents, and the closer they become to you, the bigger the challenge you will face in managing the process. Such challenges include:

☒ resisting the urge to lead your respondents
☒ facilitating honest and open responses even though your interviewees may want to 'impress'
☒ figuring out how attributes such as race, gender, ethnicity, class and age of interviewer and interviewee alike might affect the interview process – and employing effective strategies for ensuring credibility.

Additional interview 'cons' worth considering include:

☒ the potential for communication miscues
☒ difficulties of working with a large or geographically dispersed sample
☒ a lack of anonymity

Interview options

Words can conjure up images. What pops into your mind when you think 'interview'? Well I think most would probably conjure up the image of a job interview. You know, that formal scenario where the interviewee has to get all dressed up, do the firm handshake, use a formal presentation of self – all while feeling quite nervous. Meanwhile, the interviewer sits behind a big desk or on the opposite side of a conference table, holds all the cards and is definitely the power person. So I guess I shouldn't be surprised when new researchers subconsciously take this image with them into the research world. Without necessarily articulating this image to even themselves, they tend to think that this is how research interviews should unfold. But they don't have to. Yes, research interviews can be formal – but as covered in Table 6.2, there are actually lots of options that might better suit your research agenda.

Conducting your interview

Intimidating. I don't think there is a better word to describe what it feels like to conduct your first interview. No matter how well prepared you think you might be – you are still likely to feel nervous at the beginning, and wish you did things differently at the end. Now we tend to spend a lot of time in interview preparation getting our questions together or thinking about how we can cover our topics and themes. But conducting an interview is a much more complicated management task. You actually need to do three things at once. In addition to questioning, prompting and probing in ways that will help you gather the richest possible data, you also need to actively listen to, and make sense of, what your interviewee is saying – while at the same time managing the overall process so that you know how much time has passed, how much time is left, how much you still need to cover, and how you might move it all forward.

Well here's a cliché for you – practice makes perfect! I don't think anyone is born with an innate ability to conduct a good interview, but if you are aware of the key steps and can reflect on your experiences, it is a skill that will develop with time. In order to conduct a good interview you will need to do the following:

1. *Prepare questions and/or themes* – for a structured interview this will involve drafting and redrafting your questions, and making sure that you have not included questions that will be confusing, leading, offensive, or problematic for your interviewees. For a less structured interview, you will need to think about the themes you want to cover and whether you will put any boundaries on potential conversation. You may not get this just right on your first attempt – so it is essential to conduct a pilot before you construct your final draft.
2. *Consider any translation needs* – if you require a translator, you will need to consider the following:

   • will your translator translate for you and the interviewee on the spot?
   • will someone conduct the interview in the interviewee's native language to be translated at a later time?
   • are you after a literal translation or do you want your translator to use some discretion and judgement in conveying meaning?
   • how will you manage the overall process, including gaining rapport, keeping on time, exploring tangents, keeping respondents focused etc.?

TABLE 6.2 INTERVIEW TYPES

Will you conduct your interview in a formal manner – or will it be more relaxed?	
Formal: the interviewer attempts to be somewhat removed from the interviewee, and maintains distance and neutrality/objectivity. This is often done within a formal setting	➤ *This is the classic job interview. While formality can allow interviewers a high level of control – it can limit interviewee comfort, and possibly the free flow of information*
Informal: bends or ignores rules and roles associated with formal interviewing in order to establish rapport, gain trust, and open up lines of communication. The style is casual and relaxed in order to minimize any gulf between the interviewer and the interviewee	➤ *Settings are not limited to an office and might occur over a beer at a bar, or while having a cup of coffee at the local preschool. The idea is to do what you can to get your interviewee chatting comfortably*
Will your interviews be highly structured or more free flowing?	
Structured: use of pre-established questions, in a pre-determined order, with a standard mode of delivery. Prompts and probes are also pre-determined and used under defined circumstances. Interviewers often call on a formal style to help them stay on track	➤ *Best suited for interviews where standardized data is a goal. Inexperienced interviewers generally feel most comfortable with this high level of structure*
Semi-structured: use of a 'flexible' structure. Interviewers can start with a defined questioning plan, but will shift in order to follow the natural flow of conversation. Interviewers may also deviate from the 'plan' to pursue interesting tangents	➤ *The advantage here is being able to come away with all the data you intended – but also interesting and unexpected data that emerges. This style of interviewing can take a bit of practice*
Unstructured: attempts to draw out information, attitudes, opinions and beliefs around particular themes, ideas and issues without predetermined questions. The goal is to draw out rich and informative 'conversation'. Often used in conjunction with an informal structure	➤ *Most interviewees enjoy this type of interview because it allows them to 'talk' and really express their ideas in a way not dictated by the interviewer. Interviewer challenges here are to avoid leading the conversation and to keep it focused enough to get the data needed*
Will you interview one person at a time – or will you attempt to tackle a group?	
One on one: an interaction between an interviewer and a single interviewee. It is thought that 'one on one' allows the researcher control over the process and the interviewee the freedom to express their thoughts. 'One on one' can also involve an additional person such as a translator or note taker	➤ *One on one interviews are generally face to face, but can also be done over the telephone in order to increase geographical range or capture a 'difficult to get hold of' respondent. The lack of nonverbal cues in telephone interviews, however, can be a challenge*

TABLE 6.2 (CONTINUED)

Group: interviewing more than one person at a time. Can be done in a formal structured way, or may involve a more open process where the researcher acts as a moderator or facilitator. In this less structured approach, interviewees are often referred to as a 'focus group'	➤ *Not only can a group interview save time and money – it can really get people talking. Some, however, might feel unheard or marginalized. Group interviews can be difficult to follow, so most interviewers attempt to preserve raw data by tape recording*

There are no rights and wrongs here. It is the context of your particular research question that will determine the best course of action, and you may need to trial a couple of processes before you know which way to go.

3. *Decide how you will record responses* – recording responses can be done in a number of ways; you may need to trial a couple of recording methods in order to assess what is best for you and your research process. Options include:

- *note taking* – this can range from highly structured, e.g. filling in a form as the interviewee speaks, to unstructured, e.g. mind mapping concepts or jotting down thoughts, analogies, metaphors, etc. during or after an interview. Keep in mind that note taking is actually a preliminary form of analysis – you have thought through and made decisions about your data, e.g. what to note and how to note it. You will need to consider whether there is value in also capturing raw data.
- *audio recording* – this allows you to preserve raw data for review at a later date. Interviewers are therefore free to focus on the question/answer process at hand. Disadvantages, however, include the unease it can cause for the interviewee, an inability to capture nonverbal cues, potential equipment failure, and the cost of data transcription.
- *video taping* – offers the added bonus of being able to record visual cues, but is more intrusive, is prone to more technical difficulties and can generate data that is difficult to analyse.

In most situations you will be responsible for both conducting an interview and capturing responses, but under some circumstances you may use a note taker. Using a person to take notes or record your interview can allow you to focus and engage more fully in listening and directing your interview. But as well as considering resource implications, you need to carefully consider whether a third party is likely to have an affect on the respondent and the interview process.

4. *Decide on presentation of self* – how will you present yourself? How will you strike a balance between formality and rapport? Is your interview style/research goal better suited to officiousness or informality? What tone

of voice will you use? Will you joke around? Also consider body language. Reading nonverbal cues (while your interviewee is reading yours) is worth thinking about. Are you both making eye contact, looking down, looking around, picking your nails, coming across aggressively, looking relaxed?

As the interviewer, you are in a position of power. Attempting to negotiate this position of power in order to facilitate an interviewee's ability to answer questions with honesty and openness should be a central consideration in interview planning.

5. *Take care of preliminaries* – quite a few crucial things need to come together before you are in a position to ask your first question. You will need to:

- *make appointments* – allow for travel time, interview time and wait-around time
- *arrive on time* – building rapport can be a real challenge if you keep someone waiting; and if you miss an appointment altogether you may not get a second chance
- *set up and check any recording equipment* – you can do this in advance or, if done efficiently, when you first arrive for your interview
- *establish rapport* – this includes introductions, handshakes, small talk and expressions of appreciation
- *introduce the study* – this includes reviewing who you are, the purpose of the study, why involvement is important, and approximately how long the interview will take
- *explain ethics* – this can involve assurances of confidentiality, the right to decline to answer any particular questions and the right to end the interview upon request.

6. *Ease your respondents into the interview* – finally you can get down to business. As with surveying, it is important to ease your way into main questions and themes. If you start off with a 'sensitive' question or one that might be considered threatening, you may find yourself facing an uphill battle for the remainder of the interview. In fact, it can be easy to get an interviewee off-side, so it's well worth considering how you might handle such a situation.

7. *Ask questions that facilitate answers* – if you ask a Yes/No question, expect a Yes/No answer. Try to ask questions that open up conversations and draw out rich responses. Questions should create possibilities, open up options, dig below the surface and lower defences.

8. *Keep it flowing* – this involves the use of prompts, that is, giving the interviewee some ideas that might jog a response, and probes, which are comments and questions that help you dig for more, i.e. 'tell me more', 'really', or 'why?'. Sometimes probes can be an inquisitive look or a few moments of silence.

9. *Keep on track/explore tangents* – if you are conducting a structured interview and have a limited amount of time, you will want to make sure you are keeping your interviewee on track and moving at a good pace. If your interview is less structured, you may find yourself wanting to explore interesting tangents as they develop. The trick here is to be mindful of the time, and be sure you end the interview with the full range of data you aimed to gather.
10. *Be true to your role* – if you are using a formal process and are attempting an objective stance, you will want to consider how you can manage the process without directing responses. If, however, you accept that your own 'subjectivities' will be part of the interviewing process, you will need to consider and openly report on how your engagement might influence the conversation.
11. *Wind down/close* – winding down involves questions that 'round off' an interview and asks respondents if there is anything else they would like to cover, contribute, or clarify. The interview then ends by thanking your interviewee for their contribution and their time, and asking them if it might be possible to contact them again if you need to ask any further questions, or need to clarify any points. It's also good practice to offer something back, for example, a copy of your completed report.

TAKING IT ALL IN: OBSERVATION

> *'He plies the slow, unhonored, and unpaid task of observation ... He is the world's eye.'*
>
> *- Ralph Waldo Emerson*

It's easy to overlook observation as a potential data collection method – surveying and interviewing can tend to corner the social science research market. But I can give you three good reasons for thinking about conducting an observational study. The first is that there are times when you need to 'see it for yourself' – having it explained to you just isn't the same. The second reason is that the gulf between what people 'say they do' and what they 'actually do' can be far and wide. And finally, data collection through observation generally takes place in the real world, not a constructed research world. You are out there in the field, right at the heart of where your research problem sits.

Observation allows you entry to this real world, and invites you to take it all in; to see, hear, smell, feel and even taste your environment. It allows you to get a sense of a reality and work through the complexities of social interactions. So in the words of Emerson, why not think about being the 'world's eye'.

> *Observation:* A systematic method of data collection that relies on a researcher's ability to gather data through their senses within real-world contexts.

Observation pros and cons

Who knows, maybe I've already convinced you into thinking 'yes, a method that can

- ☑ explore what people actually do – and not just what they say they do
- ☑ allow you to take it in for yourself and
- ☑ get you out there in the field

sounds exciting.' And you may become even more convinced when you find out that observation is also a method that can:

- ☑ allow you to develop rapport and trust
- ☑ be flexible enough to let you explore tangents
- ☑ provide both rich, in-depth qualitative data and standardized, quantifiable data
- ☑ allow for nonverbal as well as verbal data

But because we're familiar with the general concept of observation, there's a tendency to think that using this technique as a research tool will be pretty straightforward. There is a real challenge, however, in taking something we do on a daily basis and converting it into a rigorous research method. In relation to observation, these challenges include:

- ☒ designing a protocol that can credibly capture the data you require
- ☒ making sure your biases do not colour your observations
- ☒ avoiding the dilemma of having an impact on the researched
- ☒ building trust and getting people to act naturally
- ☒ protecting confidentiality and/or anonymity

Observation options

When talking about options in observation studies, the two ends of the spectrum could not be further apart. At one end, you might have a psychologist who is holding a clipboard and watching a series of interactions from behind a one-way mirror. At the other end is your anthropologist who has lived in a remote Papua New Guinea village for the past 15 years and is dedicated to understanding the reality of this village from the perspective of the observed.

Now, on the surface, similarities may seem few and far between. In fact, these extremes are often treated as two distinct methods of data collection derived from diverse paradigms and disciplines. But when you get down to the brass tacks of researching real-world problems, I think you'll find that these extremes do sit on a continuum. Table 6.3 covers the key issues you will need to negotiate in order to determine how your own observation processes can best unfold.

TABLE 6.3 OBSERVATION TYPES

As an observer will you attempt to be removed or immersed? In other words, will you become a participant in the environment you are studying?	
Non-participant: researchers do not become, nor aim to become, an integral part of the system or community they are observing. The observer is physically present but attempts to be unobtrusive	➢ *Non-participant observations tend to occur over a fixed time period and are often highly structured*
Participant: researchers are, or become, part of the team, community, or cultural group they are observing. The goal is to preserve a natural setting and to gain cultural empathy by experiencing phenomena and events from the perspective of the observed	➢ *Participant observation can involve large emotional and time commitments. Observers may be outsiders who attempt to become insiders, or they can be insiders who decide to study their own, e.g. a member of a workforce, community, or church*
Will you conduct your observations in a covert fashion, or will you offer full disclosure?	
Candid: researchers offer full disclosure of the nature of their study; the role the observations will play in their research; and what they might expect to find through the observation process	➢ *While being candid allows observers to take notes on site, the observed can feel under surveillance, and may not act 'natural'*
Covert: researchers do not disclose the nature of their study to those they are observing; they may not even disclose that they're undertaking a study at all	➢ *It can be difficult to get ethics approval for covert studies since they breach the core ethical principal of informed consent*
Will you use highly structured or unstructured observation techniques?	
Structured: predetermined criteria related to people, events, practices, issues, behaviours, actions, situations and phenomena are used to collect data in a highly systematic fashion	➢ *Checklists or observation schedules are prepared in advance, and researchers attempt to be objective, neutral and removed in order to minimize personal interactions*
Semi-structured: observers use, but are not limited to, predetermined criteria	➢ *Observation schedules or checklists are used to organize observations, but observers also attempt to record the unplanned and/or the unexpected*
Unstructured: observers attempt to observe and record data without predetermined criteria	➢ *Observers can record all observations and later search for emergent patterns, or they make judgement calls on the relevance of initial observations and attempt to focus any subsequent observations and reflections*

Figure 6.1 actually takes this a step further and combines candid and covert strategies with varying levels of participation to offer four major strands of observation studies. Keep in mind that while these four options cover the basic

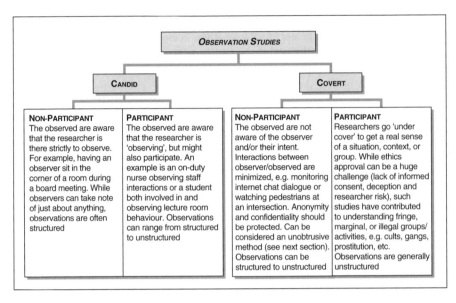

FIGURE 6.1 FOUR MAJOR STRANDS OF OBSERVATION STUDIES

possibilities, the subtleties of managing the process sit squarely with the researcher. It won't always go smoothly and you need to be ready for the unexpected. For example, you will need to have a plan you can put into place if your covert study suddenly becomes exposed. And what if, as a non-participant, you can't help yourself and start to participate? Or what if you get too immersed in the culture you are studying and begin to have second thoughts about your research role? These can be huge challenges and may require you to rethink your methodological design.

Now there is a bit of a paradox here. The more entwined you become with the researched, the richer and more meaningful the data you might generate. But this entwining is also likely to make it a more difficult process to navigate. The key to gathering credible data through observation is your ability to think through such issues, to plan with care, and to exercise *considered* flexibility.

The observation process

Okay, a common feature of all observational studies is that they attempt to document what people actually do, rather than what they say they do; observational studies rely on actual behaviour. That means there are no tools that you can use to generate particular responses from the observed. There are no 'questions'; it is simply the observed doing what they do, and observers taking that in, noting it and making sense of it.

Now the perceived advantage here is 'genuineness', but people don't always act the same when they know they're being observed. How genuine any behaviours might be can depend on both the role of the observer and the nature of the study. So as discussed below, you will really need to think this through, weigh all the pros and cons, and understand the intricacies of the process.

Planning

As in any data collection method, observation begins with planning. The following questions may assist you in preparing to 'do' observation.

- Do your goals and context lend themselves to an observational study that is candid or covert; participant/non-participant; structured/unstructured?
- Do you have/can you get required access? Can you arrange admittance and acceptance into the groups/situation/activities you wish to observe? Are there any potential language and/or cultural issues likely to affect the process? Can you get past 'gatekeepers'? Will you be welcomed? Will you be able to build trust?
- Have you considered details? What timeframe will you be working towards? Will you observe on one occasion, multiple occasions, or will your study involve prolonged engagement? How will you record your data? Do you need to prepare an observation schedule/checklist? Or if unstructured, do you need to articulate any relevant themes you wish to capture?
- Will you need to seek ethics approval? The potential for ethical irresponsibility exists in any data collection method, and observation is no exception. But the potential covert and/or participatory nature of an observation study brings certain issues directly to the fore. For participant studies, you will need to consider whether immersion will have a physical, mental or emotional toll on the observed and/or you as the observer. For example, observers may find themselves immersed in a culture that may be dangerous; they may feel pressured to become involved in immoral/illegal activities; and they may feel stressed when they need to leave the setting and report findings.
- Issues related to covert studies include justifying and getting approval for a study where there is a lack of informed consent. While some ethics committees are loath to do this under any circumstances, others will consider such studies if the researcher can give convincing assurances related to the physical, mental and emotional welfare of the observed and observer, protection of confidentiality, and perceived societal benefits.

Observing

When it comes time to begin your observations, the exact protocol you will use will be highly dependent on the type of observational study you plan to conduct.

Most candid observations, however, begin by attempting to build rapport and gain trust. The idea is to try to make the observed feel as comfortable as possible; in fact, comfortable enough to carry on as if you weren't even there.

The next step is opening your eyes, ears and mind to all that is going on around you. What do you see, what do you hear, what do you sense? We tend to be a visual society, so it's important to make sure you're taking it in through your full range of senses. And this can take time. Because you're not directing the process, you need to be prepared to make a significant investment in order to get the data you need. In fact, unless your design sees you observing for a predetermined period of time, it pays to look for saturation (your observations no longer yield new knowledge) before ending the process.

Now keep in mind that we don't all take in or perceive the world in the same way. Some of us are tuned into the bigger picture, while some of us concentrate on separate components. Some like to take in the world by looking around, some like to listen. Others understand best by moving, doing and touching. So when it comes to observation, it's not only possible, but in fact probable, that two observers in the same situation will take things on board in quite different ways. Attempting to control for this is important. If your observations are structured, an observation schedule that requires information to be gathered through a variety of senses can ensure you don't miss any potential sources of data. In a less structured study, the key will be your ability to critically reflect on your data collection processes and make any necessary modifications.

Recording

There are actually two quite different strategies for recording observations. The first involves the capture of raw data by things like photography, audio and/or video recording. This approach allows observations to be 'preserved' in a raw form so that they can be reviewed and used at a later date. These methods, however, demand the use of 'equipment' and can be considered intrusive. The second strategy is note taking or journaling. These methods can capture anything from descriptive and formal accounts of space, actors, acts and events – to much more interpretive narrative accounts that include goals, feelings and underlying 'stories'. The form also varies and can range from coded schedules and quantitative tallying – to pictures, concept maps and jotted ideas.

The recording method (or methods) you will need to adopt will vary depending on the level of participation, openness and structure in your observational processes. For candid studies, the use of an observation schedule that you fill in as observations occur might be appropriate, as would the use of photography, audio and video recording. For studies that involve high levels of immersion and are perhaps covert, you might want to note, journal, doodle, or map your observations when you are removed from your observational setting and have a level of privacy. Your circumstances may also see you looking to employ a combination of the above strategies. Now whatever recording methods you choose to adopt, it will be important to record your data in as systematic a fashion as possible. After all, this is data you will need to analyse in the future.

Reflecting

While not always conducted as a 'pilot', there is still a need to review, reflect on and modify your observational methods. Such modifications are generally based on difficulties you encountered in your initial observation work, for example difficulties with access, timing, cultural 'ignorance', comfort zones, recording/note taking, roles, objectivity, etc. It also pays to review your observation records and assess if they make sense, and are logical, rich and complete.

You should also look for 'bias'. It's very easy to see the things you expect to see and hear the things you want to hear. That's why doctors conduct double-blind studies in drug trials where neither the doctor nor the patient knows whether they have been given a placebo or the real thing. It is the only way to control for expectations.

Before you go out in the field, it's well worth consciously brainstorming your own expectations. You can then brainstorm a range of alternatives, so that you're less likely to observe and reflect on your observations in ways that confirm what you already suspect.

Authenticating

It can be hard to assess whether you've been able to control for your biases and generate credible data by reflection alone. There are, however, a number of strategies that can be used to ensure thoroughness in data collection, and confirm the authenticity of reflections.

Thoroughness of observational methods can be facilitated by working towards:

- *well-designed method* – rigorous protocols are essential
- *broad representation* – observing multiple events and various people
- *prolonged and persistent engagement* – getting credible observational data takes commitment
- *crystallization and saturation* – observing until a 'story' comes together or until new data ceases to emerge

Strategies for authenticating data include:

- *triangulating your observational data with other data sources* – assessing whether data generated from interviews, surveys or documentary review 'gels' with your observations

- *checking in with an insider* – this is particularly useful if observing within an unfamiliar culture or environment
- *asking another observer to compare notes* – while not always possible, this is an interesting exercise that can allow you to asses your ability to 'control for' your own worldview

COLLECTING DATA WITHOUT INTERVENTION: UNOBTRUSIVE METHODS

'The secret of my influence has always been that it remained secret.'

- Salvador Dali

I can tell you – it is no easy feat to find a quote related to unobtrusive methods. So I was pretty excited when I came across Dali's words on the power of secret influences. You see, most forms of data collection, for example, interviewing, surveying, experimentation and most forms of observation, actually introduce foreign entities into real-world situations. And these entities, namely the researcher and the research process, cannot help but have some impact on the reality of the situations, events, or people being explored; researchers and researching have an influence on social environments. Yet the influences implicit in traditional research strategies often go unrecognized, unacknowledged and/or ignored. In other words, or in Dali's words, they have 'remained secret'.

The main advantage of unobtrusive methods is that researchers, and the research processes they adopt, are removed from those who provide the data. There is no disruption to the social environment. The influence of researchers is controlled for.

Unobtrusive methods: Methods of data collection in which researchers and research processes are removed from the researched; direct interaction is avoided. As well as some forms of observation, unobtrusive methods include the exploration and review of pre-existing government data and records, corporate data, personal records, the media, the arts, as well as social artefacts.

Unobtrusive research pros and cons

We've pretty much covered the main advantage of unobtrusive methods; that is, they are 'non-reactive'. The potential for research participants to be influenced by the research process or the presence of the researcher is taken out of play. But there are other advantages as well. Unobtrusive research methods:

- ☑ explore evidence of what people have actually done
- ☑ allow you to acquire real-world data from the real world
- ☑ allow you to capitalize on the vast amount of data already out there
- ☑ allow for nonverbal as well as verbal data collection
- ☑ can provide both rich, in-depth qualitative data and standardized, quantifiable data
- ☑ can be time- and cost-efficient
- ☑ can eliminate the need for physical access to research subjects
- ☑ can minimize stress for both researchers and research subjects
- ☑ can eliminate worries related to: building trust; getting people to act naturally; role playing; and figuring out how attributes such as race, gender, ethnicity, class and age of researcher and researched might confound data collection
- ☑ allow you to be neutral and not a force for change

Well, that's a pretty long list, and hopefully the discussion so far has piqued your interest in exploring what I think are highly underutilized methods. But there are some challenges associated in working with 'pre-existing' data. In conducting unobtrusive methods, you will need to:

- ☒ work through data not expressly generated to answer your particular research question(s)
- ☒ overcome any shortcomings that might exist in the original records you are exploring, for example, bias, inaccuracies, incompleteness
- ☒ make sure your own biases do not colour your interpretations and understandings
- ☒ avoid taking records out of context
- ☒ protect the needs of an uninformed researched, that is, protection of privacy, anonymity and/or confidentiality
- ☒ overcome the expectation that 'real' research demands interviews and surveys

Unobtrusive research options

There is so much data already out there: records abound; research is done on a daily basis all around the globe; and the day-to-day evidence (the social artefacts) of what people think, do, believe and feel surrounds us in art, poetry, music and even our rubbish. And I, for one, don't think we do enough with this 'data'.

Now before primary data collection begins, most lecturers (including me) expect their students to have at least started a literature review. We do this because we know that to be in a position to contribute to a body of knowledge you need to be conversant with it. But before my students go down the interview/ survey path, I also ask them to look for data sources that might be out there already.

Sure, some students come back and say there isn't very much, or what's out there isn't very useful – and these students continue on with their original methodological plan. But others get quite excited by the possibility of 'data mining' or working with different forms of 'non-elicited' data, and they go on to design fully unobtrusive methods. Others still go on to use some form of unobtrusive data to triangulate their main interview or survey data – adding much to the credibility of their study.

The range of unobtrusive data types available for exploration is almost endless. Table 6.4 attempts to capture the possibilities.

Gathering relevant data by unobtrusive means

Ask a question, get an answer. That's the advantage of surveys and interviews. The answers, whether tainted by the process or not, are right there on the table for you. You get to direct the process and collect only the data relevant to your research question. Not so with data collected by unobtrusive methods. With unobtrusive methods, you are working with data not expressly generated for your particular research purposes. So this means you will really need to: (1) know what you are looking for; (2) know where it is likely to be found; (3) know whether or not you can trust it; and (4) have some sense of what you can do with it.

Knowing what you're looking for

It might sound a bit strange, but clearly and succinctly articulating what you are after in terms of 'data' is something that can actually be overlooked when using unobtrusive methods. When you conduct a survey, the process of designing and developing your questionnaire demands you work through your data needs. The same is true of interviewing. Question development is actually an exercise in clarifying what you think your respondents can offer. But with unobtrusive methods, because you are working with documents, records, data sets and artefacts not produced expressly for your purposes, it's easy to skip this articulation step and take a somewhat haphazard approach to data collection.

Unobtrusive methods demand the same consideration as any other data collection method. You need to assess your research question and/or hypothesis and ask yourself, 'What data am I after, and how will it contribute to my understanding?' You need to know what you are looking for – and think through it with the same rigour you would put into developing a questionnaire, interview schedule or observation checklist.

TABLE 6.4   UNOBTRUSIVE DATA TYPES

What type of data will you be exploring through your unobtrusive methods?

'Official' data and records – while you may have to work at getting access, it's worth exploring:

- *International data* held by organizations such as the United Nations, World Bank, or World Health Organization
- *National data* held by many federal or national governments and government departments, e.g. national census data
- *Local government data* such as State of Environment reports, community surveys, water quality data, land registry information, etc.
- *Non-governmental organization data* collected through commissioned or self-conducted research studies
- *University data*, which is abundant and covers just about every research problem ever studied
- *Archival data* such as records of births, deaths, marriages etc.

Organizational communication, documents and records – generally official communication that includes, but is not limited to:

- Press releases
- Catalogues, pamphlets and brochures
- Meeting agendas and minutes
- Inter- and intra-office memos
- Safety records
- Sales figures
- Human resource records
- Client records (this might be students, patients, constituents, etc. dependent on organization type)

Personal communication, documents and records – personal and often private communication that includes, but is not limited to:

- Letters and emails
- Journals, diaries and memoirs
- Sketches and drawings
- Poetry and stories
- Photographs and videos
- Medical records
- Educational records
- Household records, e.g. chequebook stubs, bills, insurance documents etc.

The media/contemporary entertainment – data here is often examined in relation to questions of content or portrayal, e.g. the content of personal ads, how often male characters are shown crying, or how often sexual assault has made the national news over the past two years. Data can come from:

- Newspaper or magazine columns/articles/advertisements
- News programmes and current affairs shows
- TV dramas, sitcoms, and reality shows
- Commercials
- Music videos
- Biographies and autobiographies

(Continued)

TABLE 6.4 (CONTINUED)

What type of data will you be exploring through your unobtrusive methods?

The arts – the arts have captured and recorded the human spirit and condition over the ages in every corner of the globe, making it perfect for comparing across both culture and time. Societal attitudes are well captured in:

- Paintings, drawings and sketches
- Photography
- Music
- Plays and films

Social artefacts – this can be quite fun and owes much to the seminal work of Webb et al. (1966), who identified a number of social 'traces', including those related to:

- **Erosion**, which looks at wear and tear in relation to preference. For example, looking at how worn seats are to determine where people most prefer to sit on the train, or determining patient reading preferences by examining the condition of waiting room magazines
- **Accretion**, which aims to understand society by examining what people leave behind. For example, looking through waste disposal bins in a hospital to see if staff are conforming with waste disposal policy, or examining attitudes to promiscuity by looking at toilet door graffiti

Knowing where data sources can be found

Once you know what you are looking for, you will need to know where you can find it and how you can get your hands on it. Now, as you saw in Table 6.4, unobtrusive methods are capable of collecting a huge array of data types and each type of data will demand quite distinct protocols for collection. For example, your data might be held by an organization, by an individual, or by a family. It might be on the television, at the movies, at a school, museum or park. It may be in the public domain, or it might be private. It may be held by other researchers, local government, national government or international agencies. And getting your hands on it may involve writing away for it, going to the library, making a personal appeal, or going into the field.

Given this diversity, the key to success is being prepared. You will need to know well in advance where your data sources are located; who the gatekeepers might be; how to best approach them; whether or not you will need to use a sampling strategy; and whether the collection of sensitive or private data will require ethics approval.

Assessing credibility

Because you're working with existing data, assessing credibility is essential. Ask yourself if the pre-existing data you are working with is unbiased, complete and accurate. Does it give a full account? You also need to be able to recognize whether your data was produced with a particular agenda in mind (for example, political campaign paraphernalia, promotional materials, or even surveys that have been produced by those with a vested interest). It may be tempting to treat the printed word as truth, and to treat artefacts as conclusive evidence, but all data needs to be viewed with a critical pinch of salt.

Credibility will also rest on how well you are able to manage your own subjectivities. How you 'read' and make sense of your data will be coloured by your own researcher reality. You need to ensure that your biases do not colour your interpretations and understandings, and that your data is interpreted within its original context.

Strategies for ensuring credibility are similar to those used to authenticate observations and include: well-designed and reviewed methods; broad representation that explores multiple sources of data; crystallization and saturation that sees a full 'story' come together; triangulation of unobtrusive data with other data sources; and, if possible, checking in and comparing notes with an insider or other researcher.

Working with your data

When using unobtrusive methods, the data as you find it may not be 'ready for use'. Your sources, whether they be quantitative data sets or a series of qualitative documents, will need to be explored in order for you to draw out relevant information. Now the first step here is to ask yourself questions *about* the 'data'. Who produced it? Who did they produce it for? What were the circumstances of production? When, where and why was it produced? What type of data is it? Basically, you want to explore any background information that is available (sometimes called the latent content or unwitting evidence).

The next step involves exploration of the meaning of the 'data' itself (the manifest content or witting evidence). There are a few ways you can do this. The first is highly applicable to qualitative data and involves using an *interview technique* to 'ask' your data a series of questions. As with an interview, you will need to develop and 'ask' each question, and then find the answer within your documents.

The second method, also applicable for qualitative data, involves *content* ces. This process quantifies the use of particu-
r concepts within a given situation, text or doc-
es what is being 'looked for' and notes the
t of the occurrence (this is covered more fully

analysis and is applicable to quantitative data.
analysis (see Chapter 11) of existing data sets
ed form, for example, linking census data and
there is a plethora of existing quantitative data

131

available at local, national and international scales, just sitting on the answers to many of our research questions.

MANIPULATING THE ENVIRONMENT: EXPERIMENTATION

'It is inexcusable for scientists to torture animals;
let them make their experiments on journalists
and politicians!'

- Henrik Ibsen

Experimentation: **Searching for cause and effect by varying an independent variable (something you believe is a key determinant in your study) in order to see if it has an impact on your dependent variable (the main object of your inquiry). In other words, you manipulate X to see if it has an effect on Y.**

You might not have been able to define 'experiment' before reading the above, but it's probably a term you were at least familiar with. After all, it's the main-stay of medical researchers, crime scene investigators and mad scientists alike – and would be a method of choice if your goals included: evaluating the effects of pharmaceutical drugs; looking at the connection between suspect heights and bullet trajectories, or creating the perfect human–monster hybrid.

Now in terms of practical real-world experiments, you are unlikely to be working with cells, DNA, inanimate objects or laboratory animals. The likely object of your inquiry will be people in all their complexity. You will probably explore what people do, why they do it and how the things they do affect aspects of the real world. It's also unlikely that your experiments will take place in the controlled confines of a laboratory. Your research is likely to take place in real-world settings, with all the advantages and shortcomings thereof.

Nevertheless, experimentation offers tremendous potential when researching real-world problems. For example, say the problem you were interested in was bored students who had difficulty engaging in learning. Real-world experimental design can allow you to manipulate classroom layout (the independent variable) to see how it affects student attentiveness (the dependent variable).

Or say the problem within a particular company is the high number of sick days taken. Your experimental design might involve introducing a workplace exercise programme (independent variable) to see if the number of sick days taken decreases (dependent variable). Finally, if the problem was high levels of domestic waste in a particular county or municipality, you might 'experiment' by introducing free household recycle bins (independent variable) to see if this leads to a reduction in household waste levels (dependent variable).

Experiment pros and cons

There is something very appealing about saying, 'I wonder what would happen if I were to …', and then be able to set up and assess the effects of that exact scenario. You would get to see it unfold for yourself. You would get to manipulate the environment and both witness and record the results. You would be in control. And these are just a few advantages of conducting experiments.

Experiments also allow you to:

- ☑ assess cause and effect
- ☑ compare groups
- ☑ explore real actions and reactions; and if so designed, in real contexts
- ☑ avoid reliance on respondent's memory or reactions to hypothetical situations
- ☑ generate both in-depth qualitative data and standardized, quantifiable data
- ☑ generate nonverbal as well as verbal data

Sounds pretty good. But as you might already suspect, there's no guarantee of smooth sailing. Unless you're 'Big Brother' from the 'Big Brother' house, it's hard to control it all. When experimenting on real-world problems, in real-world contexts, you will need to consider whether:

- ☒ there is equity in your design (for example, will the manipulation of your independent variable advantage or disadvantage any individuals/or groups?)
- ☒ your design will allow you to get informed consent from participants
- ☒ participants will stay involved for the duration of the experiment
- ☒ you can control for your own biases
- ☒ your design can control for extraneous, confounding or intervening variables (the things that effect your study that are not a part of your methodological design)

Experiment options

There are three basic criteria for 'pure' or 'true' experimental design:

1. that independent variables are manipulated by the researcher
2. that control groups are used, and there is random assignment to both control and target groups
3. that experiments are conducted under controlled circumstances

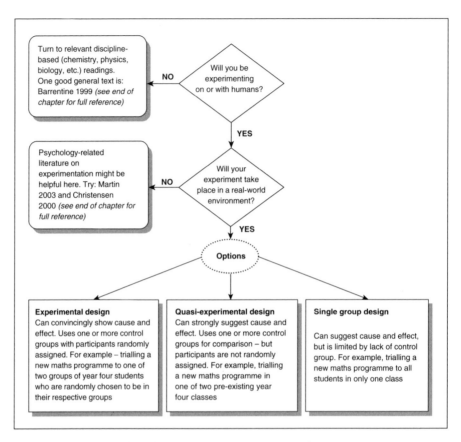

FIGURE 6.2   FOCUSING IN ON HUMAN-CENTRED REAL-WORLD
EXPERIMENTAL DESIGN

As you can imagine, these criteria, are easiest met in traditional laboratory-based research. But it's a different story when you are dealing with real-world problems. Okay, at this stage you might be thinking, 'Well actually, I'm pretty sure I am heading down the path of a more traditional lab-based experiment.' And yes, there are plenty of real-world problems where 'lab-based' experimentation on 'nonhuman' objects of inquiry can be central to research design. For example, if your interest is in skin cancer, you may want to manipulate levels of UV light to see how they affect malignancy in human cells. Or if you are interested in the benefits and dangers of fad diets, you might start your investigation by seeing how changes in levels of dietary protein affect kidney functioning in laboratory rats.

Now while the basic elements of these types of experiments mirror those of human-centred real-world experiments, they tend to require more technical expertise and advice than is available within the scope of this text. So while I do offer a few readings at the end of this chapter that can help get you started on this path, the main focus of this chapter (as highlighted in Figure 6.2) is human-centred, real-world experimental design.

The search for cause and effect

On the radio the other day I heard that 'eating fish increases your IQ'. The story reported on the latest research that found that children who eat fish at least once a week have higher IQs than their non-fish-eating peers. Hence the 'eat fish and get smart' headlines that led the story. But as I listened, I found out that the study looked at children's IQs and compared them to a number of factors including diet, education, socio-economic status, age of the parents, parental marital status, parental education level, etc. etc. And *one* of the correlations they found was between eating fish and IQ. As fish consumption rose, so too did intelligence – but then again you could also say that as IQ rose so did fish consumption. Does eating fish make you smart or do smart people eat more fish? Correlation is simply *not* cause and effect.

An intervening or confounding variable might also come into play. Maybe it's not the fish that makes you smart – maybe what's going on is that smart parents feed their children fish, and their child's IQ is determined by genetics.

Okay, let's say you really want to get to the bottom of the great fish debate and you decide you want to determine cause and effect by conducting an experiment (after all, you've read that experiments really are the best way to work through this type of research problem). So how do you go about it?

Well, initial planning will involve lots of decision making. As you work through your methodological design you will need to decide on:

1. *Your dependent and independent variables* – you will need to identify the main focus of your study or what you are trying to assess (the dependent variable), as well as the variable you will manipulate in order to cause an effect (the independent variable). In this case, you are hypothesizing that IQ depends on fish consumption, thereby making IQ the dependent variable and fish consumption the independent variable that you will manipulate. This identification of variables by type is central to moving from correlation to cause and effect.

2. *Assessment of change* – in order to determine whether the manipulation of your independent variable has affected your dependent variable, you will need to be able to assess change. The most effective way to do this is by both pre- and post-testing, which in real-world contexts may mean collecting or having access to good baseline data and being able to collect comparable data after the experimental intervention. In our case, assessing change is

relatively straightforward and would involve administering standardized IQ tests.

3. *Research setting* – consider whether you will be conducting your study in a controlled environment such as a laboratory or if you will use a natural setting. In this case a lab may give you total control, but as is the case for many real-world problems, it may not be practicable. Other options in our scenario are to ask parents to vary diets at home, or to make arrangements with maybe a day care centre to change their weekly menu.

4. *Number of participants* – the number of participants you will use is also crucial. Think about how many participants will be necessary for you to make any conclusive or statistically significant judgements. For example, if you find a pattern in five children, is it enough? (Chapter 5 covers the basics of determining sample size.)

5. *Number of groups* – you will also have to decide if you will use a control group. In our fish example, using a single group would involve testing the IQ of all the children, feeding all of them fish a set number of times a week, and testing them at some period thereafter to see what happens. With a control group you would test all of the children at the start, put half the children in a control group and the other half in a target group, and only give fish to the children in the target group. You would then test both groups again at a later date and compare findings.

6. *Assignment strategy* – if you are using a control group you will need to determine how you will assign your groups. Will children be randomly selected for fish consumption or will you use different criteria for selection? While randomization will provide you with stronger cause and effect arguments, you might find it more practical to select children based, for example, on the days of the week they're in a day care centre.

7. *Number of variables* – will you test just one independent variable or will you test for others as well? For example, will you simply look at fish consumption or are there other aspects of the children's diet you will explore, such as vegetable intake.

8. *Ethics* – consider whether you will need informed consent. In our fish consumption case, you will need parental consent. You will also need to consider if there are any advantages or potential threats to group members based on their inclusion in either a control or a target group. Now while there may not be high risks associated in eating or not eating fish, issues of equity represent a huge ethical dilemma in drug trials, treatment programmes and educational initiatives.

9. *Controlling the environment* – finally, you will need to consider how you will negotiate the balance between the practicalities of working in real-world situations and the need to control the environment. In other words, you need to consider how you can ensure your findings can be attributed to a true

cause and effect relationship between your independent and dependent variables. Now the more controls you embed into your experimental design the more convincing your arguments will be. But without such controls, arguments can be spurious. For example:

- without a controlled environment it can be hard to ensure that the only variable that has been changed, shifted, manipulated, or introduced is your particular independent variable, for example, other dietary changes, changes in sleep patterns, personal stress, etc. may be happening outside your experimental design
- without adequate numbers it will be hard to show statistical significance or that results are more than coincidence
- without a control group it's hard to ensure that there is not some other factor that might account for changes in your target or dependent variable, for example, that improvements in IQ scores cannot be attributed to things like additional attention that the children might be receiving, practice in taking IQ tests, or the coincidental commencement of a new educational programme
- without a random assignment strategy (which is often impractical in real-world research) you will need to argue that differences between the two groups are non-existent or at least minimal. In our case, if there is an innate difference in the learning abilities of the two groups, it would be impossible to attribute increased IQ to dietary habits.

In short, the bottom line in human-centred, real-world experiments is trade-offs. There are always tradeoffs. The benefits of real-world contexts need to be weighed up against the benefits of a controlled environment. I think the best advice I can give to those who want to go on and conduct experiments is to read. Not only do you need to be familiar with the basic issues presented here, you also need to be familiar with the plethora of design options open to you. The readings offered at the end of this chapter should help get you started down that path.

COMPARING METHODS OF DATA COLLECTION

I thought I'd end this fairly long chapter by offering a few quotes related to the challenge of data collection (Box 6.4) and a summary table that compares the data collection methods we've discussed (Table 6.5). The table looks at how each method deals with or treats: populations, data, relationship with respondents, perspectives and ethics. While you need to build an understanding of each of these methods before you finalize, a quick design – a side-by-side comparison can be really useful.

Box 6.4   Collecting Data – Dealing with Facts

The importance of gathering facts and data …

> *'Facts are the air of scientists. Without them you can never fly.'*
>
> Linus Pauling

But on the other hand …

> *'Facts are stupid things.'*
>
> Ronald Reagan

> *'Data is not information, information is not knowledge, knowledge is not understanding, understanding is not wisdom.'*
>
> Cliff Stoll and Gary Schubert

Perhaps even more important …

> *'You can use all the data you can get, but you still have to distrust it and use your own intelligence and judgement.'*
>
> Alvin Toffler

> *'Don't become a mere recorder of facts, but try to penetrate the mystery of their origin.'*
>
> Ivan Pavlov

> *'Science is facts; just as houses are made of stones, so is science made of facts; but a pile of stones is not a house and a collection of facts is not necessarily science.'*
>
> Henri Poincare

TABLE 6.5 COMPARING METHODS OF DATA COLLECTION

	Surveying	Interviewing	Observation	Unobtrusive	Experiments
Population					
Can readily reach a large number of respondents	+	+			
Can readily represent a population	++	+	+	+	+
Best with smaller accessible populations		+	++		
Data types					
In-depth qualitative data	+	++	++	++	+
Quantifiable data	++	+	++	++	++
Nonverbal as well as verbal data		++	++	++	++
Data generated expressly for your study	++	++	++		++
Use of existing data				++	
Respondent relationships					
Can build trust and rapport		++	++		+
Can come back for additional data		++	++	++	
Nonreactive				++	
Perspective					
Can see cause and effect					++
Can explore tangents/ interesting directions		++	+	++	
Can observe it for yourself			++	++	++
Evidence of what people actually do/produce			++	++	++
Real-world environments		+	++	++	+
Control/manipulate the environment					++
Allows for comparison	++	++	++	++	++
Ethics					
Can be anonymous	++		++		
Can be confidential	++	++	++	++	++
Non-Interventionist			+	++	

++ A strength of this approach
+ While not a defined strength, the process can be managed such that this goal can be acheived

FURTHER READING

While this chapter should give you a good idea of what is involved in each data collection method, getting right into the details will require you to do a bit more reading. The following list contains some of the most recent and accessible readings on the data collection methods discussed in this chapter.

Surveying
Fowler, F. J. Jr (2001) *Survey Research Methods.* London: Sage.
Groves, R. M., Fowler, F. J., Couper, M. J., Lepkowski, J. M., Singer, E. and Tourangeau, R. (2004) *Survey Methodology.* New York: John Wiley & Sons.
Oppenheim, A. N. (1999) *Questionnaire Design, Interviewing and Attitude Measurement.* London: Pinter.
Schuman, H. and Presser, S. (1996) *Question and Answers in Attitude Surveys: Experiments on Question Form, Wording, and Context.* San Diego: Academic Press.

Interviewing
Fielding, N. (2002) 'Qualitative Interviewing' in N. Gilbert (ed.), *Researching Social Life.* London: Sage. pp. 135–53.
Fontana, A. and Frey, J. H. (2000) 'The Interview: From Structured Questions to Negotiated Text', in N. K. Denzin and Y. S. Lincoln (eds), *Handbook of Qualitative Research.* Thousand Oaks: Sage. pp. 645–72.
Gubrium, J. F. and Holstein, J. A. (2001) *Handbook of Interview Research: Context and Method.* London: Sage.
Kvale, S. (1996) *InterViews: An Introduction to Qualitative Research Interviewing.* Thousand Oaks: Sage.
Rubin, H. J. and Rubin, I. S. (2004) *Qualitative Interviewing: The Art of Hearing Data.* Thousand Oaks: Sage.

Observation
Angrosino, M. V. and Mays de Perez, K. A. (2000) 'Rethinking Observation: From Method to Context', in N. K. Denzin, and Y. S. Lincoln (eds), *Handbook of Qualitative Research.* Thousand Oaks: Sage. pp. 673–702.
Bakeman, R. and Gottman, J. M. (1997) *Observing Interaction: An Introduction to Sequential Analysis.* Cambridge: Cambridge University Press.
Jablon, J. R., Dombro, A. L. and Dichtelmiller, M. L. (1999) *The Power of Observation.* Florence, KY: Thomson Delmar Learning.
Lofland, J. and Lofland, L. H. (2003) *Analyzing Social Settings: A Guide to Qualitative Observation and Analysis.* Belmont, CA: Wadsworth.

Unobtrusive methods

Holder, I. (2000) 'The Interpretation of Documents and Material Culture', in N. K. Denzin and Y. S. Lincoln (eds), *Handbook of Qualitative Research*. Thousand Oaks: Sage. pp. 703–16.

Kellehear, A. (1993) *The Unobtrusive Researcher: A Guide to Methods*. St Leonards: Allen and Unwin.

Lee, R. M. (2000) *Unobtrusive Methods in Social Research*. Buckingham: Open University Press.

Prior, L. (2003) *Using Documents in Social Research*. London: Sage.

Webb, E. J., Campbell, D. T., Schwartz, R. D. and Sechrest, L. (1966) *Unobtrusive Measures: Nonreactive Research in the Social Sciences*. Dallas: Houghton Mifflin.

Webb, E. J., Campbell, D. T., Schwartz, R. D. Sechrest, L. and Grove, J. B. (1981) *Nonreactive Measures in the Social Sciences*. Dallas: Houghton Mifflin.

Experiments

Barrentine, L. B. (1999) *An Introduction to Design of Experiments: A Simplified Approach*. Milwaukee, WI: ASQ Quality Press.

Campbell, D. T. and Stanley, J. C. (1966) *Experimental and Quasi-Experimental Designs for Research*. Dallas, TX: Houghton Mifflin.

Christensen, L. B. (2000) *Experimental Methodology*. Boston, MA: Allyn & Bacon.

Martin, D. W. (2003) *Doing Psychology Experiments*. Belmont, CA: Wadsworth.

Trochim, W. M. (2005) *The Research Methods Knowledge Base*. Web page at http://www.socialresearchmethods.net/kb/index.htm

Chapter Summary

- Data collection possibilities are wide and varied, with any one method of collection not inherently better than any other. Each has pros and cons that must be weighed up in view of a rich and complex context.

- All methods of collection require rigorous and systematic design and execution that include thorough planning; well considered development; effective piloting; weighed modification; deliberate implementation and execution; and appropriate management and analysis.

- Surveying involves gathering information from individuals using a questionnaire. Surveys can reach a large number of respondents; generate standardized,

141

quantifiable, empirical data – as well as some qualitative data; and offer confidentiality/anonymity. Designing survey instruments capable of generating credible data, however, can be difficult.

- Surveys can be descriptive or explanatory; involve entire populations or samples of populations; capture a moment or map trends; and can be administered in a number of ways.

- Survey construction involves formulating questions and response categories; writing up background information and instruction; working through organization and length; and determining layout and design.

- Interviewing involves asking respondents a series of open-ended questions. Interviews can generate both standardized, quantifiable data, and more in-depth qualitative data. However, the complexities of people and the complexities of communication can create many opportunities for miscommunication and misinterpretation.

- Interviews can range from formal to informal; structured to unstructured; and can be one on one or involve groups.

- When conducting your interviews you will need to question, prompt and probe in ways that help you gather rich data, while actively listening and making sense of what is being said. At the same time, you will need to manage the overall process.

- Observation relies on researchers' ability to gather data though their senses – and allows researchers to document actual behaviour rather than responses related to behaviour. However, the observed can act differently when surveilled, and observations can be tainted by a researcher's worldview.

- Observation can range from non-participant to participant; candid to covert; and from structured to unstructured.

- The observation process is sometimes treated casually, but is a method that needs to be treated as rigorously as any other. The process should include planning, observing, recording, reflecting and authenticating.

- Unobtrusive methods involve researchers and research processes that are removed from the researched. Unobtrusive methods are 'non-reactive' and capitalize on existing data. But researchers need to work through data not expressly generated for their purposes that may contain biases.

- Unobtrusive methods include the exploration of official data and records, corporate data, personal records, the media, the arts, as well as social artefacts.

- In order to gather data by unobtrusive means you need to know what you are looking for; where you can find it; whether it can be trusted; and what you can do with it.

- Experimentation explores cause and effect relationships by manipulating independent variables in order to see if there is a corresponding effect on a dependent variable.

- Pure experimentation requires both a controlled environment and the use of a randomly assigned control group. This can be difficult to achieve in human-centred experiments conducted in the real world.

- There are many experiments that can only be carried out in the messy uncontrolled environments of the real world, so the search for cause and effect will require tradeoffs between real-world contexts and a controlled environment.

Part Three
Researching Problems

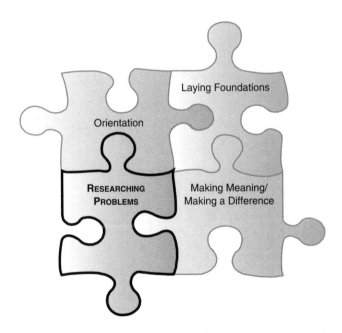

Chapters 7–10 are structured by the actual goals and objectives that drive research into real-world problems. This generally involves: (1) gaining a better handle on problem situations; (2) trying to find a solution to a particular problem; (3) engaging in actual situation improvement through research; (4) evaluating change initiatives and/or; (5) a combination of the above. The chapters address each of these goals in turn and offer specific methodological techniques and strategies that can help you achieve these objectives.

7
Understanding Problems

> *'The better off you become at analyzing complex problems,*
> *the better off you are for solving them.'*
>
> *- Tom Morris*

WHEN THE RESEARCH GOAL IS 'TO FIND OUT MORE'

In order to solve problems, you need to understand them. Without knowing prevalence ... it's impossible to argue the need for, or target, solutions. Without understanding cause ... you can't work on prevention. Without understanding effects ... you can't work on remediation. Without understanding who's at risk ... you won't know who to help. Put simply, you need to understand problems before you can begin to deal with them.

Sounds pretty logical, right? Well, then why is it so easy to think of examples where governments, consultants, bosses etc. come up with absolutely absurd ideas that we know will never work. Why is it so easy to say, 'That's ridiculous ...', 'They're dreaming ...', 'Don't they realize ...'

Well, I think it really is that simple ... they don't realize. In fact, those in charge of problem resolution often 'assume', an as the truly wise Mike 'Brady Bunch' Brady once said, 'When you assume, you make an "ass" out of "u" and "me".' There is a clear difference between assumption and fact. And as researchers working on real-world problems, what we are after is data that supports facts; compelling data that can be used in problem resolution.

> *Data:* **Factual information, especially information organized for analysis or used to reason or make decisions. (*The American Heritage Dictionary of the English Language*, 2000)**

When researching real-world problems, a clear, consistent and worthwhile goal is 'to find out more'. In other words, to gather credible data necessary for facilitating evidence-based decision making.

Acknowledging complexity, searching for clarity

> *'Everything is complicated; if that were not so, life and poetry and everything else would be a bore.'*
>
> *- Wallace Stevens*

As touched on in Chapter 1, problems are complex. They are multi-faceted and have embedded within them a plethora of dimensions, including the economic, bio-physical, cultural, political, social and personal. But the complexity does not stop there. As shown in Figure 7.1, problems have: (a) a reality – the who, what, where and when of the problem situation; (b) multiple and complex causes; and (c) both short- and long-term effects. And all of these sit within a set of (d) societal assumptions that help construct our understandings through ideological frameworks, common values, shared norms, our education systems, the media, etc.

FIGURE 7.1 UNDERSTANDING PROBLEMS

Now the first thing you might notice about Figure 7.1 is that it captures a wide array of elements. So I guess it's not surprising to find so many important problem-based research questions centring on some aspect of problem understanding. It's important to remember, however, that you don't need to do it all. Your job here is to supplement a body of knowledge and add illumination where it is needed. Some information is probably known – and your review of relevant literature should help you narrow and clarify your focus for 'finding out more'.

So as discussed in Chapter 2, the first challenge in understanding problems is knowing precisely what aspects of your problem need further exploration through research. The second challenge is to set your clarified and focused quest to find out more in a context that can help you determine the most appropriate and useful methodological approaches for your study. Not an easy task when possibilities are so wide open. So how do you begin to organize your thinking around appropriate methodological approaches? What research strategies should you turn to in your quest 'to find out more'?

Quick sketch or detailed portrait

As you begin to work through methodological options, one of the dimensions worth considering is the extent, depth and level of thoroughness you will aim for in your research process. Now credibility is a must. If your findings are not 'believable', why bother to do any research at all? But when it comes to researching real-world problems, the thoroughness of your research can actually fall on a continuum that ranges from 'quick sketch' to 'detailed portrait'. This is particularly true in research that aims to explore 'place'; that is, research that explores the context or settings of real-world problems. Rapid appraisal and in-depth case studies represent two ends of this spectrum.

Rapid appraisal strategies

Rapid appraisal strategies such as *rapid rural appraisal* (RRA) and *participatory rural appraisal* (PRA) are often used to generate an overview of a community, context, or setting in a short period of time. Rapid rural appraisal, which is actually somewhat misnamed since it can be applied to urban as well as rural settings, refers to a set of informal techniques used to collect and analyse community-based data. RRA is generally seen as an efficient and cost-effective way to look at settings and is often used in community development research. It relies on multiple sources of triangulated data in order to provide a broad-brush picture of the context or setting in which a problem may sit. Secondary sources of data, direct observation, key informant interviews and a scan of local media collected over a limited period of time, generally by a research team, are pulled together to understand a context in a way that values local knowledge.

Participatory rural appraisal evolved from rapid rural appraisal and differs in that data collection and analysis are undertaken by local people, with outsiders staying in a facilitative role. The purpose of PRA is to enable researchers, practitioners, government officials and local people to work together in ways that empower community members. As with RRA, PRA can be employed successfully in a variety of settings, including urban areas, and it is generally done within a tight timeframe.

When you're working in the real world, you might not always have the time, resources, or expertise for a full-blown academic research study. But you may still recognize the importance of data and evidence in informed decision making. If this is the case, rapid assessment strategies can be worth exploring, particularly if: (a) the exploration of your problem demands a broad brush understanding of both the environmental and cultural nature of your community or setting and/or (b) you plan to work *with* your 'community' on the development of change initiatives.

The various data collection strategies used in RRA and PRA are pretty much covered in Chapter 6, so I won't say too much more about them here. But at the end of this chapter I do offer a few key readings that can help you explore this area a bit further.

Case studies

At the other end of the spectrum are in-depth case studies that often involve prolonged engagement and even cultural immersion in order to build a rich picture. Exactly how deeply you delve into a case will depend on your objectives, your timeline and your resources. As in rapid appraisal strategies, the data generated from a case study needs to be both useful and credible. As long as these criteria are met, the options associated with the exploration of cases are wide open.

Now case studies are often referred to as a methodology, but the methodological approaches associated with case studies are actually eclectic and broad. Not only can they involve any number of data gathering methods, for example, surveys, interviews, observation, quasi-experiments and a range of unobtrusive methods; they can also be used to meet a wide variety of research goals. In fact, many of the applied examples offered in this and the following chapters are case-based.

If you think about the term, this actually makes sense. Case studies refer to the form and shape of 'participants', which is precisely why the concept is discussed in Chapter 5, 'The Quest for "Respondents"'. So while case studies have some commonality in that they generally:

- allow for in-depth exploration
- are an examination of subtleties and intricacies
- attempt to be holistic
- explore processes as well as outcomes
- investigate the context and setting of a situation

they actually cut across a number of methodological approaches discussed in both this and the following chapters. Research into real-world problems is often case-based – but the methods and techniques used to understand a particular case can vary widely.

Looking out vs. looking in √

Another simple framework that can help get you started in determining appropriate methodologies involves asking yourself whether your question is one that leads you to look outward or inward. As indicated in Box 7.1, a question that leads you to look outward is one where you believe answers lie in broad societal attitudes and opinions, or in general trends; in other words, the answers lie in researching popu-✳ lations. On the other hand, a question that leads you to look inward is one where the quest for answers will see you delving quite deeply into the intricacies and cultural reality of your problem situation. And of course, in a bid for rich and full understanding, you may opt for multiple approaches that allow you to analyse a problem situation through a combination of outward and inward exploration.

Box 7.1   Looking Out and Looking In

Looking Outwards:
Researching populations

Looking Inwards:
Delving into problems

LOOKING OUTWARD: RESEARCHING POPULATIONS

Analysing problems by looking outward means turning your attention to data gathered or generated by a population. It refers to problem analysis through exploration of the experiences, attitudes and opinions of the 'many'. Questions such as:

151

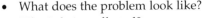

- What does the problem look like?
- Who is being affected?
- When and where does the problem occur?
- Why is it happening?
- What are the consequences?

Can all be answered by looking outwards.

There are actually two broad methodological strategies that can help you 'look outward'. The first is to review existing evidence; that is, exploring and capitalizing on data that already exists. The second is to gather primary data; that is, generating data from a population for the express purposes of your study. Each is discussed below.

Reviewing existing evidence

A review of existing data is actually a form of unobtrusive method, which is covered in Chapter 6. So rather than repeat myself here, I'll simply refer you to that section and jump right into an example from some time I spent in Palau, a small island nation in middle of the Pacific Ocean.

Applied Example 7.1   Bento Boxes and Belly Ache – Food Poisoning in Palau

The islands of Palau

When I was asked if I would be interested in going to Palau to be part of a team working on the development of the country's National Environmental Health Action Plan, I have to admit I'd never heard of the place. Palau which has recently been used as a *Survivor* location, is but a speck in the middle of the Pacific Ocean, somewhere near Guam. It is made up of over 300 limestone rock islands, has a population of about 19,000, and it has to be one of the most amazing natural environments I have ever seen. Up until 1994 it was an American Protectorate, but it is now a new nation trying to stand on its own two feet. With its unparalleled snorkelling and diving, its economic future relies on building its tourism sector.

The bento box

My colleague and I arrived a day early and decided to take a snorkel tour of the islands, which I have to say was pretty spectacular. The following day we related our adventure to the team we were to work with at the Division of

Applied Example 7.1 (Continued)

Environmental Health. I was quite surprised when one of their first comments was 'I hope you didn't have a bento box!' Now a 'bento box' is basically a Japanese-influenced packed lunch, and I did indeed have one. Mine contained rice, vegetables, chicken and cake. It had been placed unrefrigerated on the boat in a stinking hot tropical climate at 7am, and was not eaten until after 1pm. At the time, I was torn between being worried and being hungry – but as any-one who knows me could guess, my stomach won out over common sense. I have to admit, however, I realized I might have made a mistake when I saw that my chicken was still quite red at the bone.

The challenge of ensuring safe food

Well, I was told by the team that bento boxes are actually made in private homes and are delivered in the evening where they sit out overnight without refrigeration – so this chicken of mine could have been sitting out for up to 24 hours. Delicious! Anyway, my ironclad stomach was fine, and I was able to participate in a really interesting conversation about food safety and the challenges the Division faces in ensuring restaurants and supermarkets engage in safe practices.

In the West, we tend to take fresh food for granted. But in Palau, almost everything is imported, and stores are full of 'out of date' items (McCreadie and O'Leary 2005). International manufacturers tend to use Palau as a convenient dumping ground for near-date foods, and there seems to be little recognition or appreciation of the importance of temperature control.

Finding out more

The area of food safety was one the Division wanted to include in their planning processes, so we asked if food poisoning was a big problem. The answer was a definitive 'Yes'. We then asked how big, and the most specific answer we could get was 'pretty big'. So we decided to design a method for finding out more. We grappled with how we could find out about: numbers of cases; severity of cases; who is affected; if there are seasonal variations; and potential causes.

After working through a number of options, we decided to turn to existing records. The plan was to have the team go to every hospital, doctor and med-ical facility in the country and identify and explore records for all reported cases of food poisoning (which might sound bigger than it was. Remember this is a very small place; in fact, the Governor of one state invited me to dinner where I could meet the residents – all 36 of them!)

(Continued)

Applied Example 7.1   (Continued)

We understood that this review of records would have its limitations. For one thing, it would be a review of reported cases, not all cases. Secondly, it would be reliant on getting access to records (which the team did not think would be too difficult). Thirdly, it was reliant on the accuracy and thoroughness of the records reviewed.

The Pay-off

Even with these limitations, this study would make a contribution. It would allow the team to: (a) generate a 'reported' food poisoning figure; (b) look at distribution by season, race, tourist vs. local, etc.; (c) begin to look at recorded causes; (d) write more effective food safety policy; and finally (e) produce recommendations about systematic data collection within the medical sector.

Now personally, I think I've been scared off the bento box for good. But I'd certainly recommend a trip to Palau for anyone who has the opportunity. Just remember – pack your own lunch!

Data is everywhere. Resist falling into the trap of thinking that the only data you can use is data you generate. The data you find may not be in a form that directly answers your question, but therein lies the challenge. Remember, refining the wheel will often get you further than reinventing it.

Gathering primary data

Existing data and records related to your specific topic are not always available, or perhaps not available to you. So there will be plenty of times when you'll need to generate primary data. Now when the challenge is looking out at problems by gathering primary data, the answer is generally 'conduct a survey'.

The main challenges in conducting a survey are sampling, which is covered in Chapter 5, and survey construction and administration, which is covered in Chapter 6. So, as in the last section, I'm going to jump right into an applied example.

**Applied Example 7.2   Recommendations to
Stop Bullying – The Need for Data**

Sorry, but I can't find any research here ✓

It may sound a bit strange, but I sometimes get student research proposals that
don't contain any 'research'. In fact, I'd say this happens just about every semester.
So what are in these 6–10 page 'research' proposals? Well, these students want
to jump straight into 'development'. They want to produce something; perhaps a
set of recommendations, some guidelines, or a new/revamped programme. In
other words, they want to produce a 'deliverable'. And the proposal they produce
for me is related to the development initiative they wish to undertake, not the
research that is needed to undertake that development.

The need for foundations for development

This was the case for a student of mine who was once a primary school
teacher. The main objective in her proposal was to develop anti-bullying guidelines appropriate for Australian rural primary schools. She proposed the development of her guidelines based on her years of experience, anecdotal evidence
about a lack of effectiveness of current anti-bullying strategies and her personal
insights into the problem. What her research proposal lacked, however, was
recognition of the importance of 'data' as a foundation for developing an effective anti-bullying campaign.   *I DO HAVE THIS, DON'T I? → Value Genesis + Avance*

Given that data collection was required for this assignment, I tried to help this
ex-teacher understand how a research process could help her meet her objective.
I asked her, 'Do you know all you need to know in order to write these guidelines?'
'Do you have all the data you require?' 'Do you have an evidence base to work
with?' She then took some time to think about all the issues that could inform her
guidelines and decided that while she did have some valuable insights, there was
indeed a need for some 'data'. I then asked her if the data existed somewhere. Had
relevant studies been conducted that would provide her with what she needed to
know? She was unsure, so she had a look at the literature and found that while
any number of studies into bullying had been conducted, she did not find many
that addressed the problem within the context of rural Australian schools.

Gathering primary data

Now we were on to something. In order to produce effective guidelines our
ex-teacher had identified a need for data. And once she'd thought about it, she

(Continued)

155

Applied Example 7.2   (Continued)

---

realized she wanted the data to come from students themselves. So she went back to the drawing board and wrote a two-phase proposal. Writing the guidelines became phase two. Phase one involved collecting data. She proposed to survey approximately 300 students selected by sampling rural 'clusters' in Australia, randomly selecting primary schools within those clusters and finally distributing surveys to students within these schools (see cluster sampling in Chapter 5). She planned to collect data related to the following:

- How common is bullying?
- What form does bullying take? Verbal, physical, threats, intimidation? Does this vary according to gender, race, class, year, academic achievement levels?
- Who are the 'bullies'? Are they evenly distributed according to gender, race, class, year, academic achievement levels?
- Who are the 'victims'? Are they evenly distributed according to gender, race, class, year, academic achievement levels?
- Where and when does bullying occur?
- How do victims currently handle bullying?
- When do victims feel comfortable 'telling'?

This phase one problem analysis would then provide her with a solid foundation for the phase two development of her guidelines. And she was quite excited about this. She had come to realize that the key to developing an effective anti-bullying campaign was data; in this case data gathered directly from the source. She was determined to write and disseminate guidelines that were truly evidence-based.

Have you ever heard the term 'data-free environment?' It refers to environments where decisions are made without data to support those decisions. Those with power hold the cards and those without often pay the price. Understanding real-world problems by collecting data across relevant populations can be an effective tool in ensuring that decisions are well informed and based on more than personal preference, anecdotal evidence or biased opinions.

LOOKING INWARD: DELVING INTO COMPLEXITY

As well as looking outward towards a population, your quest to find out more may see you turn your view inward. You may believe that true understanding of a problem situation requires you to get in there amongst it; to delve into intricacies and complexities; to understand what it feels like for those in the midst. In your quest to understand a problem situation, rather than seek hard population data, or maybe to complement this data, you may seek richer, more empathetic understandings gathered through in-depth engagement and even immersion into the problem situations you are studying.

This can open up some really interesting windows in problem analysis. In addition to studying the reality of problems – the who, what, where and when – inward exploration can help build rich understanding of complex causes and both long- and short-term effects. Inward exploration can even provide a window into the broader cultural ideologies that can act to shape and define problem situations.

The in-depth interview

By far the most common approach used in inward exploration is *in-depth interviewing*. As discussed in Chapter 6, this type of interviewing involves researchers generating a list of question or themes and attempting to get their respondents to open up and give more than pat answers. The researcher and respondent often engage in a 'conversation' that attempts to allow full expression.

Many methodological designs for 'finding out more' start and stop with the use of this tool. And that's fine. In-depth one on one interviewing and/or the use of focus groups can be very effective in problem analysis. In this chapter, however, I thought I'd take this a bit further and introduce you to a couple of methodological frameworks commonly used in the humanities, anthropology and psychology that are expressly designed for looking inward. They often call on in-depth interviewing – but offer a more defined context for using this data collection method.

Exploring cultural realities: using ethnographic techniques

We don't always understand why people do the things they do, or why they react in certain ways. And I think this is because we don't all share the same frame of reference, or have the same reality. I remember one tutor who was brilliant at drawing this out. He asked our students, 'What do you think of pigs? Good or bad?' He then got them fiercely debating and defending their porcine opinions – and just as people started to get frustrated, he yelled out 'Stop! Now picture your pig – what do you see?' Well, some saw Porky, and quite a few pictured Babe or Wilbur. Others pictured wild boars, or fat, dirty, smelly farmyard swine rolling in the mud. Another told us of the evil pigs from an animated version of George Orwell's *Animal Farm*. Another had his Vietnamese potbelly in mind. He then asked the students how they could expect to argue and end up on the same page, if they (a) didn't start on the same page and (b) didn't recognize the highly distinct frames of reference in operation even for a simple concept like 'pig'.

157

key concept ✱

Realities, particularly cultural realities, can be distinct – and building empathetic understandings is sometimes difficult – but I'd argue essential. Think about the goals associated with researching real-world problems. What we are after is problem understanding that can aid in problem resolution. What we are after is data or information that can help us target strategies for change. But to be able to do this, and be able to do this well, we need to appreciate a problem situation as it is understood by the people most affected by it.

Take, for example, the custom of arranged marriages. Many Westerners are quick to judge and see such marriages as bizarre and even backward. Marriage without a foundation of love and free choice seems unfathomable. But cultural realities can differ and in certain cultures, economic, educational, social and cultural compatibility are seen to be as important to a marriage as is love and attraction. There is even a presumption that parents might know best (now you know you're not in the West; most Western teenagers don't trust their parents to choose their day's outfit, let alone their lifelong spouse).

Now this doesn't mean that arranged marriages are not problematic. But it does highlight that if your goal is understanding the difficulties associated with such marriages, you would need to recognize and control for your own culturally derived biases and assumptions. If you wanted to work towards change, you would need to understand the situation from within the cultural framework in which it sits.

A really good book or a good movie can do this. It will take you inside a world or a culture you have not experienced and do not understand. But when you leave the theatre, or shut the cover, you feel a new sense of appreciation for the distinct reality of others. In the world of research, our attempt to get to this level of understanding is 'ethnography'.

> *Ethnography:* To 'write a culture'. Exploration of a cultural group in a bid to understand, discover, describe and interpret a way of life from the point of view of its participants.

Using ethnographic techniques

Ethnographers attempt to understand the realties of a particular cultural group through deep, persistent and prolonged engagement within a natural setting. Credible ethnographic studies require researchers to go below the surface, and break through the pleasantries, and this requires a high level of access as well as the ability to build trust and rapport. It's therefore not unusual to find ethnographers working with groups, environments or communities that they belong to or have established connections with.

The goal of ethnography is thick description and rich interpretation, so few ethnographers would limit themselves to only one method of data collection. Most will use an array of tools, including participant observation, in-depth unstructured interviews (often conducted as conversation) and unobtrusive methods such as document analysis (see Chapter 6 for full discussion of data collection methods). In ethnography, data collection often continues until 'saturation' – that is, until new data no longer sheds new light.

Now while it's possible to generate quantitative data (perhaps collected through a small survey), most ethnographic data is likely to be qualitative so that the richness of the cultural realities being explored can be fully described.

Applied Example 7.3 provides an insight into the use of ethnographic techniques to build a rich and empathetic picture of a 'problem' situation.

Applied Example 7.3   A View from the Inside – Life in a College Dorm

Freedom at last

Life in a college dorm. Name me one living arrangement that could be less conducive for study. You are away from home, often for the first time, you have virtually unlimited freedom and you are surrounded by people your own age – who have one common purpose … no not study, but to have a really good time. Sounds perfect doesn't it?

The culture that exists within some college dorms, residential halls, fraternities and sororities, however, can be a real worry. Hazing (humiliating initiation rites and practices), sexism, racism, binge/forced drinking and sexual assault can somehow exist within a culture that is still highly appealing to students.

A female student of mine certainly found this to be the case when she moved into a residential hall in her first year of university. Now in this particular environment, the culture was strongly influenced by a long, rich and celebrated history of life on the land, mateship and rugby. The place was steeped in agricultural heritage and the glory of past and present sporting victories. The first women entered the university in the early 1970s, yet the culture remained one that most would consider highly patriarchal.

Life in this student's first year at university was great – new friends, parties every night and even a new boyfriend on the rugby team. But as rich and rewarding as this experience was, there were things about the culture that began to niggle, and then worry, and as time went on even offend, her. Yet loyalties to the place, and to the culture, remained strong. And by the end of her undergraduate career she was a young woman torn.

(Continued)

Applied Example 7.3   (Continued)

Outsider judgement

Now understanding and judging this culture from the outside had been done many times, but any attempts to work towards radical change had consistently failed. It was as though people from the outside and those on the inside spoke two different languages. Those on the outside could only see and discuss a dangerous, racist and misogynist culture. While those on the inside defended a culture of mateship and loyalty with ferocity and passion. Insiders felt misunderstood and threatened. And when you feel that way two things tend to happen. First you become defensive. Second, internal bonds can strengthen as you face a common enemy.

Insider insights

In what can only be described as an exceptionally brave move, this student decided to undertake an Honours thesis exploring the richness and complexity of this culture from a highly privileged position on the inside. And while her desire to explore the culture was driven by what was becoming more clearly defined to her as a 'problem', she was determined to suspend judgement, and use an ethnographic approach that could help her understand the culture and the situation from the perspective of those within it. Her goal was to look at the reality of the culture as it was lived by its members.

So she engaged in 'participant observation'. She lived and learned through both intuitive and systematic observation and reflection. She kept a journal, conducted in-depth informal conversational interviews with key informants, and really listened. Her goal was to build a rich picture that could help outsiders understand a distinct cultural reality.

A rich picture emerges

The understandings she was able to offer at the conclusion of her study were highly interesting and full of critical insight. She richly and empathetically described: a distinct culture with a powerful belief system that values what outsiders so often judge and condemn; processes of socialization highly effective in inculcating its members; the power of outside threats to simultaneously raise defences and strengthen commitment; as well as a lack of both insider and outsider empathy.

A word of caution

You have to go into this type of study with your eyes wide open. This study certainly had its fair share of challenges for our student. There were times when she felt highly disloyal, times when she felt threatened, and many times when she felt distressed. But she persevered because she knew she could make an original and valuable contribution to problem understanding.

The strengths and challenges of ethnographic approaches

Ethnographic techniques offer an approach for delving into the values, beliefs and practices of cultural groups through thick description of real people in natural settings. It also highlights the importance of multiple worldviews and can help build understandings from the perspective of the researched.

There are, however, a number of challenges associated with ethnographic approaches. As a researcher using ethnographic techniques, you will need to reflexively consider and skilfully negotiate: any preconceived notions or biases you may hold; potential difficulties in gaining a high level of access; the challenge of building trust; the potentially high emotional costs for both you and the 'researched'; and the potential for you to have an effect on research participants. You will also need to guard against 'homogenization', which is the tendency to give minimal recognition to divergences within a particular group. Now while there are no easy answers for overcoming such challenges, Chapter 4 does offer some strategies for enhancing your ability to ensure integrity, and thus credibility, in the research process.

Ethnography vs. ethnographic approaches

I don't know how many of you will aspire to become true 'ethnographers', but I do know that problem understanding can be enhanced by everyday real-world researchers taking some of the theory and techniques of ethnography on board. We have a tendency to think that the rest of the world operates as we do – but ethnographic approaches help us stay true in representing the reality of cultural groups that may not be well understood. Surely a worthwhile goal when attempting 'to find out more'.

Understanding lived experience: drawing on phenomenology

Is it worth knowing what it feels like to win ... or to lose? Is it worth understanding the lived experience of struggling with breast cancer? Is it worth knowing what it feels like to be at the bottom of the class? Now I'm not talking about cause and effect. I'm not asking why someone won or lost, or the implications of cancer, or why someone might struggle at school. I'm strictly talking about 'phenomenon' or 'lived experience' – what it feels like for them.

My answer? Well I think understanding lived experience is absolutely vital. Look, one of the key premises of adult education is that you need to start where people are. And I have certainly found this to be the case – not only in my own teaching, but in conflict mediation, change agency, situation improvement and problem resolution. If you want to be truly effective in getting people to move from A to B you need to start at A, to understand A and to appreciate A. And not just intellectually, but emotionally as well.

I have a niece who suffers from anorexia nervosa. I don't see her very often, but we got together at a wedding a few years ago and she told me a bit about her struggles, her self-image, her counselling and her various therapists. Something about the conversation led me to ask, 'If there was a magic pill that could cure you overnight – would you take it?' She thought about it for a few seconds and said 'No, I wouldn't … they all think I want to get better'.

Well then, what I want to know is how can 'they' help her? There doesn't seem to be any appreciation for her lived experience. They've got A wrong, so there isn't really any chance of helping her move from A to B.

If you want to know why athletes are willing to take steroids – you need to understand the lived reality of winning and losing. If you want to help someone through breast cancer – you need to know how they are experiencing the phenomenon. If you want to understand how you can help motivate struggling students – you need to know what the lived experience is like for them at the bottom of the class. And if you want to help my niece in her struggle to overcome anorexia, you need to appreciate her headspace – even if it makes no sense to you.

This is the goal of phenomenology. Rather than ask what causes X, or what is X, phenomenology explores the lived experience of X.

> *Phenomenology:* **Study of phenomena as they present themselves in individuals' direct awareness and experience.**

Drawing on phenomenological approaches

The key outcome of phenomenological studies is rich phenomenological descriptions. In fact, the goal is to produce descriptions so full of lush imagery that it allows others to share in how a particular phenomenon is experienced.

The process of generating such descriptions generally involves sourcing people who have experienced a particular phenomenon and conducting one or more in-depth interviews with each participant. The number of respondents can vary – but given that there is likely to be more than one way to experience any particular phenomenon, you generally need to conduct a sufficient number of interviews for drawing out variation. Interviewers often look for 'saturation', that is, additional interviews no longer add new perspective.

The goal of the interviews, most often conducted as a 'conversation', is to draw out rich descriptions of lived experience. In other words, you want your respondents to tell you what a phenomenon feels like, what it reminds them of, and how they would describe it. Respondents are then encouraged to further reflect on various aspects of their descriptions. This often involves digging below the surface of words to understand the meaning behind them. For example, the phenomenon of 'winning', first described as 'fantastic', might be further described as 'like being on the top of the world' or 'I know I have worth'. In this way, the researcher and the researched create a narrative that is both descriptive and interpretive; and is often rich, poetic and full of metaphor.

It is worth mentioning that in addition to, or instead of, conducting interviews, researchers can also explore pre-produced texts. Beautiful, rich phenomenological descriptions abound in letters, journals, books, movies, poetry and music. Take for example, the phenomenon of 'going into battle'. Imagine the rich, candid and chilling descriptions you might be able to gather just from reading letters home.

Now once you have generated (or located) your descriptions, and you feel you have reached a point of saturation, the next step is synthesis. The goal here is to explore commonalities and divergences in the experience of the same phenomenon. You are looking for the range of experiences related to the phenomenon itself. This is generally done by cycling between the texts and eventuating themes in a bid to reduce unimportant dissimilarities and integrate the essential nature of various descriptions.

I know this might sound a bit confusing, but I'm hoping Applied Example 7.4, which is drawn from my own PhD study, will shed some light here.

Applied Example 7.4   Losing Faith: Understanding the Phenomenon of 'Apostasy'

Off to the Emerald Isle
When I was an undergraduate in the mid '80s, I decided I needed a break from my life at Rutgers University, so I became an exchange student to Ireland. I attended University College Galway for a term and made some terrific friends. Now I was actually raised Catholic (I am an O'Leary after all), but I was somewhat jaded by years of Catholic schooling. I no longer believed in God, but then again neither did many of my friends back home. It wasn't that big a deal.

The reality of 'God'
But I found that Catholicism was a very big deal in Galway. I found myself in a culture where God really did seem omnipresent. My new friends not only believed in God, he was actually a part of how they processed almost everything going on in their world. I remember one of my friends saying, 'You must think us quite daft – with all this God and religion shite!' And I thought, 'No, actually I don't.' I said something like, 'Just because I don't believe in God, doesn't mean he isn't real for you. You go to his house every Sunday. You talk to him every night. He comforts you when you're sad. He even manages to keep you a virgin! What could be more real?'

Now I wouldn't have been able to articulate it at the time, but living with these girls (as they called themselves) and attempting to understand their lived experience, was a phenomenological study. The truth of God didn't matter. That could be put aside, or as they say in phenomenology, 'bracketed'. All that mattered – what was real – was their lived experience.

(Continued)

Applied Example 7.4   (Continued)

Exploring 'apostasy'

My interest in religion continued into my graduate studies and I decided to explore the process of giving up faith (apostasy) for my PhD dissertation. I was determined to use both quantitative data (my training and comfort zone) and qualitative data (I recognized the limitations of quantitative data in capturing the rich descriptions I was after). I wanted to really understand what it felt like to lose faith.

Data collection

In order to understand the disaffiliation process, I conducted in-depth interviews with 80 individuals who were raised Christian but had become atheists ('apostates'). Forty of these apostates had given up faith prior to 1967, while the other 40 had given up faith after 1982. My premise was that the experience of losing faith had changed over time. Those who gave up faith prior to the cultural revolution of the '60s would have had a different and more significant type of struggle than those who had given up faith more recently. As they say, changing your religion is now as easy as changing your socks.

Data analysis

While I found the interviews easy to conduct (there were some fascinating stories), I had a hard time figuring out what to do with the data. Finding helpful and consistent advice related to phenomenological 'methods' wasn't easy. In the end, I simply read my transcriptions and listened to my tapes over and over again. I was looking for themes ... and eventually I found them.

Findings

At some stage I realized I was listening to three distinct experiences of apostasy. The first was a journey of resentful reaction ('anomic' apostasy). For individuals who went through this experience, the phenomenon of losing faith was steeped in anger and hostility. They were mad at God, angry at the church, and had decided that enough was enough. Interestingly, the majority of these apostates came from the older generation. The second experience of losing faith was a more introspective journey ('egoistic' apostasy). Individuals who had this experience had lost their faith because they could not see the point. They were lost and confused in a world full of injustice, inequity, suffering and a lack of humanity. Many described a journey that spiralled into depression. Apostates who had this phenomenological experience

Applied Example 7.4   (Continued)

were equally distributed across both cohorts. Finally, there were apostates whose journey reflected spiritual exploration ('postmodern' apostasy). These apostates, drawn mainly from the younger cohort, did not go through the angst described above. The process was more intellectual and involved a quest for meaning.

Significance

Now you may debate whether apostasy is a problem or an answer, but the Christian Research Association of Australia, which still sells a short monograph of this work on the Internet (O'Leary 1999), certainly sees disaffiliation as a problem. And they very quickly recognized the contribution that such phenomenological understandings might make in their attempts to reverse Christian disaffiliation trends.

The strengths and challenges of phenomenology

I think the main strength of phenomenology is that it offers a way of exploring this thing called 'phenomena'; something I believe is highly important in a bid 'to find out more'. Yet phenomena are often ignored when researching real-world problems. But think about the value of being able to understand and describe lived experience. How much more insightful could change initiatives or problem resolution strategies be if we had this level of understanding? Whether working with students, patients, staff, teenagers, the elderly, etc., if we could capture the essence of their lived experience, we would have a real advantage in working towards situation improvement.

But as with anything worth doing, it's not necessarily easy. Literature on phenomenology tends to be thick and philosophical, and doesn't offer a lot of clear guidance on actual 'methods'. You probably won't get much advice from research textbooks either. Few texts cover the topic at all, and those that do, don't do it very well. This leaves you with two options. The first is to delve into the literature (I offer a few starting points at the end of the chapter) and really embrace this approach. The second is to do less reading but practise thinking phenomenologically. I did not come across and delve into literature on phenomenology until after I realized I had already designed it in my own study. Sometimes practical real-world insights and the ability to think outside the square can be enough to get going in new and exciting directions.

FURTHER READING

Readings related to **looking outward** include works on *sampling* (see end of Chapter 5), *unobtrusive methods* (see end of Chapter 6) and *surveying* (also offered at the end of Chapter 6). Readings related to **looking inward** include literature that covers *in-depth interviewing* (see end of Chapter 6) and *case studies* (see end of Chapter 5). Readings on *rapid appraisal, ethnography* and *phenomenology* are offered below.

Rapid appraisal strategies
Cornwall, A. and Pratt, G. (eds) (2004) *Pathways to Participation: Reflections on Participatory Rural Appraisal.* Warwickshire: ITDG Publishing.
Estrella, M. (ed.) (2000) *Learning from Change: Issues and Experiences in Participatory Monitoring and Evaluation.* Sterling, VA: Stylus Publishers.
Kumar, S. and Chambers, R. (2003) *Methods for Community Participation: A Complete Guide for Practitioners.* Warwickshire: ITDG Publishing.

Ethnography
Fetterman, D. M. (1997) *Ethnography: Step-by-Step.* London: Sage.
Geertz, C. (1973) *The Interpretation of Cultures.* New York: Basic Books.
Grills, S. (ed.) (1998) *Doing Ethnographic Research.* London: Sage.
Schensul, J. and LeCompte, D. (eds) (1999) *The Ethnographer's Toolkit* (7 vols). London: Sage.

Phenomenology
Berger, P. and Luckmann, T. (1967) *The Social Construction of Reality: A Treatise in the Sociology of Knowledge.* New York: Anchor.
Moran, D. (2000) *Introduction to Phenomenology.* London: Routledge.
Moustakas, C. (2000) *Phenomenological Research Methods.* London: Sage.
Sokolowski, R. (2000) *Introduction to Phenomenology.* New York: Cambridge University Press.

Chapter Summary

- When researching real-world problems, a clear, consistent and worthwhile goal is 'to find out more'. Data derived through problem analysis can be central to evidence-based decision making.

- Because problems tend to be so complex, it can be a challenge to narrow down methodological options. Consider whether your research question is suited to a 'quick sketch' as offered by rural appraisal strategies, or a more 'detailed portrait' as offered by a case study.

- Research questions can also lead you to look outward towards broad societal trends, attitudes and opinions, or inward where you will need to delve into the intricacies of your problem situation.

- A question that has you looking outward may see you turning your attention to the exploration of existing data and archival records. The challenge here is getting the data into a shape and form that will allow it to address your research questions.

- Outward exploration might also see you generating primary data. This is often done through a survey process that involves sampling a population and distributing, collecting and analysing questionnaires.

- Inward exploration is often reliant on the use of in-depth interviews. Such interviews may be the heart of the research design – or they may sit under ethnographic, phenomenological, or case study approaches.

- Building rich, empathetic, problem understandings from the perspective of those facing problems should be a central goal in real-world research. Ethnographic research techniques can help you in this endeavour.

- The goal of ethnographic research is thick description reliant on multiple methods such as participant observation, in-depth unstructured interviews and unobtrusive methods such as document analysis.

- An important goal in finding out more is attempting to understand how individuals experience phenomena. Rather than ask what causes X, or what is X, the goal of phenomenology is to explore the lived experience of X.

- The key outcome of phenomenological studies is rich phenomenological descriptions that allow others to share in how a particular phenomenon is experienced.

167

8
The Quest for Solutions

Chapter Preview
When the Research Goal is 'To Search for Solutions'
Assessing Needs and Visioning Futures
Exploring Potential Programmes, Interventions and Services
Examining the Feasibility of Change Initiatives

'If politics is the art of the possible, research is surely the art of the soluble.'

– Sir Peter Medawar

WHEN THE RESEARCH GOAL IS 'TO SEARCH FOR SOLUTIONS'

Do you remember the Rubik's cube? Well it was one of the fantastic fads of the early 1980s (also the decade responsible for the 'pet rock'). They sold millions of the things, which is quite amazing since it didn't come with a solution and it was virtually impossible to figure out for yourself. You could play with the stupid cube for hours on end, day after day, and basically go around in circles. Most gave up – but some were determined to beat the cube.

Now to complete the cube you actually had to work through three distinct steps. First, you had to know your goal. You had to be able to vision the solution and picture the completed cube. No problems here – everyone knew that the six sides of the completed cube would be a single colour each – if memory serves, blue, green, yellow, red, orange and white.

The second step involved finding a solution. Now given that teams of mathematicians from the most prestigious universities struggled to come up with the answer – you probably weren't going to get very far on your own. So you had to get your hands on a proven solution. Now this fad predated the Internet, so most had to resort to buying one of the many solution books that popped up on the

168

market. Another possibility was to have someone who had bought and mastered a solution give you a hands-on demonstration.

The third step was assessing the feasibility of adopting and using your solution. Even with the answer in hand, most gave up before mastering the cube; too confusing, too frustrating, not enough patience. If you had a solution, then yes it was possible to complete the cube – but certainly not practical for the majority. In fact, a much more feasible solution was to get out your tweezers, peel off the coloured stickers and attempt to meticulously get them back in place. Of course this doesn't work so well when you drop one of them on the carpet and it's suddenly full of dirt, dust, and dog hair!

The point here is that questions can sometimes revolve around solutions rather than problems. You may feel you know all you need to know about the problem situation at hand. As with the Rubik's cube, it is laid out in front of you. The bigger challenge is finding 'answers'.

So a legitimate goal in researching real-world problems is 'to search for solutions'. A well-designed solution-based research study can support the three steps generally involved in working towards answers. They can help:

1. Determine what others want to accomplish or what is being strived towards. In researching real-world problems, this might involve assessing needs, visioning solutions and futures, and asking what the situation would look like if problems were resolved.
2. Assess what answers and solutions might already be out there. This can involve asking if there are any tried and true options or if there are any exciting new and/or original prospects. Success stories, as well as pitfalls, can also be explored.
3. Assess practicality and feasibility. The goal here is to figure out whether particular solutions will work in your context. This may involve asking if a solution is appropriate, if it is workable, or if it is likely to be accepted by relevant stakeholders.

Possibilities and practicalities

The aim of this chapter is to work you through research strategies that can help you search for solutions by assessing needs, visioning futures, exploring options and assessing feasibility. Now in many ways it would be nice if each of these goals directly aligned itself with a particular methodological approach, but that's simply not the case. Researching real-world problems means that contingencies are many and possibilities are broad. So as discussed in the earlier chapters of this book, it's really a matter of you as a researcher being able to clearly articulate what it is you want to know, that is, your research question (see Chapter 2), who might hold the answer to that question, namely, your potential respondents (see Chapter 5), and working through logical, feasible and practical methodological design (see Chapters 3 and 6), in an ethical and credible manner (see Chapter 4). Without a doubt, your ability to think both creatively and strategically will be the key to defining the approach that is best for your particular question, in your particular context.

That said, there are certain research approaches that have proven themselves to be particularly effective in meeting research goals related to the search for solutions. So in this chapter, I will endeavour to offer some relevant examples and highlight some of the strategies that experienced researchers tend to call on to assist them in this quest.

ASSESSING NEEDS AND VISIONING FUTURES

'I know what's best for you.' Whether that statement comes from a parent, doctor, boss, or teacher, it is a highly annoying phrase that no one wants to hear. But for most of modern history this is how those with power interacted with those 'under' them. It may not have always been articulated – but it was a far-reaching sentiment. Governments, teachers, parents and doctors knew best. And they knew what was best for you.

Thankfully, this is starting to shift. Those in power are starting to recognize the importance of listening and respecting the voices of those for whom they have some responsibility. But change can be slow, so we still bump up against the tendency of those in power to know what is best and to propose solutions for others without bothering to ask and without bothering to listen. From aid agencies to the medical profession, from school systems to the home front, there are endless examples of top-down, imposed answers that simply don't work because those at the receiving end are misunderstood or ignored. No one asked, no one listened.

But it is well worth listening – especially if you're after sustainable change. Sure, we can tell others what we 'know' they should do, but the chances are they won't do it; they'll make a token or half-hearted effort; or they'll make a start but they won't keep it up. If it's not part of *their* vision or *their* goals, it probably won't be taken up for the long term – and shouldn't that be an overarching goal in the search for solutions?

Two of the most common approaches for working towards solutions that reflect the needs, desires and goals of relevant stakeholders are assessing needs and visioning futures:

1. *Assessing needs* – if you want to value the voice of those who will be affected by solutions, you need to explore perceived or felt needs. Now you might think that if you really understand a problem, you will automatically understand the needs of those affected by it. But this isn't always the case. For example … she says, 'I feel fat, Sam is now six months old and I still can't get into my old clothes.' He assumes her need is 'to go on a diet' and foolishly

tells her this. Not a wise move. If he had asked, he might have found out that her needs are to have a sympathetic ear or to hear how good she still looks – saving them both from a nasty little domestic situation.

The same is true when working within an organization or a community group. The problem may be defined, say high turnover at a workplace. But this doesn't mean you necessarily know and understand the needs of those who are thinking about leaving. You might assume that the most pressing need is higher pay. But employees might be looking for more flexible hours, on-site child care facilities, career advancement opportunities, or a change in management (style and/or personnel).

2. *Visioning futures* – in order to work towards solutions, it's important to have a vision or picture of the future. In other words, to know what you're striving for. This means exploring the overarching goals and desires of those at the coalface. What image of a problem-free environment do your stakeholders hold?

Keep in mind that visioning futures not only explores possibilities, it can also build commitment to a common goal. For example, at Yanuca in 1994 the Ministers of Health from island nations across the Pacific came together and explored their vision of a healthy future. They explored opportunities and concepts of the future related to family, social and physical environments, lifestyles and health. Together they created, and became committed to, the first 'Healthy Islands' vision:

> Healthy islands should be a place where children are nourished in body and mind, environments invite learning and leisure; people work and age with dignity; and ecological balance is a source of pride. (World Health Organization Regional Office for the Western Pacific 1995)

Using appropriate tools

You can assess needs and vision futures in any number of ways, but the key is finding the right tool for both your goals and your context. I'm going to concentrate here (and in Applied Example 8.1) on three distinct research strategies that experienced researchers often call on when attempting to understand stakeholder needs and vision futures. These methods are surveys, focus groups and public forums.

Conducting a survey

Surveys are quite common in needs assessment and can be highly effective if your aim is broad representation of a community, organization, or cultural group. It allows you to ask a range of stakeholders to name, confirm and prioritize their needs. They thereby provide 'hard data' that researchers can use to:

- make convincing arguments to governments/funding bodies
- settle any controversy about needs
- raise community awareness

Chapter 6 covers the survey process is some detail, so I will not rehash that here. But I will stress the importance of thinking through how you will capture needs in your survey. For example, say you did want to know what would make people more content in a workplace with a notoriously high turnover rate. Your insights might lead you to believe that relevant needs include higher pay, more flexible hours, on-site child care facilities, career advancement opportunities, change in management personnel and a change in management style.

Your options for confirming these insights and capturing other needs include:

- listing 'needs' and asking your respondents to tick those they agree with
- listing 'needs' and asking your respondents to put them in rank order
- listing 'needs' and asking your respondents if they agree/disagree using a Likert scale: 1 = strongly disagree, 2 = disagree, 3 = unsure, 4 = agree, 5 = strongly agree
- leaving the question open so that respondents can write down anything they choose

Now each of these approaches has advantages and disadvantages. The first three use lists that can give respondents ideas and spur on thinking. Using such a list in conjunction with a simple tick is quick and easy for respondents, but does not provide an indication of prioritization. Rank ordering accomplishes this, but respondents can find items difficult to rank if lists exceed six or seven. Likert scaling can overcome both of these above dilemmas – but there's often a tendency for respondents to choose the same response throughout a question set. A further dilemma with all 'lists' is that they can limit the imagination of your respondents. Even with the inclusion of an 'other' option, responses will tend to centre around your own preconceived notions rather than the range of possibilities open to your respondents. To overcome this, you have the option of leaving the question open so that preconceived notions do not impact on the survey. But this does not allow you to give prompts, and you may find responses lacking in breadth and depth.

So what should you do? Well, it really depends on the context, your respondents and the circumstances at play. There are, however, two strategies you can call on to help you make your decision. The first is to do your homework and know your background. Having strong contextual knowledge can give you insights into the best way to proceed. For example, if you are familiar with the literature on a particular topic, you may feel comfortable and confident in providing a list of options. On the other hand, if little is known about current needs for your particular situation, you may decide that open answers are most appropriate.

The second strategy is to run a pilot – something advised for all surveys. A pilot gives you the opportunity to try a few options and debrief with a trial group of respondents in order to get a sense of what will work best in your main survey.

Facilitating focus groups

While focus groups can be used for any number of research purposes, they are highly effective when your goal involves getting a group of individuals to work together towards a common purpose. So while they can certainly work if you're conducting needs assessment, they really come into their own when attempting to work with a group to vision a future.

Focus groups can range in size. They generally have more than three members (anything less and the advantages of the one on one interview tend to outweigh the advantages of using a group) and less than 15 (anything more and it can be really difficult to manage). The idea is to facilitate discussion and provide a comfortable forum for contributions from all.

When used in market research (something quite common) focus groups are generally asked a series of questions in an interview format with group members encouraged to debate and discuss each issue, topic or question raised by the interviewer/facilitator. When focus groups are used in visioning futures, however, it is quite common to go beyond traditional interview techniques and use more creative tools for illuminating vision. The interviewer, whose main role is to facilitate, may ask key questions, but this is often done in conjunction with strategies designed to encourage creativity. Such approaches can include:

- *Visualization* – researchers ask group members to close their eyes and visualize the future. Researchers attempt to facilitate the process by asking question such as: what does it look like; what are people doing; how does the place/situation feel? Visualization can be a very effective tool at the start of a visioning process.
- *Brainstorming* – researchers attempt to capture all thoughts without judgement. This is often done using a whiteboard with researchers asking group members to put all ideas forward no matter how silly or trivial they may seem. Everything is noted, anyone and everyone is heard, and nothing is discounted.
- *Mind mapping* – often a step that follows on from brainstorming, mind mapping also calls for a wide array of ideas, but organizes ideas and 'maps' them in order to draw out connections and build themes. This process can be facilitated by the researcher or can be facilitated solely within the group. As shown in Figure 8.1, words, ideas, pictures and symbols can all be used to capture a rich picture.
- *Poetry, song, story and metaphor* – who says academic writing is the fount of all knowledge? Researchers who want to encourage creativity will often offer respondents the option of capturing their ideas using more creative forms of writing.

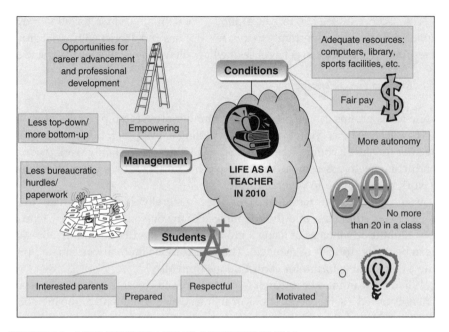

FIGURE 8.1   MIND MAPPING LIFE AS A TEACHER IN 2010

Holding a public forum

While public forums can be useful in problem identification, they can also be highly effective in gathering and capturing the needs, hopes, desire and vision of a residential, cultural or workplace oriented 'community'. Public forums are particularly effective for situations where interest and even passion in your issue or topic already exists. And if well publicized, they allow a range of interested parties to have a voice.

The potential for a large turnout, however, means you will need to call on all your organizational skills to pull it off. Holding a public forum involves:

- finding and organizing an appropriate meeting place
- reaching your 'community members' through adequate publicity and advertising
- training strong, yet sensitive facilitators
- engaging discussion leaders who are willing to listen to and respect opinions that might conflict with their own
- sensitively introducing your issue/agenda
- using a range of tools for capturing discussion and gathering rich data

Once the meeting is under way you can use any number of strategies and tools for assessing needs and visioning futures. Surveys, focus groups and interviews can all be conducted within the parameters of a public forum.

Applied Example 8.1   *Using a Variety of Methods to Assess Needs and Vision Futures*

Conducting a needs assessment survey

I once had a Master's student who was interested in removing a prolific noxious weed from a local community. He was passionate, as were many of his friends and community contacts. His goal was to do something about the problem. So he organized a community forum. The turnout, however, was really disappointing. He persisted and decided to organize a well-publicized community clean-up, but again turnout was low – hard to understand when he knew just how pressing the issue was. If the community did not get a handle on this weed soon, several native species were going to be under threat. Why wasn't the community responding?

Well, this student was a passionate environmental activist, as were many of his friends – yet his expectation was that the general community would prioritize this issue as much as he did. I suggested he might be working under a false assumption and that he consider conducting a community needs assessment for his research methods project in order to shed some light on the issue. He agreed.

The student ended up sending out a survey that covered needs related to education, health care, employment, housing, transportation and environment (including the removal of noxious weeds) to every household (approx. 400) in the target community. Only 33 surveys were returned, so he decided to canvass people coming out of the local post office. He eventually gathered 157 completed surveys.

When he compiled the results he was surprised to find that environmental concerns were relatively low on the community agenda. The need for better public transport, something he only added to the survey in a late draft, actually headed up community concerns. He also found that those who did prioritize environmental issues gave local needs, such as removal of noxious weeds, lower prioritization than more global needs, for example controlling greenhouse gas emissions. In fact, noxious weed removal was cited as a top three priority by only 12 households – and this student estimated that he probably knew someone in at least 10 of these households personally, which he realized could be why his community perception was so skewed.

(Continued)

Applied Example 8.1   (Continued)

Using focus groups

Empowerment. The opportunity and ability to contribute to one's own future should not be underestimated. Having some say in your own destiny is an essential ingredient in a search for fulfilment and well-being.

As well as a strong sentiment in social psychology literature, this is also the belief of one of my students who works with adults with acquired brain injury (individuals who have experienced trauma to the brain resulting in physical, cognitive, and/or emotional effects including fatigue, memory loss, lack of fine motor skills and depression).

This student was quite frustrated by the patronizing approaches to care she saw utilized by both medical and government sectors when dealing with community-based individuals (those who are living outside a hospital setting either in shared homes, supported homes, with a family, or on their own) with acquired brain injury (ABI). She believed that the practice, programmes and policy currently dictating approaches to care did not take the perceived or felt needs of those they were trying to help into account. When working with these individuals she sensed, and was told, of both frustration and disempowerment.

She firmly believed that the inclusion of individuals with ABI in both the assessment of needs and the development of care plans was an essential ingredient for a fulfilling existence within a community setting. Accordingly, she decided to explore whether the use of focus groups that included a range of stakeholders (including individuals with ABI) could better identify needs leading to more effective, sustainable and self-empowering care plans.

She facilitated a number of focus groups that centred on empathetic listening. All stakeholders were given an opportunity to be heard and all opinions were valued – particularly those of the ABI individual. Needs were first identified and the groups then worked together to develop (and action) appropriate and sustainable plans.

Holding a public forum

For her PhD dissertation, a friend of mine wanted to explore the impact of tourism on local communities and decided to focus her study on the Southern New Jersey coast. In the course of her study, she found out that one shore town was planning to hold a public forum to better understand community needs and discuss a new community vision. She offered to work with the forum committee on various aspects of data collection and was able to negotiate the use of the data in her thesis.

The town's leaders, most of whom owned local businesses supported by the tourism sector, organized the forum under the theme 'a new town vision'. The sessions included perceived community needs such as:

Applied Example 8.1   (Continued)

- increasing the young adult market
- attracting young families
- keeping the tourism dollar in town
- promoting a longer season (e.g. Indian summer)
- making the town's gateway more attractive
- changing liquor licensing laws
- improving public transportation to and from the town

The forum was well publicized and there was a fairly large turnout at the town civic centre. The mayor welcomed all, gave some background to the forum, and explained that the forum would use a number of facilitators and focus groups to discuss particular topics before a more general session would come together to discuss a town vision.

Well, according to my friend, the mayor was quite taken aback when his call for initial comments opened up a barrage of criticism. As it turns out, a number of community members were quite fed up with the 'tourism' agenda, and how completely it was reflected in the organization of the forum. While they could see the importance of tourism to the local economy, they wanted the forum to reflect a broader range of concerns and needs. They were dedicated to developing a vision that would respect and value the local host community as well as the town's natural environment. They argued that tourism should be but one dimension of the town's vision.

The mayor was quick to respond and immediately called for new thematic areas to be added to the agenda. New focus groups were organized and many in the community felt that the forum came to reflect broader community concerns and needs – and not just the needs of the business sector.

EXPLORING POTENTIAL PROGRAMMES, INTERVENTIONS AND SERVICES

You know, chances are you're not the first person to tackle the problem you want to address. Someone, somewhere, someplace has probably tried something. Whether it be different types of practice, new and innovative programmes, cutting-edge policy, or even bold legislation, there's a good chance that an attempt has been made to alleviate and address the problem at hand.

This means you don't always need to start at square one; you don't have to reinvent the wheel. Sometimes your focus will be on finding out what others have done – and if possible, whether or not it worked. A legitimate, yet sometimes underutilized research question, is 'What solutions are already out there?'

Drawing on 'traditional' methods

Okay, as with any research goal there are a number of ways you can collect the data you need. In fact, four of the five data collection methods discussed in Chapter 6 can be readily called on in your quest to find out about potential solutions. What will be most appropriate for your study will be determined by your own context and circumstances. Now while details of these methods can be found in Chapter 6, I'll briefly discuss each here in relation to the opportunities and challenges they present when searching for solutions.

- *Interviewing* – a good way to find out what others have attempted is to ask. If you have the opportunity to sit down and talk with someone who has tried something you think might work in your context, an interview can be highly effective for gathering the data you need. There are, however, two prerequisites here. The first is that you are able to identify those who have attempted a relevant solution. Second, you will need to have access to those individuals – which can limit your geographic range.
- *Surveying* – conducting a survey is one way to get around geographic constraints and reach a larger number of individuals or organizations, but you still need to be able to identify this population. Another difficulty here is getting people to respond. Some will not want to tell you what they've been doing – they may think it's none of your business. Others simply couldn't be bothered. A survey is not likely to work in this context unless you do a lot of homework and groundwork. Grease the wheels, so to speak, and try to make personal contacts. You'll need to gain some commitment to the survey's completion.
- *Observation* – if you are looking at physical solutions, for example, how a new playground is set out, or perhaps alternative classroom layouts, observation can be an effective tool. You will, however, have geographic constraints. So it is a method best suited to studies where the solutions being explored are both physical and local.
- *Document analysis* – I think this is a particularly effective method in the search for solutions. The bureaucratic world in which we live means that most of us are swamped with paperwork. There is a good chance that an attempt at a solution has been documented. As discussed in Chapter 6 and the section that follows, the trick here will be finding, accessing and finally evaluating these documents.

Utilizing the Internet

I cannot believe what is out there on the information superhighway. In short, everything; an unbelievable amount of data. The Internet has, in fact, become the fount of all knowledge. Students spend less and less time at the library and more and more time online. And whether I like it or not, each year more student references start with 'www'. If it's not online, it's not in their essay.

So how effective is the Internet for gathering primary data in a research context? Well, while you'll need to exercise a fair bit of criticality (there is a lot of crap out there on the Net), it can be an exceptional tool. You see, interviewing, surveying and observation rely on a local context and/or groundwork in finding the right people. Looking at documentary evidence on the Internet, however, is unobtrusive. What you are after is already out there in the public domain. In fact, the Internet is largely responsible for the creation of a global village. It still amazes me that from my own home I can access local government meeting minutes from around the world. Think of the potential in the search for solutions. As highlighted in Applied Example 8.2, you can unobtrusively search for answers that have been implemented across the globe.

Gaining access to more 'data' than you can possibly imagine will require you to:

- *Hone your search skills* – the skills discussed in searching for literature (Chapter 3) are similar to those used when searching the Internet. Basically, you need to play detective. There is no search engine that can hone in precisely on what you are after. But learning how to identify and explore potential leads is a skill worth developing. Now when it comes to non-specialist search engines, I consistently find *Google* the most powerful. *Dogpile* is also good because it accesses a number of search engines simultaneously.
- *Wade through a lot of garbage* – the fact that it's all out there on the Web is both a strength and a weakness. In any one search there are likely to be the things you are after, as well as a whole lot of stuff that's simply not relevant. As well as attempting to narrow your search, having clear criteria, being able to quickly identify sources and assess their legitimacy, can help you wade through it all.
- *Critically assess the agenda and bias of what you find* – because the Internet has no quality control, assessing credibility is essential. Look for any biases and consider whether your sites have an agenda. Your ability to credibly draw on the data you find will be dependent on how well you can critically assess the information you come across.

Applied Example 8.2   The Sticky World of
Syringe Disposal – The Search for Solutions

The dilemma

One of the major problems with re-usable syringes, whether for legal use (e.g. immunizations or insulin) or illegal use (e.g. morphine or heroin injecting), is the spread of infections such as HIV and hepatitis. One answer to this dilemma is the mass production of disposable syringes. But of course, disposable syringes need to be disposed of. And this can be a real dilemma, particularly in developing countries where contaminated medical waste can find its way into municipal garbage dumps where people are known to scavenge and recycle. The health risks, both in terms of direct exposure and environmental contamination, are huge.

Finding solutions

The World Health Organization recently commissioned a study (with which I was involved) on options for the destruction and disposal of used injecting materials. The idea was to explore existing options and compare the strengths and weaknesses of each. Those in need of a solution could then quickly assess these options and work towards a solution.

The method

The research team decided that the best way to proceed was to source and analyse documents that discussed options for syringe disposal, as well as broader issues related to general health care waste management in developing countries. The documents selected for inclusion were broad and were chosen to represent the following contexts:

- public health and safety
- practitioner exposure to injury and/or disease
- waste management and disposal
- pollutants generated through health care activities
- alternative technologies and/or practices

Documents included published research articles, reports and conference proceedings, as well as documents produced by disposal manufacturers. Given that there were no pre-existing relationships in place with the producers of the relevant documents, the research team felt the best way to access materials was through the Internet. Searches were conducted using both general and specialist search engines.

Assessing credibility

As the authors explain, assessing the credibility of each of the documents sourced through the Internet was a high priority. They state:

Applied Example 8.2   (Continued)

---

the credibility of each document was assessed with particular attention paid to any perceived bias on the part of the author(s). The peer-review system was generally seen as a satisfactory guard against potentially biased and unreliable information from journals and conference proceedings. In the case of information provided by manufacturers, however, the authors often found themselves limited to gleaning only data related to technical specifications.

... systematic reviews made by various international coalitions such as the **World Health Organization** and **Health Care Without Harm** were treated as reliable and representative because of the largely bipartisan nature of the organizations that produced them. Potential bias that may have come from historical endorsements of any number of particular practices and technologies was overcome by viewing the materials in relation to published data from peer-reviewed sources. (Tamplin et al., 2005)

Reflections

While I was well practised at using the Internet to gather background information, this was the first study I'd been involved in that used the Internet as its main data gathering tool. And I did find it a challenge. For one, if the information you were after was somewhere on the Internet, you had to find a way to locate it. There were plenty of times when we felt like detectives following up on leads, wading through the 'hits' and assessing the evidence. Second, if a document was referred to, but was not online, we had to go back to the painstakingly slow snail mail approach. Finally, if a relevant piece of information was not even referred to on the Net, you obviously weren't going to come across it using this tool.

While no data gathering tool is perfect – Internet included – we did feel that for our particular research question, making use of the Internet was the most effective and efficient way to gather the data we were after.

EXAMINING THE FEASIBILITY OF CHANGE INITIATIVES

For every problem, there is one solution which is simple, neat and wrong.

– Henry Louis Mencken

Eureka! You have found the answer. It sounds perfect. And besides they've been doing it over in Wales for more than eight years with great success. Let's do it!

Not so fast ... just because it worked in Wales doesn't mean it will work for you. The fact of the matter is – no two contexts are identical. Both physical and cultural environments will differ. There is no guarantee that a practice, programme, intervention, or policy that worked in situation A, will work in situation B.

For example, in Fiji, an aid consultant's simple, crystal-clear answer to a village's waste management dilemma was to recommend the installation of pit toilets. He had successfully made such recommendations in the past, and felt this would solve the problem in a relatively inexpensive fashion. So the aid agency expended the necessary funds and dug the pit toilets as specified by the well-paid consultant. But as it turns out, the well-paid consultant didn't bother to assess feasibility. He didn't check with the village chief and villagers; for if he had, he would have discovered that the location he recommended for the toilets was in an area that the villagers felt was 'out of bounds'. The toilets were put in and simply not used; the project's resources were expended and the problem remained. If only someone had assessed 'feasibility'.

Feasibility studies attempt to assess solutions by determining their potential value, usefulness, suitability, feasibility, efficiency, efficacy, practicality, appropriateness, cost-effectiveness or any other relevant measures of success. It's worth noting that the most successful interventions tend to:

- show respect for cultural values and identity
- be appropriate for the physical environment
- be seen as relevant by stakeholders
- engage participants and foster involvement
- be affordable and cost-effective

Assessing potential solutions along these lines is a crucial step in the search for workable and sustainable solutions.

Comparing strategies

The methodological approaches you can call on when assessing feasibility are, once again, quite wide-ranging. But they do tend to sit under two general strategies:

1. *Contextual investigation* – this involves assessing feasibility and attempting to predict success by exploring the initiative or intervention within its proposed context. Contextual investigation can involve comparing the context in which a potential initiative sits with the context that is being proposed, as well as seeking opinion on appropriateness and practicality from a range of relevant stakeholders.

2. *Running a trial* – rather than a data collection method in its own right, a trial is better understood as a framework under which data can be collected. A trial involves piloting an initiative in order to gauge its potential for full use in your context. It allows you to assess how well it will meet its objectives or a set of criteria. Trials can be embedded into a number of research strategies, including quasi-experimentation (see Chapter 6), action research (see Chapter 9) and evaluative research (see Chapter 10).

Drawing on management tools

While any number of traditional data collection methods can be called on when assessing feasibility, there can also be a place for management-based tools such as: criteria-based assessment; cost–benefit analysis; force field analysis; and SWOT analysis. These tools can be used by researchers and stakeholders when exploring context or when running a trial.

- *Criteria-based assessment* – criteria-based assessment involves data collection through surveys, interviews, or focus groups that are directly related to set criteria. Such criteria can be drawn from project objectives, the main threats and opportunities associated with the initiative, management mandates or any other issues of concern. For example, an assessment criterion related to the introduction of electronic assignment submission in an external university programme might be to 'decrease turnaround time by a minimum of one week'.
- *Cost–benefit analysis* – cost–benefit analysis is best suited for initiatives with clear *financial* costs and benefits, and involves summing the benefits of a course of action and subtracting the costs associated with it. While this bottom-line approach can be quite useful when dealing with bottom-line managers, the difficulty comes when subjective costs, such as environmental degradation or workplace stress, and subjective benefits, such as well-being or even human life, need to be calculated mathematically.
- *Force field analysis* – as shown in Figure 8.2, force field analysis involves making decisions about a course of action by exploring and comparing the strength of forces for and against change. The idea here is that clearly articulating and quantifying the forces at work can help an individual or an organization move out of equilibrium and inaction. The analysis can also give an indication of what might need to shift before a change initiative is likely to be accepted.
- *SWOT analysis* – SWOT stands for Strengths, Weaknesses, Opportunities and Threats and is a strategic planning tool generally used to assess or audit an organization's resources and capabilities in relation to an external environment. It can, however, be a highly useful framework for assessing the feasibility of change initiatives. Internal analysis centres on an initiative's strengths and weaknesses, while external analysis focuses on outside opportunity and threats.

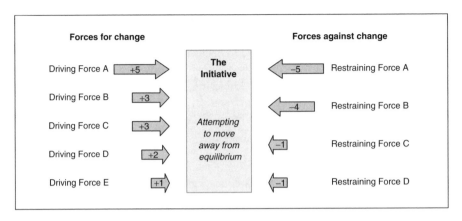

FIGURE 8.2 FORCE FIELD ANALYSIS

> ### Applied Example 8.3 Running a 'Blue Eyed' Trial in Australia

Attempting to teach more than just concepts of race

In my undergraduate teaching, I never really found discussing concepts related to race, ethnicity, or discrimination an insurmountable challenge. But what I did find difficult, what was a real challenge, was moving beyond concepts towards empathetic understanding. Each semester I struggled to find the best way to break through, to get students to really understand what discrimination feels like for those at the receiving end. So I was constantly on the look-out for teaching materials that would help me make the point and leave my students with an understanding that would run much deeper than simple concept understanding.

'Blue Eyed'

A few years ago, I came across a documentary entitled 'Blue Eyed' by Jane Elliott, who I since discovered is a pioneer in racism awareness training. At the time of Dr Martin Luther King Jr's assassination in 1968, Jane Elliott was teaching third grade in an all-white school. In order to give her students a true sense of racism she conducted an exercise in which students were treated as inferior or superior based on eye colour. She continued to use this exercise in primary teaching until she moved into corporate training.

Applied Example 8.3   (Continued)

The documentary shows the use of her 'blue eyed' exercise in a corporate training session, as well as snippets of Jane's life where she discusses the personal price she paid for addressing discrimination in the 1960s. In the corporate exercise highlighted in the film, Jane Elliott divides participants into two groups based on eye colour and discriminates against the blue eyed group by treating them in any number of soul destroying ways. She then draws comparison to the daily experience of African Americans in the United States. I found it incredibly powerful and knew it might be the tool I was looking for.

The Australian context

The dilemma was that the context for the documentary was the United States and the history of racism and discrimination in that country. There was a strong focus on African Americans and the day-to-day struggle they face in the land of opportunity. Now I'm originally from the States, but live and work in Australia, and I find Australian stories of racism to be quite distinct from those of the US. Rather than a 'slave' history, aboriginal history is one of invasion/colonization. As well, the 'White Australia Policy' that ran from the 1850s until 1973 means that immigrants of colour are a fairly new phenomenon. To this day, immigrants from, say, Asia and the Middle East are not always considered 'real' or 'true' Australians, but at best, 'new Australians'.

The Australian 'larrikin' culture can also act to mask racism. For years I have heard my students call on the Australian sense of 'fun' to justify the use of racist language and comments. Students would tell me that Australia's not like America, and that racist comments aren't really racist. They'd say: 'it's all in fun'; 'we're just messing around'; 'they call us "skip" and we call them "wogs"'; 'if they can't take a joke, it's not our problem'; and 'that's the way Australians are'. Of course, I would have felt more comfortable if I had heard that from students of colour rather than white Australians – but that never happened.

Assessing feasibility – would 'Blue Eyed' work in Australia?

So here I was with the 'Blue Eyed' video – which I felt could offer much to understandings of racism, but only if students felt they could relate to it. What I needed was a feasibility study, so I decided to offer the project to a final year student who agreed to run a trial as part of his final year practicum.

(Continued)

185

Applied Example 8.3   (Continued)

The student decided to assess the video by trialing it with three groups of eight students of varying backgrounds who were studying at the University of Western Sydney. The students were asked to watch the video and then participate in focus groups that would discuss the impact of the video and its usefulness in Australian undergraduate teaching. What he found was both interesting and useful.

He found that all bar one of the 24 students found the video interesting and quite a few (18) found it riveting. Over half felt that the context of the video mirrored that of Australia. What was interesting, however, was that virtually all of the students who believed the video was *not* relevant were of Anglo origin (9/10). Of the 14 that did think the stories and experiences rang true for an Australian context, only two were of Anglo descent. The remainder were made up of eight 'new' immigrants from Asia, Greece and the Middle East, and two were Aboriginal students. All of these students claimed that the experiences of racism they had faced in Australia left them with feelings as expressed in the video.

The conclusion

After the trial and assessment, I did decide to use the video. As I expected, some students stated that the context was not relevant to Australia, which is when I promptly told them about the trial, the focus group and the discussions that followed. This then seemed to give current students of colour permission to tell their stories and open up the minority voice. And I can tell you – it was extremely rewarding to see a new-found sense of respect for people's experience and pain develop in a classroom right before your eyes.

FURTHER READING

Assessing needs, visioning futures, searching for solutions and assessing feasibility are all considered elements of *applied research*, and the readings below should give you a good start in sourcing such material. *Searching the Internet* as a rigorous research tool is a relatively new addition to research literature, and I have included two recent references worth exploring. Finally, I have offered two key sources from the huge array of *change management literature* that can help you explore highly useful data gathering tools not generally considered mainstream in social/applied science research.

Exploring 'applied' research

Bickman, L. and Rog, D. J. (1998) *Handbook of Applied Social Research Methods*. Thousand Oaks: Sage.

Gupta, K. (1998) *A Practical Guide to Needs Assessment*. San Francisco, CA: Pfeiffer.

Witkin, B. R. and Altschuld, J. W. (1995) *Planning and Conducting Needs Assessments*: A Practical Guide. London: Sage.

Witkin, B. R. and Altschuld, J. W. (1999) *From Needs Assessment to Action: Transforming Needs into Solution Strategies*: London: Sage.

Internet searching

Best, S. J. and Krueger, B. S. (2004) *Internet Data Collection*. Thousand Oaks, CA: Sage.

Hock, R. and Price, G. (2004) *The Extreme Searcher's Internet Handbook: A Guide for the Serious Searcher*. Medford, NJ: Cyberage Books.

Change management tools

Beitler, M. A. (2003) *Strategic Organizational Change*. Dayton, OH: Ppi Publishing.

Cameron, E. and Green, M. (2004) *Making Sense of Change Management: A Complete Guide to the Models, Tools and Techniques of Organizational Change*. London: Kogan Page.

Chapter Summary

- The quest for solutions involves determining what others want to accomplish; finding out about the answers and solutions that might already be out there; and assessing the practicality and feasibility of those solutions.

- Methodological options used in the quest for solutions are quite broad and will be driven by your own research agenda. Certain research approaches, however, have proven themselves to be particularly effective when searching for solutions.

- Assessing needs and visioning futures highlights the importance of listening to stakeholders. Assessing needs values the voice of those who will be affected by solutions, while visioning futures allow you to share in your stakeholders' pictures of the future.

- Methods appropriate for assessing needs and visioning futures include surveys, focus groups and public forums.

- Exploring potential programmes, interventions and services allows you to avoid reinventing the wheel. Plenty of solutions have been tried with varying levels of success – some of which might even be right for your context.

- When exploring a solution you may draw on any number of 'traditional' data collection methods, including interviewing, surveying, observation and document analysis.

- While not a traditional data collection strategy, using the Internet can be an exceptional tool when looking for answers. Successfully navigating the Net is reliant on: honing your search skills; wading through garbage; and being able to critically assess the agenda and bias of what you find.

- Examining the feasibility of change initiatives involves assessing an initiative's potential value, usefulness, suitability, feasibility, efficiency, efficacy, practicality, appropriateness, cost-effectiveness, or any other relevant measures of success.

- The methodological approaches that can be used to assess feasibility are quite open, but do tend to sit under two general strategies: contextual investigation and the running of a trial.

- Tools for assessing feasibility include criteria-based assessment, cost–benefit analysis, force field analysis and SWOT analysis.

9
Research that Moves from Knowledge to Action

Chapter Preview
When the Research Goal is 'To Combine Research and Action'
Change-Oriented Goals in Action Research
Issues in Action Research

'A thought which does not result in an action is nothing much, and an action which does not proceed from a thought is nothing at all.'

- Georges Bernanos

WHEN THE RESEARCH GOAL IS 'TO COMBINE RESEARCH AND ACTION'

Why research real-world problems? That's simple – to make a difference. The ultimate goal in researching real-world problems is to make a contribution that can lead to genuine and substantive change. But in most research approaches, this contribution is limited to the production of knowledge; the goal is to have knowledge produced through research become key in evidence-based decision making related to problem resolution.

But what if you want to do more than produce knowledge? What if your goals are to go beyond evidence and recommendations? What if your research goals include doing, shifting, changing or implementing?

Linking change management and research agendas

The concepts of doing, shifting, changing and implementing are certainly not foreign to anyone trying to make a difference in their workplace or in their community. Continuous improvement is part and parcel of any management framework. Whether based on: (1) informal and unstructured anecdotes and reflections; (2) more structured feedback received from clients or recipients (students, patients, community members, etc); or (3) more formal systems of total quality management, such as the International Organization for Standardization's ISO 9000, the need for reflection and learning that can assist in meeting never-ending challenges is a constant.

So how does this link to research? Well, one approach to researching real-world problems is to work at the intersection of 'the production of knowledge' and a 'systematic approach to continuous improvement'. But this has its challenges, one of which includes finding a framework that allows you to conduct rigorous research while working towards tangible change. One framework capable of meeting this dual agenda is action research.

Exploring action research

The term action research was coined in 1946 by Kurt Lewin (Lewin 1946) and represented quite a departure from 'objective' scientific method that viewed implementation as discrete from research processes. Under this traditional framework, responsibility for what happened as a consequence of the production of knowledge was not generally part of a researcher's agenda.

Researchers who were working for and with organizations, however, began to recognize that: (1) the knowledge produced through research should be used for change; and that (2) researching change should lead to knowledge. The appeal of a research strategy that could link these two goals while embedding elements of evaluation and learning was quite high, particularly in the fields of organizational behaviour and education, where continuous improvement was, and still is, a primary goal.

Action research also offered a departure from 'researcher' as expert and the 'researched' as passive recipients of scientific knowledge. It therefore had great appeal among community development workers who saw value in a collaborative research approach that could empower stakeholders to improve their own practice, circumstances and environments.

Now action research, as it developed through the disciplines of organizational behaviour, education and community development, has travelled down a number of divergent paths; each with its own priorities and emphases (for more detail here see the readings offered at the end of this chapter). There is, however, a general definition and key elements that define and characterize this genre of research.

Defining action research

> **Action research:** Research strategies that tackle real-world problems in participatory and collaborative ways in order to produce action and knowledge in an integrated fashion through a cyclical process. In action research, process, outcome and application are inextricably linked.

Because action research is quite distinct from traditional research strategies, working through the key elements in the above definition is well worth the time. Understanding the benefits and challenges of this mode of research is an essential preliminary step in determining the appropriateness of action research for any particular context.

Addresses real-world problems

Action research is grounded in real problems and real-life situations. It generally begins with the identification of practical problems in a specific real-world context. It then attempts to understand those problems and to seek and implement solutions within that context. Action research is often used in workplaces where the ownership of change is a high priority or where the goal is to improve professional practice.

Pursues action and knowledge

Action research rejects the two-stage process of 'knowledge first – change second', and suggests that they are highly integrated. Action research practitioners believe that enacting change shouldn't just be seen as the end product of knowledge; rather it should be valued as a source of knowledge itself. And we're not talking here about anecdotal knowledge. The knowledge produced from an action research study needs to be credible and must be collected and analysed with as much rigour as it would be in any other research strategy.

Action is also a clear and immediate goal in every action research project. Whether it be developing skills, changing programmes and policies, or working towards more radical change, action research works towards situation improvement based in practice, and avoids the problem of needing to work towards change after knowledge is produced.

Is participatory

The notion of research as the domain of the expert is rejected, with action research calling for participation of, and collaboration between, researchers, practitioners and any other interested stakeholders. There is an attempt to minimize the distinction between the researcher and the researched – with high value placed on local knowledge. The premise is that without key stakeholders as part of the research process, outsiders are limited in their ability to build rich and subtle understandings ... or implement sustainable change. Contrary to many research paradigms, action research works *with*, rather than *on* or *for* the 'researched', and is therefore seen as embodying democratic principles. The key is that those who will be affected by action research are not acted upon.

The nature and level of participation and collaboration is varied and based on: the action research approach adopted; the particular context of the situation being

191

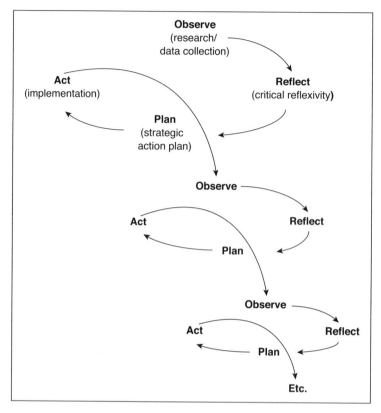

FIGURE 9.1 CYCLES IN ACTION RESEARCH

studied; and the goals of the various stakeholders. This might find different stake-holders involved in any or all stages and cycles of the process. As for those individuals driving the research process, facilitating a sustainable change process might see them acting as planner, leader, catalyser, facilitator, teacher, designer, listener, observer, synthesizer and/or reporter at various points throughout the project.

Is cyclical

Action research is not a one-shot affair. The premise here is that you learn, you do, you reflect, you learn how to do better, you do it better, you learn from that, do it better still, and so on, and so forth. In other words, you're working through a series of continuous improvement cycles that converge towards better situation understanding and improved action. The goal is to continuously refine methods, data and interpretation in the light of the understanding developed in earlier cycles.

The cycles themselves can be defined in numerous ways. But, as shown in Figure 9.1, they generally involve some variation on observation, reflection, planning and action.

The exact nature of the steps in each part of the cycle is emergent and developed collaboratively with stakeholders who form the research team. Research for the 'observation' part of the cycle is likely to be in the form of a case study, and as with all case studies, might involve a variety of approaches, methodologies and methods in a bid to gather data and generate knowledge. The 'reflection' part of the cycle can be informal and introspective, or can be quite formal and share many elements with formative evaluations, as discussed in the next chapter. The steps related to 'planning' and 'action', however, are likely to go beyond reflection and research, and may require practitioners to delve into literature on strategic planning and change management.

The decision to engage in action research

Because there can be a fair amount of diversity in action research methods, understanding what actually constitutes an action research study and whether or not you should engage in one, can be somewhat difficult. In fact, what student researchers often see as action research sometimes fits more comfortably under the heading of quasi-experimentation (see Chapter 6) or evaluation (see Chapter 10). While all three of these types of study involve evaluative and action oriented elements, as shown in Table 9.1, action research tends to be distinct in terms of its embedded assumptions, its goals and its methods.

The decision to engage in action research should be driven by a researcher's objectives. Action research is likely to be a good fit if these objectives include: engagement and involvement of stakeholders as collaborators or co-researchers; prolonged involvement in learning cycles; the production of rigorous, credible knowledge; and the actioning of tangible change.

CHANGE-ORIENTED GOALS IN ACTION RESEARCH

The nature of the potential change produced through action research is broad and, as discussed below, can involve anything from improved practice to shifted programmes, policies and systems, through to more radical 'cultural' shifts that include empowering the marginalized. While the goals of any one action research proposal may sit neatly in any one of these categories, it is not uncommon for action research studies to simultaneously work across a number of goals.

Improving practice

Action research can be an effective way of empowering practitioners to improve their own professional practice. Rather than mandates that come down from on high, or knowledge that comes from outside experts, action research, which is expressly designed to improve professional practice, recognizes that practitioners can contribute to their own learning and development. Action research recognizes the professional

TABLE 9.1 UNDERSTANDING THE SUBTLETIES AND DEFINING ELEMENTS OF ACTION RESEARCH

	Quasi-experimentation (see Chapter 6)	Evaluative studies (see Chapter 10)	Action research
Objectives	• Knowledge/truth	• Knowledge (sometimes politically charged)	• Knowledge • Change implementation
Participants	• 'Subjects'	• 'Clients' or 'Participants'	• 'Co-researchers' • 'Collaborators' • 'Team members'
Researchers	• Generally outside experts • Sometimes practitioners	• Often 'consultants' (outside experts) • Sometimes practitioners/ managers	• Research team made up of relevant stakeholders
Setting	• Can be a 'lab' or real-world setting	• Generally a real-world setting	• Always a real-world setting
Timeframe/cycles	• Timeframe varies with the nature of the experiment • Generally one cycle that might be replicated	• Timeframe will vary based on goal and evaluative methods used (see Chapter 10) • Generally one cycle	• Generally requires prolonged engagement • Requires a number of multiple learning cycles
'Manipulation' of the environment	• Done by researchers	• What's being evaluated sits outside researcher control and has not been driven by the researcher	• While not considered 'manipulation', continuous improvement is part of the research process

nature of practitioners and their ability to conduct meaningful research. In doing so, it helps break down the divide between practitioners and the 'academic elite', and brings research into day-to-day professional practice.

Improving practice through action research is quite common in the educational sector where teachers are encouraged to work in ways that develop their own skills and practice. In recent years, however, there has been an increase in action research studies in health care and nursing, where the desire for professional recognition, autonomy and respect for learned/local knowledge are high.

Now you would think that in an institute of higher learning, such as a university, the same would hold true – that there would be recognition of the value of practitioner involvement in developing practice. But as shown in Applied Example 9.1, which relates to my own university, working in ways that empower the individual can be a real challenge for any bureaucracy.

> **Applied Example 9.1   *Developing an Empowering Process for Improving Practice in a University Setting***

Recommendations to reduce assessment

A pro-vice chancellor at my university recently wrote and brought forward a discussion paper on the appropriate assessment of undergraduate students. The paper advocated a need to restrict units to no more than two items of assessment with a total equivalent of 3,000 words for introductory level units and 4,000 words for intermediate and upper level units. These recommendations were offered as a strategy for alleviating the pressures on over-assessed students and overworked staff. It was also thought they would help overcome the difficulties in timely and consistent results processing. The paper was distributed to all academic staff.

The discussion of this paper was then set as an agenda item for a meeting of the College Education Committee, of which I am a member. We on the committee were asked to canvas' and collate staff opinion from our respective academic areas and report back. So in my role as school representative, I duly sent out an email that summarized the recommendations and asked for comment.

Staff reaction

Well I certainly received comment and, as they say, the paper went over like a 'lead balloon'. Even though this was a 'discussion paper', it seemed to strike a raw nerve with many academics who stated that they were already feeling disempowered by a seemingly unending series of restructures. Academics were concerned that this paper represented:

- a fundamental misconception about the nature of assessment – that the purpose of assessment goes beyond assessing what students know; assessment can also be a tool used to drive student engagement and learning
- administrative/financial considerations overriding issues of academic quality
- a 'one size fits all' model that could not possibly recognize existing diversity in programmes, subjects, cohorts and academics
- a move towards a loss of academic autonomy and freedom

There was also concern that:

- this discussion paper would become policy regardless of staff opinion
- staff and students were not consulted about other possible solutions

(Continued)

195

Applied Example 9.1   (Continued)

Developing an action research proposal

So strong was the reaction to this paper that academics in my area came together to talk about its implications. Discussion quickly turned to the perceived lack of consultation and whether an action research process could address the paper's concerns in ways more likely to leave staff feeling empowered.

The group decided to design an action research proposal. Objectives covered both process and outcomes and included:

- working in consultative, participatory and empowering ways
- engaging in learning cycles that would move between the production of change and the production of knowledge
- increasing the timeliness and consistency of results processing
- respecting the diversity that exists in academic content and pedagogy
- striking a balance between academic workloads and outcomes
- striking a balance between student workloads and outcomes

While the exact nature of the action research protocol was to be emergent, the general process would involve:

1. Forming a committed stakeholder-based research team that included representatives from management and administration, as well as academics and students who represented a wide range of teaching and learning experiences.
2. Engaging in a participatory research process that would build richer understanding of the problem situation, that is, clarifying administration's difficulties/concerns; understanding the aims and objectives of assessment; working through staff-related workload issues; understanding workload implications for students; weighing up the implications of consistency verses diversity.
3. Exploring what staff at this and other institutions have done when faced with similar pressures/issues.
4. Developing and implementing an action plan to improve practice. This would involve taking the knowledge derived from the above steps and modifying assessment procedures accordingly.
5. Rigorously evaluating process and outcomes related to the implementation of the action plan from the perspective of staff, students, administration and management.
6. Reflecting on evaluative outcomes and modifying practice in a cyclical fashion, perhaps as part of an ongoing end of semester evaluation process.
7. Documenting the process so that findings, as they emerge, could be disseminated throughout the university community and offered as data for evidence-based policy decisions.

> **Applied Example 9.1   (Continued)**
>
> **Targeting the proposal**
> The next phase was to work on targeting the proposal. The group discussed the possibility of bringing the proposal forward to the pro-vice chancellor for university-wide action, but decided that this would see the group lose control. They therefore decided it would be more productive to work at a smaller departmental level. They felt that real outcomes would be better achieved if they concentrated their efforts on developing their own practice by exploring assessment procedures within their own subjects.
>
> **An ongoing process**
> At the time of writing, opportunities for funding for the modified proposal was being sought. But even without funding, several academics have indicated that they would be willing to facilitate such a study. As it turns out, dedication to improved practice through strategies that empower, rather than disempower, are viewed by these practitioners' as valuable and worthwhile.

Shifting systems

Sometimes it begins and ends with developing your own professional practice, but other times you may want to work at the organizational level. Beyond practice, you may be interested in working within an organizational setting to improve programmes or policy. In fact, in the above example a higher-level goal was to have the findings from an action research study aimed at developing professional practice contribute to the development of effective policy.

Personally, I can't think of any organization that couldn't be improved in some way or another. Inefficient systems, ineffective management and outdated policy, provide action research opportunities for those working in and with businesses, government and non-government agencies, community groups, etc. But while action research has been around for the better part of 60 years and can offer much to the management of organizational change, it is not generally a core management strategy. Action research literature certainly addresses organizational change, but change management literature rarely tackles action research.

Nevertheless, terms such as learning, education, facilitation, participation, negotiation and collaboration that are core in action research are also core in change management-speak. This is particularly so in organizations that have recognized the value of on-the-ground knowledge, as well as the role of engagement and ownership in working towards effective and sustainable change.

As highlighted in Applied Example 9.2, action research as a strategy for driving workplace-based change can be highly effective in securing stakeholder support. It can also get a wide range of staff working together towards a common goal; provide a systematic and well-established approach to sustainable change; provide a framework for the conduct of research; and embed the concept of research into management practice. It can also be a step along the way in the development of a learning organization.

Applied Example 9.2   Shifting the System – Creating a New Workplace Environment through Action Research

Deciding to undertake an action research study
I get a fair few Master's students proposing action research studies, and I think that's because many of these students work full-time, study part-time and conduct research that is related to their workplace. These students like the idea of actually actioning change through the research process. Some like the fact that they will be able to produce something that goes beyond recommendations. Others are attracted by a process that is both collaborative and participatory and allows on-the-ground ownership of both findings and initiatives.

In the case of a student working as a manager in charge of occupational health and safety (OH&S) for an electronics manufacturer (we'll call him Ken), a trilogy of goals lead him to consider an action research process. These were:

1. Creating a healthier/safer work environment (a need created by humanitarian, financial, and legal concerns).
2. Recognition that imposed policy and procedures were not being followed. He saw the need for employees to see relevance and have ownership of any OH&S initiatives.
3. A practical need to conduct a research project as a requirement for a Master's degree.

We talked about Ken's workplace and it turns out that Ken was tired of being seen as the 'enemy', by both blue-collar workers who perceived OH&S as a huge pain in the ass, and white-collar workers who tended to see OH&S as a legal requirement that costs money and cuts productivity. In our discussions, Ken said that before any OH&S programme or polices could be successfully implemented, it was essential that embedded assumptions were broken down and that there was greater recognition of the benefits of OH&S to both labourers and management.

Applied Example 9.2   (Continued)

I told him that this goal sat nicely with action research and suggested that he do some reading related to that method. I also pointed him to the *Healthy Workplace Guidelines* produced by the World Health Organization Western Pacific Region Office (1999), which advocates a participatory approach to creating a healthy workplace.

Implementing the WHO guidelines as an action research process

I saw Ken a couple of weeks later and he was raring to go. He didn't really know much about action research prior to our conversation, but after reviewing some of the literature it dawned on him that:

- the participatory nature of action research might work well in gaining staff acceptance and commitment
- the cyclical nature of continuous improvement in action research would sit well with his goals for achieving and maintaining relevant International Standards; and last but certainly not least
- he would not have to separate this research project from his work commitments; because it had strong action elements he could conduct much of the project during work time

Ken was also impressed by the WHO guidelines. He felt they did an excellent job of articulating the benefits of a healthy workplace to both employees and organizations. Furthermore, the WHO approach sat nicely with the action research strategies he was now determined to adopt.

The process

The guideline recommended eight steps for creating a healthy workplace. Steps were described as non-prescriptive and could be modified according to circumstance and context. Ken felt that the steps, particularly if done in multiple cycles, would provide him with a strong action research blueprint. The steps, as they evolved through the action research process, involved:

1. **Ensuring management support** – Ken went to management and was told that as long as it wasn't going to cost the company anything he had their support.
2. **Establishing a coordinating body** – using more action research oriented terms, he established a 'research and implementation team' and volunteered to be the facilitator, rather than the leader.

(Continued)

199

Applied Example 9.2   (Continued)

---

3. **Conducting a needs assessment** – Ken volunteered to put together a workplace profile and to summarize the company's health and safety records. Meanwhile, other team members spoke to a range of staff about their perceived needs.
4. **Prioritizing needs** – this actually presented quite a challenge because the needs prioritized by Ken were not the same as those prioritized by the group. After a bit of an internal struggle, Ken realized he needed to let this go. He now recognized that there was a downside in working collaboratively, particularly for someone used to being in charge.
5. **Developing an action plan** – while there was much debate amongst the team, Ken was pleased because he could see a sense of ownership building as team members put forward and debated their ideas.
6. **Implementing the plan** – the team came up with a plan that addressed practice, programmes, and policy, which was implemented over a three-month period.
7. **Evaluating process and outcomes** – because he was undertaking this study as part of his Master's degree, Ken volunteered to design and run the evaluation with team advice.
8. **Revising and updating the programme** – the team became part of the company's OH&S framework and now regularly meets to review and revise OH&S programmes and policy based on evaluative outcomes.

Reflections on the process
I spoke to Ken a while back and asked him how it was going. He said the biggest challenge he faced was learning how to facilitate rather than lead. When he started down this path he didn't realize that there might be a tradeoff between his control and their ownership. Before he started, he imagined that it would all unfold as he wanted/expected. But as the team grew in confidence, the direction they took sometimes surprised him. On the upside, he said that while there were still some problems with full compliance, there had been an improvement in knowledge, attitudes and practice, and that he was pleased there was now a strategy in place for continuous improvement.

Working towards empowerment

As highlighted in both of the above Applied Examples, a large part of action research's appeal is the empowering nature of the process itself. While action research aims to produce credible knowledge while working to change practice, programmes and/or policy, it also aims to empower those whose role has traditionally been limited to being the subject of research or the beneficiary/victim of change. This is particularly important when the problem situation being addressed is impacting on those who don't generally have a voice.

Now while empowerment is a central theme in almost all action research studies, it is even more explicitly drawn out in what is known as participatory action research (PAR). As in other modes of action research, PAR works with real problems in a cyclical and participatory fashion in order to produce knowledge and action directly useful to stakeholders. PAR, which grew from rural community development work, however, puts a stronger emphasis on the empowerment of the 'marginalized'. A central goal is to help those who have traditionally been acted on to construct their own knowing, and attempt to create and action their own strategic plan for a better, less oppressed future.

PAR recognizes that the knowledge and experience of the 'marginalized' should be respected and valued, and it attempts to capitalize on capabilities and cultural practices that are often ignored. The aim is to strive towards social transformation by strengthening a group's capacity to generate knowledge and action from their own perspectives, and in their own interests.

Applied Example 9.3, which tells the story of an action research process aimed at improving the livelihood of farmers in South Sulawesi, Indonesia, provides a nice example of a community development oriented PAR project.

Applied Example 9.3   From Technology Transfer to Active Learning – Using PAR as a Tool for Change and Empowerment in Tombolo Village

When one of our international students began her PhD, she had been working as a senior extension officer for the Farming Systems Division of the Indonesian Department of Agriculture for some years. During this time she became increasingly frustrated by the Division's operations. She began to question not only their practices but some of the underlying assumptions that drove that practice. In particular, she became wary of:

- research projects that did little to change the situation of those under study
- the use of top-down approaches to solve farmers' production problems

(Continued)

201

Applied Example 9.3   *(Continued)*

- technology transfer models in which researchers' develop technology and then use extension agents to transfer that technology to farmers
- lack of recognition of local knowledge and the importance of political context

She decided to facilitate a participatory action research process that could improve a specific problem situation (livestock production) while empowering stakeholder groups, particularly farmers themselves. The following excerpt from the conclusion of her thesis tells the story quite well.

> This study was conducted using participatory action research and a systemic approach to improve the livelihood of some smallholder livestock farmers in a rural area of South Sulawesi, Indonesia. In this context, action provided changes and research provided understanding. The PAR methodology also provided rigour through the spiral of cyclical processes.
>
> Previously, development workers and extensionists approached the farmers in this study area through the employment of only technical interventions, and the farmers' knowledge and circumstances were not taken into account. I brought the idea of AR and a systemic approach, and the general idea of participative learning into this study based on my strong passion to undertake research that would be of benefit to the local people and bring about changes for the better within the situation of concern.
>
> I began action researching with the notion of first understanding the situation being studied, and also having participants (farmers and development workers) directly involved in the inquiry process. This was considered vital to generate collective action as well as to develop participants' skill through 'learning by doing' (experiential learning) as a means to promote their self-reliance. Forming a learning group of farmers enacted this, and I believed that this self-reliance would enable farmers to solve the complex issues for themselves …
>
> I as the facilitator of this learning process benefited from having a specific problematic situation to deal with explicitly, with participants gaining from the experiential learning processes and action learning concepts. Through this process I could provide a focus for learning about such things as *developing forage technology* to demonstrate to participants how learning occurred in the groups, and how they could share their experience with others for collective action to improve the wider situation (livestock production) …
>
> Within the livestock development context, this study enabled my colleagues and myself to work participatively and collaboratively with farmers, prompting significant changes in our practice of facilitation. My colleagues and I developed a more congruent practice of participation and collaboration through the action researching of our practice of facilitating farmers to improve the situation of concern …

Applied Example 9.3   (Continued)

As a trainer and supervisor I have the opportunity to implement this learning approach to agricultural development to South Sulawesi through facilitation of and participation in the development of the cognitive maps of development workers in concert with other stakeholders, with the purpose of informing both methods of livestock production and to enhance the livelihood of smallholder farmers. I also have the opportunity to educate and train my colleagues and farmers to enable them (a) to develop a participative worldview, and (b) to develop their capability to be self-critical and reflective of their own knowledge and action. This may produce a 'new generation of agricultural practitioners' who are willing to share power with their peers and other stakeholders, and who are willing to learn from and with other stakeholders as equals. (Reprinted with permission; Habibie 2003, p. 234–6)

ISSUES IN ACTION RESEARCH

Yes, action research can produce knowledge and change in empowering ways. But anyone who has ever facilitated the process can tell you that it's far from easy. The participatory, cyclical and multi-goaled nature of action research can make it a difficult process to navigate. And a team approach means you will not have full control. Nevertheless, you are likely to be responsible for overall management and will probably need to work to tight timelines and budgets. Hence, being practical and realistic is critical to the success of any action research project. In short, the project must be manageable.

Some of the issues you will need to negotiate as an action researcher include:

- *Facilitating rather than directing* – because of its participatory nature, the ultimate direction of the project is not fully in your hands. Decisions made about the project's direction and its probable outcomes should be collective.
- *Managing the scope* – action research projects can get very big, very quickly. New researchers can be surprised to find that a rigorously conducted needs assessment or the conduct of an evaluative study within just one action research cycle can be a large research project in its own right.
- *Assuring rigour in methods* – while continuous improvement strategies often rely on anecdotal evidence and general reflections, action research demands a higher degree of rigour. Perhaps the best advice here is to identify the key

research questions within each action research cycle and treat each of these as a small research study in its own right. While these studies will certainly need tight, realistic boundaries, they still need to be conducted so that they meet indicators of good research, that is, validity, authenticity, reliability consistency etc. (see Chapter 4).

- *Managing the pace* – getting stakeholders together, getting consensus and actioning real change can be slow, particularly in multiple cycles. Action research takes time and tends to work best when embedded in day-to-day practice.
- *Keeping momentum* – in a long-term project, many things can go astray. Key stakeholders may come and go, change initiatives may not get off the ground and the conduct of rigorous research may become overwhelming. And while this is the nature of action researching real-world problems, realistic planning, acceptance of the unexpected and being prepared to be flexible can help keep momentum going.
- *Managing people* – facilitating collaboration is not always easy. Some stakeholders may feel unheard, ignored and/or marginalized; some may be overbearing and pompous; others may be pushing their own agenda. As a facilitator, you will need to call on negotiation, facilitation and, potentially, conflict resolution skills.
- *Acting ethically* – researchers carry the burden of ethical responsibility for both the production of knowledge and for the welfare of the researched (see Chapter 4). In action research, the involvement of stakeholders in the research team, combined with the agenda of actioning change, make for very high levels of participant involvement. Protecting the welfare of these participants is paramount.
- *Needing a range of skills* – in addition to being a methodological 'expert', the action researcher must also be a consummate organizer, effective communicator, skilled negotiator, conflict resolution specialist, well-organized time manager, strategic planner, efficient documenter and be willing to get their 'hands dirty' as an on-the-ground implementer – all of which might require the development of specialist skills.
- *Ownership* – finally, the researcher needs to negotiate ownership of research outcomes, which may include rights to publish, issues of authorship etc.

When it comes to knowledge and change, action research attempts to let you have your cake and eat it too (which actually make sense – after all, what good is a cake you can't eat …). It also allows you to work with others in empowering ways. And, while action research can be quite challenging, for individuals and organizations whose goals match those of action research, it can be a challenge well worth taking up.

FURTHER READING

The field of action research (AR) is quite diverse and can be delineated by both discipline and approach. The literature, however, tends to reflect disciplinary distinctions. I have reflected this in the list below by offering a range of general references as well as readings targeting education, health care and community development.

General AR readings
Coghlan, D. and Brannick, T. (2004) *Doing Action Research in Your Own Organization*. London: Sage.
McNiff, J. and Whitehead, J. (2002) *Action Research: Principles and Practice*. London: Routledge.
Reason, P. and Bradbury, H. (2001) *Handbook of Action Research: Participative Inquiry and Practice*. London: Sage.
Stringer, E. (1999) *Action Research*. Thousand Oaks, CA: Corwin Press.

Health care oriented AR
Morton-Cooper, A. (2000) *Action Research in Health Care*. Oxford: Blackwell Science.
Winter, R. and Munn-Giddings, C. (2001) *A Handbook for Action Research in Health and Social Care*. London: Routledge.

Education oriented AR
Sagor, R. (2004) *The Action Research Guidebook: A Four-Step Process for Educators and School Teams*. Thousand Oaks, CA: Corwin Press.
Stringer, E. (2003) *Action Research in Education*. Englewood Cliffs, NJ: Prentice Hall.

Community development oriented AR
Fals Borda, O. and Rahman, M. A. (1991) *Action and Knowledge: Breaking the Monopoly with Participatory Action Research*. New York: Intermediate Technology/Apex.
Smith, S., Willm, D. G. and Johnson, N. A. (eds) (1997) *Nurtured by Knowledge: Learning to Do Participatory Action-Research*. New York: Apex Press.
Whyte, W. F. (ed.) (1991) *Participatory Action Research*. Newbury Park, CA: Sage.

Chapter Summary

- Researching real-world problems is about making a contribution that can lead to real change. In most research approaches, however, this contribution is limited to 'knowledge'. Enter 'action research', which embeds the actioning of change into the research process.

- Action research covers a broad array of research strategies that are dedicated to the integrated production of knowledge and the implementation of change. Action research addresses practical problems; generates knowledge; enacts change; is participatory; and relies on a cyclical process.

- In business, education and health care, action research can be a practical means for improving practice, policy and programmes. In community development work, action research is also expressly used to empower community members.

- Because action research shares some key elements with quasi-experimentation and evaluative research, it is important to understand how its dual agendas and its participatory and cyclical nature set it apart.

- A common goal in action research is to empower practitioners to improve their practice by recognizing how they can make a contribution to their own learning and development.

- Action research is also utilized at the organizational level in order to improve programmes, policy and even organizational culture. But while action research can offer much to the management of organizational change, it is generally seen as a research strategy rather than a core management strategy.

- Participatory action research (PAR) is explicit in its agenda of empowerment. A central goal is to help community groups construct their own knowing in order to create and action their own plan for a better future.

- Facilitating a participatory process can be both rewarding and challenging. Challenges include: facilitating rather than directing; managing a project's scope, pace and momentum; managing people; working ethically; being multi-skilled; and negotiating ownership.

10
Evaluating Change

'Change means movement. Movement means friction. Only in the frictionless vacuum of a nonexistent abstract world can movement or change occur without abrasion.'

- Saul Alinsky

WHEN THE RESEARCH GOAL IS 'TO EVALUATE CHANGE INITIATIVES'

I agree with Alinsky, change does mean movement … and in the real world, movement does not happen without repercussions. Whether they are intended or unintended, positive or negative, change has its consequences. And understanding the nature of these consequences is the main objective of evaluative research.

Evaluative research: Research that is undertaken in order to determine the relative value of some initiative, for example a product, procedure, programme, or policy. Evaluative research studies can be used to identify both an initiative's consequences as well as opportunities for its modification and improvement.

The need for evaluative research studies that can assess the effectiveness of change intervention programmes and policies is ever-increasing. The findings

207

offered by such studies are considered more and more crucial to rational, informed, or evidence-based decision making. In fact, a well-conducted evaluative study is now a key strategy for supplying decision makers the data they need to determine:

- whether an initiative was successful in meeting its objectives
- whether it had any unintended effects
- whether it was cost-effective
- whether it was 'popular'
- whether it should be continued as is, modified, expanded or scrapped

Whether it be evaluation of new teaching strategies, the effectiveness of anti-obesity campaigns, or the impact of new child-friendly workplace policies, data derived from rigorous evaluative studies is considered necessary in effective change management. In fact, change intervention proposals increasingly require evaluative components so that assessment is embedded into the management of change from conception.

Now there are many questions that can be asked in an evaluative study, but they generally fall into two main categories: those questions that ask about *outcomes*, in other words 'did it work?', and those questions that ask about *process*, or 'how can the design and implementation of the initiative be improved?' And as highlighted in Applied Example 10.1 at the end of this section, it's not uncommon for an evaluative study to include questions that cover both outcomes and process.

Assessing real outcomes

Outcome evaluation, also referred to as *summative evaluation*, aims to provide data and information related to the effectiveness of the change strategy in question (that goals, aims and objectives have been met) and its efficiency (that the effects justify the costs). The idea here is to investigate whether an initiative is responsible for outcomes that would not have occurred if it were not for the initiative, and this should include both intended and unintended effects. Now in the real world, the financial bottom line is almost always a factor, so many outcome evaluations also include data related to cost-effectiveness, often in the form of a cost–benefit analysis.

The results of outcome evaluations are expected to inform decision making related to programme funding, continuation, termination, expansion and reduction. While findings are often case-specific, results can be of interest to any number of stakeholder groups. And depending on the nature of the change intervention, might be of interest to the wider population as well.

Evaluating the change process

Process evaluation, also referred to as *formative evaluation*, aims to provide data and information that will aid the development of a particular change initiative. Such studies investigate an initiative's delivery and ask how, and how well, it is being implemented. These studies can assess strengths, weaknesses, opportunities and threats; and often work to assess the factors acting to facilitate and/or block successful implementation.

The results derived from process evaluations are expected to inform decision making related to programme improvement, modification and management. And while these studies also tend to be case-specific, 'transferable' findings will allow other organizations interested in the use of any similar initiatives to apply 'lessons learned'.

Applied Example 10.1 Evaluating Community Participation in a Healthy Islands Setting

Background

In response to the WHO's 'New Horizons in Health' policy framework that emphasized wellness, positive health and community participation, Ministers of Health from Island Nations across the South Pacific met in Yanuca in 1994 and established the concept of 'Healthy Islands'. Not only did Healthy Islands work to promote better health in 'settings', e.g. local schools, villages and hospitals, it also worked to empower both community members and health practitioners.

In Fiji, enthusiasm for developing new ways of operating through Healthy Islands was high, and the use of 'settings' became central to Fiji's national environmental health planning process. In fact, in 1998, the Fiji government developed the Pacific's first national environmental health action plan (NEHAP) using two settings projects (Kadavu and Makoi) as a focal point for changing environmental health policy and practice.

In 2002, the revised NEHAP reported the use of over 100 settings projects throughout Fiji. The plan indicated that Healthy Islands settings now formed a significant part of the practice of environmental health practitioners. This significant change in both policy and practice, however, occurred in the absence of any rigorous evaluation.

(Continued)

Applied Example 10.1 (Continued)

The need for community participation evaluation

Of significant concern were goals related to community participation. Some practitioners sensed that the settings approach was empowering people at the local
level. Others, however, felt that negotiating community participation was difficult
even through the use of settings. It was decided that a study that would explore:
(1) the effectiveness of settings in engaging community participation; and (2) how
settings approaches could be enhanced to improve participation, might inform
further development of Fiji's environmental health policy and practice.

The Makoi setting

In 1997, the Fiji School of Medicine, the WHO and the Fiji Ministry of Health
collaborated in applying the Healthy Islands vision and settings approach in
Makoi – a multi-racial, urban fringe community of some 1,046 households situ-
ated near Fiji's capital, Suva. A community Health and Environment Promotion
Centre was established in the early stages of the project. The community could
access the centre for meetings and a range of health promotion services,
including screening for non-communicable diseases, advice on health matters
and environmental health issues. It was also hoped that community-based projects aimed to improve environmental health, such as area clean-ups, could be
organized through the centre. The centre ran for five years and was considered
an appropriate target for an evaluative study.

Evaluating community participation

The first phase of the study involved assessing community participation. To
that end, a questionnaire was distributed to 200 Makoi households in June of
2002. Three language choices were available: English, Fijian and Hindustani,
with respondents asked to indicate both awareness and participation in centre
activities.

The study found that awareness of health promotion interventions was quite
high, but not evenly distributed across various sectors of the population. Similarly,
community support structures were not being accessed by the full range of
community members. One of the more interesting findings was that Indian-
Fijians were less likely to know of, and access, Makoi's health promotion initiatives than Indigenous Fijians.

Evaluating aspects of the process

The second phase of the study was informed by the first, and focused on evaluating the process used to engage community participation. The evaluators

were interested in knowing how the process might be improved in order to increase levels of participation, particularly in the Indian-Fijian community. This phase of the study involved informal in-depth interviews with key stakeholders who were privy to the Makoi centre's planning and daily operations.

The evaluators found that in attempting to find an appropriate structure to enter the community, the Methodist church was selected as an influential structure for community organization. With the aid of the local minister, the Makoi plan was introduced to, and accepted by, the congregation. Using the church's existing organizational structure that divided Makoi into 10 sectors, environmental health practitioners conducted a range of visioning and planning meetings where community members identified and prioritized issues and developed action plans.

Evaluators found that from the initial planning phase it was recognized that utilizing the Methodist church might exclude the ethnic Indian population, most of whom are followers of the Hindu religion. It was felt, however, that the development of a new health and environment centre would open out the initiative to the Hindu community. The evaluators, however, found that this was not the case.

The use of the Methodist church in isolation from a possible range of entry points was seen as a likely contributor in not allowing for racial and cultural inclusion. It was felt that participation of one section of the community had come at the expense of the whole, leading to a dominant minority (the Indigenous Fijians) dictating the needs of the entire community (both Indigenous Fijians and Indian-Fijians). By confining initial contact to the Methodist church community, facilitators overlooked an important opportunity to develop solidarity across a heterogeneous community.

Conclusions

While the lessons learned from this study relate specifically to Makoi, the issues related to engaging community participation are common in many settings-based health promotion projects, namely:

- the need for practitioners to be aware of cultural, racial, and/or gender diversity in the early planning stages of any settings project
- the need to ensure that means of access are broad-reaching and equitable
- the need to build a sense of solidarity amongst groups labelled as communities

(Continued)

Applied Example 10.1   (Continued)

Environmental health practitioners in Fiji also responded to the results of this study by identifying a need for effective process and summative evaluation to be designed and integrated into any health promotion intervention. They recognized that systematic evaluation can point to the need for alternate strategies and modified practice if programmes are shown to be ineffective, or not optimally effective, for a significant segment of their target population. (Adapted with permission from Brear, Powis, O'Leary and Davidson 2004)

THE METHODS OF EVALUATION

So what methods are best suited to an evaluative study? Well, rather than be defined by any particular methodological approach, evaluative research is distinguished by its evaluative goals, and it is these goals that determine appropriate methodology. But this can get quite complicated since the goals of evaluative research can be quite varied. As discussed, some goals will be related to measuring effects, outcomes and change, while other goals will be related to understanding the process of a particular initiative and how it might be improved. Added to this is the question of perspective. Is success to be measured from the perspective of the provider, the recipients, or the wider community? And of course when it comes to opinions related to an initiative's strength, weaknesses and potential improvements, each of these groups might have a very different point of view.

In fact, in order to design appropriate methodology it is essential that those undertaking an evaluative study work out: (1) precisely what they want to know and (2) whose perspective they seek. As shown in Table 10.1 (and Applied Example 10.2), the answers to these questions can point the way down a particular methodological path.

Methods appropriate to outcome evaluation

In outcome evaluation, the main goal is to find out if an initiative worked. In other words, did it meet its objectives? Now initiatives often have multiple objectives that are likely to vary for each stakeholder group. As an evaluator exploring outcomes, you will need to determine and prioritize which outcome objectives are to be explored and whose perspectives you seek. Your methods will then vary accordingly (detailed discussion of each of the methods highlighted below can be found in Chapter 6).

TABLE 10.1 EVALUATIVE METHODS

	Provider perspective	Recipient perspective	Wider perspective
OUTCOME	Was it cost-effective/beneficial to the provider?	Was there a real change in the target group?	Did it meet a wider community need?
Did it work?			
The questions that providers, recipients and the wider community would answer generally differ …	• Document review • Key informant interviews • Focus groups	• Experimentation/ quasi-experimentation using control groups or before/after data • Exploration of post group only by survey/interview	• Surveys • Focus groups
PROCESS	What were the strengths/weaknesses; how could the process be made more efficient/effective?	What were the strengths/weaknesses; how could the process be made more efficient/effective?	What were the strengths/weaknesses; how could the process be made more efficient/effective?
How could it be improved?			
Providers, recipients and the wider community often answer similar questions but from distinct perspectives …	• Interviews with key organizational stakeholders • Focus groups • Observation • Document review	• Surveys • Focus groups • Interviews	• Surveys • Focus groups • Interviews (often key informants/ stakeholders)

- *Provider perspective* – when designing methods, there are two general ways to find out if providers believe an initiative is a success. This first is to ask. *Interviews* and *focus groups* allow you to talk to those responsible for design, delivery, implementation, as well as those with a higher level of organizational responsibility. The second method is to look at *documentary evidence.* This is particularly relevant for questions that focus on cost-effectiveness, or anywhere that evidence of success is likely to be in 'records'.

- *Recipient perspective* – this is where you really get down to brass tacks and see if the initiative's change oriented outcome objectives have been met. Now many (including myself) would argue that the best way to do this is through *experimental* or *quasi-experimental* designs (see Chapter 6) that allow for comparison across groups and time. There are three possibilities here:

  1. *Case/control design* to see whether an initiative has made a difference for a target group, you can use a control group to compare those who have undergone an initiative with those who have not.

2. *Before/after design* – sometimes called 'time series analysis', this approach allows for comparison of the same group of individuals before and after an initiative is implemented.
3. *Case/control – before/after design* – allows for even more definitive results by combining the two methods above.

Now all three of these approaches require forward planning, something not always possible (this is discussed in more detail in the next section). The alternative is to evaluate perceptions of change, rather than change itself, by *surveying* or *interviewing* recipients after implementation. The goal here is to see if recipients *believe* that change has occurred (the decision between surveying and interviewing will depend on both sample size and depth of answers sought).

- *Wider community perspective* – initiatives often include objectives related to stakeholder groups who are not direct recipients. For example, a school initiative to curtail bullying may include an objective related to decreasing parent/community anxiety. Or a health care initiative may include an objective related to improving an organization's reputation in the community. The methods of choice here are *surveys* and *focus groups*. And while such approaches generally ask community members to report on their perceptions and recent changes in those perceptions, the collection of similar data prior to the initiative will allow you to engage in direct comparison.

Methods appropriate to process evaluation

As highlighted in Table 10.1, the main objective in process evaluation is assessing an initiative's strengths and weaknesses and asking how the process could be made more efficient and effective. While stakeholder perspectives will certainly vary, the question at hand is quite similar (detailed discussion of each method highlighted below can be found in Chapter 6).

Important factors

- *Provider perspective* – the methods you will use here will be highly dependent on the complexity and diversity of the groups responsible for provision. For example, at one end of the spectrum you might be asked to evaluate a classroom initiative driven by a particular teacher. In this case, an *in-depth interview* would make most sense. At the other end of the spectrum, you may be evaluating a new government health care policy whose design, development and implementation might have involved individuals working at various levels of government and private industry. With this level of complexity you may need to call on multiple methods, for example, *interviews*, *focus groups* and even *surveys* to gather the data you require. There may also be value in direct *observation* of the process or in *document review* that finds you trolling through and examining records and minutes related to the process being explored.

214

- *Recipient perspective* – initiatives are often full of assumptions related to various stakeholder groups, including recipients, so a good process evaluation will go beyond provider perspective and seek recipient opinions on strengths, weaknesses and potential modifications. As with providers, target groups also vary in size and complexity, and you may find yourself calling on a variety of methods, including *interviews, focus groups* and *surveys* to gather the data you require.
- *Wider community perspective* – the first question you need to ask here is, do you or your 'client' want wider community opinion? You may not feel that the wider community is a relevant stakeholder, or that broader community groups have the prerequisite knowledge necessary for providing an informed opinion. On the other hand, the initiative under review might have far-reaching implications that affect the community or might be related to a problem where the community sees itself as a key stakeholder; say, for example, an initiative aimed to stop neighbourhood graffiti. In this situation, canvassing wider opinion on an initiative's strengths and weaknesses may be of value. The methods most likely to be called upon here are *surveys, focus groups* and possibly *key informant interviews*.

Applied Example 10.2   Fiji's National Centre for Health Promotion – Establishing Evaluative Protocols and Methods

The need for systemic and rigorous evaluation

How do you divvy up a limited budget? This was the question that led the newly appointed director of Fiji's National Centre for Health Promotion to ask for assistance in embedding evaluative strategies in the Centre's health promotion activities.

The director realized that a key part of his role was determining what initiatives and programmes should be funded. Sure he had plenty of anecdotal evidence, political directives and a list of pet projects with long histories, but what he realized he didn't have was hard data that showed effectiveness of the centre's projects. He felt he didn't have the data he needed for informed decision making.

(Continued)

Applied Example 10.2   (Continued)

Embedding evaluative practice

I was asked to go to Fiji to help the Centre embed evaluative practice into their day to day activities. I very quickly said 'absolutely' (after all, there are worse things in life than spending a week in Fiji). We discussed the possibilities and agreed that the best approach would be learning by doing. So in August 2004 we arranged a workshop in Suva for key staff from the National Centre as well as key staff from across Fiji's districts.

Training by doing

After an initial orientation to evaluative research, we began the process of embedding evaluative practice in centre activities. The workshop was very hands-on and involved: agreeing on a national pilot project; developing SMART (specific, measurable, achievable, relevant, time-bound) project objectives; designing methods; and developing data collection tools. A second workshop was arranged for February 2005 in order to work through data management, analysis and reporting.

The project

The Centre's director suggested the national pilot campaign align with the 2003 Tongan agreement's call for the development of environments that support healthy lifestyles. Workshop participants agreed and decided to develop a healthy lifestyles campaign in schools. While it was envisaged that the programme might eventually become national, they decided to pilot the programme and its evaluation in four primary and four secondary schools across Fiji.

Articulating project objectives

Initially, participants felt that coming up with SMART objectives related to this project was relatively easy. They were quite experienced in generating objectives and thought that after 20 minutes they had the task licked. But I then asked them to work through each of the objectives to see if they really were SMART. Participants felt that the objectives were indeed 'specific', 'achievable' and 'relevant', but they hit a roadblock when it came to 'measurable'. In fact, it took the better part of a full day to move towards our final four SMART objectives.

Designing methods

Given this was a learning exercise, participants were asked to propose diverse methodologies for measuring the extent of each objective's success or failure.

216

Applied Example 10.2   (Continued)

After much learning, discussion and debate, participants came up with the following methods for their SMART objectives.

1. **To increase the percentage of children within the WHO healthy weight range**

   Sample: All primary school students in pilot schools in years 5 and 7, and all high school students in pilot schools in forms 3 and 5.

   Method: 'Before and after'. (1) Collect demographic and weight-related baseline data at the beginning of the 2005 school year; (2) initiate and run programme; (3) collect follow-up/comparative weight-related data at the end of the school year.

2. **To increase physical activity levels of children in schools by working in partnership to review and strengthen physical education (PE) curriculum and work with/offer support to existing PE teachers**

   Sample: All primary school students in pilot schools in years 5 and 7, all high school students in pilot schools in forms 3 and 5, and a control group made up of similar students from schools not involved in the campaign.

   Method: 'Before and after' and 'case/control'. (1) Assess the students' school-related activity levels at the beginning of the 2005 school year in both the control and pilot groups; (2) initiate and run new PE programme in the pilot schools; (3) collect follow-up data related to activity levels at the end of the school year in order to compare the pilot groups over time, as well as compare the pilot groups to the control groups.

3. **To improve eating habits of children during school hours by working in partnership to improve canteen choices, provide school lunch inspections and foster school gardens**

   Sample: As in 2 above.

   Method: 'Before and after' and 'case/control'. (1) Assess student's food intake at the beginning of the 2005 school year in both the control and pilot groups; (2) work with staff to implement new lunch programme in the pilot schools; (3) collect follow-up data related to food intake at the end of the school year in order to compare the pilot groups over time, as well as compare the pilot groups to the control groups.

4. **To improve attitudes and practices of children and parents in relation to healthy eating habits and physical activity**

   Sample: Minimum of 50 randomly selected primary school students in years 5 and 7 from the pilot schools and their parents, plus a minimum of 50 randomly selected high school students in forms 3 and 5 from the pilot school and their parents.

(Continued)

Applied Example 10.2   (Continued)

Methods: 'Post test only survey'. Administer two post test only surveys (one for parents and one for children) that asks questions related to healthy eating knowledge, attitudes and practice.

Tool development

Tool development, for example, writing the survey, developing data collection sheets, constructing observation checklist etc., came next and was a challenging but necessary exercise. Not only did it prepare the teams to go out and collect consistent data, the preliminary design of these tools highlighted flaws and difficulties in the proposed methodologies that were then modified accordingly.

Designing process evaluation

Finally, on the last day of the workshop we discussed potential protocols for process evaluation. While detailed discussion was deferred until the next workshop (yet to be held at the time of writing), the participants felt that a broad array of methods might work best in gathering stakeholder opinions on strengths and weaknesses of their initiatives. Appropriate methods might include:

- a survey for parents
- focus groups for school children
- key informant interviews with school staff
- a workshop/forum for themselves as implementers

ISSUES IN EVALUATIVE RESEARCH

'Honest criticism is hard to take, particularly from a relative, a friend, an acquaintance, or a stranger.'

- Franklin P. Jones

The goal of any research study is to produce useful and credible results. In evaluative research, however, this goal can be quite problematic. Researchers attempting to conduct an evaluative study need to recognize that:

TABLE 10.2 EVALUATION IN AN IDEAL WORLD ...

Evaluation in an ideal world would mean ...	Unfortunately, in the real world ...
Politics	
• Full stakeholder cooperation	➤ Cooperation can be hard to obtain. Programme initiators may not want to invest time and resources ... and they may resent feeling judged
• True desire for unbiased results	➤ Not everyone will want a candid assessment of their initiatives. Some will, but others will be looking to meet requirements, or simply receive validation
• No pressure from vested interests	➤ Whether overt or subtle, pressure to find success can come across loud and clear
Direction	
• Clear client directives	➤ A need to evaluate might be recognized, but there is often little consensus on the exact nature of the evaluation to be undertaken
• Realistic expectations	➤ Expectations are often unrealistic – especially when initiative effects can be: (a) difficult to measure; (b) difficult to attribute to the initiative under study
The initiative	
• Evaluation planned from the initiative's onset	➤ The decision to evaluate often comes after implementation, which means solid baseline data and/or comparable control groups can be hard to find
• Clear and measurable aims and objectives	➤ Objectives can be (a) implicit and not clearly articulated and/or (b) not measurable
• Well established, mature initiatives	➤ Interventions rarely show immediate success, yet they can be subject to deadlines that might come before you would expect to see any real change
Resources	
• Adequate time and funding to undertake the study	➤ As in any study, time and resources can be in short supply
• Researchers with insider knowledge, political nous and outsider objectivity	➤ There is almost always a need to balance political and research agendas

- *Evaluative research is highly political* – there are many vested interests and the pressure on researchers to find 'success' can be high.
- *There is nothing clear-cut or controlled in evaluative research* – when conducting an evaluative study researchers are absolutely immersed in the complexity and chaos of a real-world setting.

In fact, as shown in Table 10.2 and teased out in the following sections, credibility in evaluative research would be much easier to assure in an ideal world.

Negotiating politics, pressure and vested interests

'In criticism I will be bold, and as sternly, absolutely just with friend and foe. From this purpose nothing shall turn me.'

- Edgar Allan Poe

Clearly Poe's sentiments should apply in evaluative research. Integrity and objectivity should be transparent objectives. But there's no getting around the fact that evaluative research is political. It would be naive to pretend otherwise. Evaluative research means working with real people; and working with real people requires diplomacy.

So how do you begin to negotiate and balance the sometimes divergent political and scientific goals of evaluative research? Well, I think the first step is to get a better understanding of researcher/researched realities and relationships. For example, not everyone undergoing evaluative studies has the same goals. Yes, some want honest and open feedback, but others might be after validation of what they've done, and others might simply be submitting to an evaluative process in order to meet requirements. And of course, some may be after a combination of the above.

The same is true of researchers, whether insiders or outsiders; not all evaluative researchers operate with the same style, skills or goals. For example, some see themselves as objective researchers whose clear and unwavering objective is credible findings regardless of political context. Others do operate at a more political level and are highly in tune with government/organization/political funding realities, and perhaps their own ongoing consultancy opportunities. There are others (in my experience often ill-trained, inexperienced, insecure and sometimes pompous and arrogant individuals) who tend to be overcritical and need to show their intelligence by picking holes in the work of others. Finally, there are those that see themselves as facilitators or even mentors who are there to help.

When I first began doing evaluative research I came across and learnt from all of these styles. And I assumed that my way forward would be as an objective researcher. But I soon realized that the political end of evaluative research cannot be ignored and that the key to real-world evaluation is flexibility. Now my main grounding objective, which is tied to my own professional ethics, is to produce credible and useful findings. But how those findings are presented, what is emphasized, what is best left unsaid, is undeniably influenced by both politics and context.

Table 10.3 looks at the intersection of researcher/researched goals in terms of researcher credibility and researcher/researched relationships. While the matrix cannot capture all possibilities, it should provide you with some insights into the

220

TABLE 10.3 RELATIONSHIPS IN EVALUATIVE RESEARCH

'Clients' who seek ... / Evaluators whose style tends to be that of ...	Honest feedback	Validation	To meet funding requirements
The Critic Credibility: can be difficult to build trust, thereby influencing data/findings. Findings tend to overemphasize the negative and not point out the positive	While the client may appreciate knowing their initiative's shortcomings, they can be left feeling deflated and undervalued by the critic	This relationship spells trouble. Clients are likely to be demoralized, disheartened and even angry. Critics are likely to burn their bridges here	Those who do not appreciate the value of evaluation are likely to be further put off by the critic. There is a good chance here of weakening trust and building resentment
The Unbiased Scientist Credibility: best odds of credible data/findings, particularly if the approach is one that attempts to build trust while collecting unbiased data	**A good match**, but still no harm in the 'scientist' honing political skills. Even those who want honest feedback appreciate diplomacy	While findings might be fair, how they are accepted and acted upon by those seeking validation often depends on a researcher's sensitivity and communication skills	Relationships tend to be enhanced by supportive findings and a researcher's interpersonal skills – communication skills can be instrumental in 'selling' the value of evaluation
The Facilitator/ Mentor Credibility: likely to result in credible findings if the initiative is a success. There can be a tendency to gloss over shortcomings and emphasize the positive. Can lead to thorough process-related recommendations	While relationships are generally positive, clients can be frustrated if they feel they are not getting the feedback/hard data they need for effective decision making	This is actually a **good match** that can leave clients feeling their work is valued. Good chance that process-related recommendations will be taken up	Mentors might be able to build trust and instil the value of evaluation. But if clients remain cynical, they may not put high value on the mentor's recommendations
The Politician Credibility: findings need to be explored in light of the political context – there is a need to read between the lines. Findings may support the agenda of those commissioning the research	Generally not too problematic as long as expectations are clear. Researcher and client objectives should be made explicit and negotiated so that they are not at cross-purposes	If politician and client goals are the same, i.e., validation, the relationship is likely to be good, even if feedback is uncritical. If, however, goals are at cross-purposes, client satisfaction can be low	This tends to be a **good match** because goals are usually aligned with a particular agenda. Levels of critical feedback should be discussed and negotiated

realities of evaluative research and the skills required to work effectively in such a politically charged environment.

I've worked with quite a few evaluators and I think the best ones are politically astute but always work under a code of professional ethics and integrity. Some will adapt their style dependent on the client and context, while others will stay true to a certain way of working. But almost all good evaluators understand the need to negotiate clear expectations that meet both client and researcher needs and goals with integrity.

Unfortunately, such expectations are not always easy to negotiate. Say, for example, you are commissioned to conduct an evaluative study and you sense there is an unspoken expectation that your results will confirm the client's hard work and large investment. Their expectation of you may be at odds with your professional ethics that see you need to produce credible results. If this is the case, it may be best to decline the opportunity to engage in that particular evaluative study. In the end, if expectations remain divergent, you are highly unlikely to meet your client's needs in a comfortable way.

Negotiating real-world challenges of evaluative research

In the conduct of evaluative research, political realities are not the only challenge to the production of credible data. As highlighted in Table 10.2, evaluative research is set within messy and chaotic real-world settings, and you will need to skilfully negotiate this level of complexity if you want to produce solid, valuable results.

Now if it were up to me, all of the initiatives I would be asked to evaluate would be mature and well established with clear and measurable aims and objectives. But rarely is this the case. You generally need to find ways to work around circumstances that are less than ideal. Such situations include the following.

When the decision to evaluate comes after initial implementation

It would be wonderful if the need to evaluate was a recognized part of project planning from conception. You'd then have all the options. Early planning would allow you to design truly comparative studies such as randomized trials, quasi-experiments with control groups, or before and after designs. But there are plenty of circumstances where you will need to undertake evaluations where the evaluative planning was but an after-thought – thereby limiting your methodological options.

The key here is remembering that evaluative studies, particularly those studies related to outcomes, are all about comparison. And by far, the best way to compare is by using at least two data sets. Effective evaluations are based on either before and after data (data collected before the initiative that can be compared with data collected after the initiative), or case/control data (data collected from two groups, one that has undergone the initiative and one that hasn't).

Without the aid of forward planning you will need to consider if either of these options is available to you. In other words, you will need to determine whether you'll be able to collect solid relevant baseline data, or whether you'll be able to find a comparable control group. If you can, rigorous evaluation is not too problematic. But if baseline data or a comparable control group are not available, you are left with the following methodological options:

- Do a 'post group only' study in which you ask stakeholders about the effects (on knowledge, attitude and/or practice) of the initiative under review. While generally not as strong as truly comparative methods, this approach can still have value. The key here is clear expectations. Your clients need to be aware of your methodological constraints and how they might affect findings.
- Limit your study to process evaluation that centres on stakeholder's reflections on an initiative's design, delivery and implementation.

When objectives are not clearly articulated or are not readily measurable

If you want to know if an initiative has achieved its goals, then you clearly need to know two things: (1) what those goals were/are and (2) how they might be measured. Now by far the best objectives are those that are 'SMART'; as described in Applied Example 10.2, this stands for **S**pecific, **M**easurable, **A**chievable, **R**elevant and **T**ime-bound.

If your initiative has been developed with such objectives in mind, in terms of methodological design, you're half-way there. By definition, your objectives are measurable – so you just need to go out and measure. But for initiatives where objectives are not clearly articulated, or are not measurable, you have to do a bit more work. Since you simply can't evaluate non-existent or waffly objectives, you will need to:

- work with stakeholders to clearly draw out and articulate the initiative's objectives
- decide which objectives will be prioritized for evaluation

- determine and agree on how these objectives can be operationalized (for example, designing a method that can measure 'the joy of reading in children' is much more difficult than designing a method that can measure 'an increase in recreational reading of third graders by 50% by the end of the year')

When the initiative has not been going long enough to expect results

It's not unusual for the timeframe given for an evaluative study to be shorter than that needed for an initiative to produce its intended results. For example, in health promotion campaigns goals are often related to disease alleviation such as reducing incidence of lung cancer, or decreasing the incidence of Type II diabetes. But not only are such effects hard to attribute to a particular campaign, such effects might not be seen for several years.

A common strategy used by evaluators facing this situation is to negotiate short-to intermediate-term outcomes that can be (a) measured within the timeframe available, and (b) correlated to the expected long-term outcomes. For example, success might be measured by increased awareness, i.e. increased community knowledge about the dangers of smoking or increased awareness of the impact of carbohydrates on insulin. Success might also be measured by changes in behaviour, such as reducing the number of cigarettes smoked or decreasing levels of sugar consumption.

When effects of the initiative can be: (a) difficult to measure or (b) difficult to attribute to the initiative

Say you were asked to evaluate a high school sex education programme that has a clear and central goal of increasing abstinence. To evaluate this programme, not only would you need to collect sensitive data from young people (who may not feel comfortable exposing themselves), you would also need to design a research protocol that could control for any other factors that are known to have an effect on abstinence, such as parents, peers, media, etc. Remember, you're not just looking for a correlation here. You are actually trying to establish cause and effect, and your methods will need to attempt to control for any other factors that might be causal to any perceived change or difference. Controlling for extraneous factors is the only way to be able to attribute results to the programme itself.

The lesson here is that before taking on an evaluative research study, you need to clearly consider, articulate and negotiate what is, and what is not, possible. In the real world it can be difficult, if not impossible, to control for all extraneous variables that may affect change.

Remember, it's much better to have critiques of your methodology come before you undertake a study, rather than after it's been completed!

FURTHER READING

There are a number of books that can take you further into the world of evaluative research and I've tried to recommend some that give both practical advice and grounded examples. If you're after readings that get right into the nitty-gritty of evaluative *methods*, you may find you need to turn to readings more specifically related to methods of data collection (see recommended readings in Chapter 6) and methods of data analysis that you intend to use (see recommended readings in Chapter 11).

Berk, R. A. and Rossi, P. H. (1999) *Thinking about Program Evaluation.* Thousand Oaks, CA: Sage.

Chen, H. (1999) *Theory Driven Evaluations.* Thousand Oaks, CA: Sage.

Estrella, M. (ed.) (2000) *Learning from Change: Issues and Experiences in Participatory Monitoring and Evaluation.* Sterling, VA: Stylus Publishers.

Mansoor, A. F. Kazi (2003) *Realist Evaluation in Practice: Health and Social Work.* London: Sage.

Patton, M. Q. (2001) *Qualitative Research and Evaluation Methods.* Thousand Oaks, CA: Sage.

Rossi, P. H. (1999) 'Evaluating Community Development Programs: Problems and Prospects', in R. F. Ferguson and W. T. Dickens (eds), *Urban Problems and Community Development.* Washington, DC: Brookings. pp. 521–67.

Rossi, P. H., Freeman, H. E. and Lipsey, M. W. (1999) *Evaluation: A Systematic Approach.* Thousand Oaks, CA: Sage.

Chapter Summary

- Evaluative research is undertaken to determine the value of some initiative such as a programme or policy. Findings of evaluative studies are considered crucial to rational and informed decision making.

- Evaluative studies can relate to outcomes, 'Did it work?', or process, 'How can the design and implementation of the initiative be improved?'

- Rather than be defined by any particular methodological approach, evaluative goals and perspectives sought determine appropriate methodology.

- Multiple and diverse methods such as interviews, surveys, focus groups, observation and document review are often called on in process evaluation. They can also be important tools in outcome evaluations that seek provider and community perspectives.

- Methods that allow for direct comparison, such as experiments and quasi-experiments, can be highly useful when evaluating outcomes that affect target groups.

- Evaluative research is political, with both stakeholders and researchers having diverse goals and complex relationships.

- Navigating the politics of evaluation is easiest if client and researcher objectives/expectations are made clear and are openly negotiated.

- Evaluative research takes place in the real world with all its associated complexity. Real-world challenges include: when the decision to evaluate comes after initial implementation; when objectives are not clearly articulated or are not readily measurable; when the intervention has not been going long enough to expect results; and when effects of the initiative can be: (a) difficult to measure; (b) difficult to attribute to the initiative.

PART FOUR

Making Meaning/Making a Difference

11 **Analysing and Interpreting Data**
12 **Producing Research 'Deliverables'**

These final two chapters centre on the challenge of moving from raw data to an end product capable of making an impact. While research into real-world problems has an end goal of making a difference, it's easy to get lost in the production of dry and turgid reports that are often not 'heard' by those in a position to implement change. These chapters will help you use your data to tell a 'story' and to produce useful 'deliverables'. The goal is to maximize the potential for your research to make a real contribution to on-the-ground change.

11
Analysing and Interpreting Data

'All meanings, we know, depend on the key of interpretation.'

- George Eliot

FROM RAW DATA TO MEANINGFUL UNDERSTANDING

It's easy to fall into the trap of thinking the major hurdle in conducting real-world research is data collection. And yes, gathering credible data is certainly a challenge – but so is making sense of it. As George Eliot states, the key to meaning is 'interpretation'.

Now attempting to interpret a mound of data can be intimidating. Just looking at it can bring on a nasty headache or a mild anxiety attack. So the question is, what is the best way to make a start? How can you begin to work through your data?

Well, if I were only allowed to give one piece of advice, it would be to engage in creative and inspired analysis using a methodical and organized approach. As described in Box 11.1, the best way to move from messy, complex and chaotic raw data … towards rich, meaningful and eloquent understandings is by working through your data in ways that are creative, yet managed within a logical and systematic framework.

229

Box 11.1   *Balancing Creativity and Focus*

Think outside the square ... yet stay squarely on target
Be original, innovative, and imaginative ... yet know where you want to go
Use your intuition ... but be able to share the logic of that intuition
Be fluid and flexible ... yet deliberate and methodical
Be inspired, imaginative and ingenious ... yet realistic and practical

---

Easier said than done, I know. But if you break the process of analysis down into a number of defined tasks, it's a challenge that can be conquered. For me, there are five tasks that need to be managed when conducting analysis:

1. Keeping your eye on the main game. This means not getting lost in a swarm of numbers and words in a way that causes you to lose a sense of what you're trying to accomplish.
2. Managing, organizing, preparing and coding your data so that it's ready for your intended mode(s) of analysis.
3. Engaging in the actual process of analysis. For quantified data, this will involve some level of statistical analysis, while working with words and images will require you to call on qualitative data analysis strategies.
4. Presenting data in ways that capture understandings, and being able to offer those understandings to others in the clearest possible fashion.
5. Drawing meaningful and logical conclusions that flow from your data and address key issues.

This chapter tackles each of these challenges in turn.

Keeping your eye on the main game

While the thought of getting into your data can be daunting, once you take the plunge it's actually quite easy to get lost in the process. Now this is great if 'getting lost' means you are engaged and immersed and really getting a handle on what's going on. But getting lost can also mean getting lost in the tasks, that is, handing control to analysis programs, and losing touch with the main game. You need to remember that while computer programs might be able to do the 'tasks', it is the researcher who needs to work strategically, creatively and intuitively to get a 'feel' for the data; to cycle between data and existing

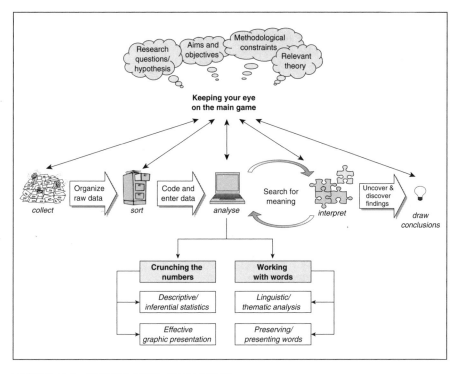

FIGURE 11.1   THE PROCESS OF ANALYSIS

theory; and to follow the hunches that can lead to sometimes unexpected, yet significant findings.

Have a look at Figure 11.1. It's based on a model I developed a while ago that attempts to capture the full 'process' of analysis; a process that is certainly more complex and comprehensive than simply plugging numbers or words into a computer. In fact, real-world analysis involves staying as close to your data as possible – from initial collection right through to drawing final conclusions. And as you move towards these conclusions, it's essential that you keep your eye on the game in a way that sees you consistently moving between your data and … your research questions, aims and objectives, theoretical underpinnings and methodological constraints. Remember, even the most sophisticated analysis is worthless if you're struggling to grasp the implications of your findings to your overall project.

Rather than relinquish control of your data to 'methods' and 'tools', thoughtful analysis should see you persistently interrogating your data, as well as the findings that emerge from that data. In fact, as highlighted in Box 11.2, keeping your eye on the game means asking a number of questions throughout the process of analysis.

**Box 11.2   Questions for Keeping the
Bigger Picture in Mind**

Questions related to your own expectations

- What do I expect to find i.e. will my hypothesis bear out?
- What don't I expect to find, and how can I look for it?
- Can my findings be interpreted in alternative ways? What are the implications?

Questions related to research question, aims and objectives

- How should I treat my data in order to best address my research questions?
- How do my findings relate to my research questions, aims and objectives?

Questions related to theory

- Are my findings confirming my theories? How? Why? Why not?
- Does my theory inform/help to explain my findings? In what ways?
- Can my unexpected findings link with alternative theories?

Questions related to methods

- Have my methods of data collection and/or analysis coloured my results. If so, in what ways?
- How might my methodological shortcomings be affecting my findings?

Managing the data

Data can build pretty quickly, and you might be surprised by the amount of data you have managed to collect. For some, this will mean coded notebooks, labelled folders, sorted questionnaires, transcribed interviews, etc. But for the less pedantic, it might mean scraps of paper, jotted notes, an assortment of cuttings and bulging files. No matter what the case, the task is to build or create a 'data set' that can be managed and utilized throughout the process of analysis.

Now this is true whether you are working with: (a) data you've decided to quantify; (b) data you've captured and preserved in a qualitative form; (c) a combination of the above (there can be real appeal in combining the power of words with the authority of numbers). Regardless of approach, the goal is the same – a rigorous and systematic approach to data management that can lead to credible findings. Box 11.3 runs through six steps I believe are essential for effectively managing your data.

Box 11.3   Data Management

Step 1   Familiarize yourself with appropriate software

This involves accessing programs and arranging necessary training. Most universities (and some workplaces) have licences that allow students certain software access, and many universities provide relevant short courses. Programs themselves generally contain comprehensive tutorials complete with mock data sets.

Quantitative analysis will demand the use of a data management/statistics program, but there is some debate as to the necessity of specialist programs for qualitative data analysis. This debate is taken up later in the chapter, but the advice here is that it's certainly worth becoming familiar with the tools available.

Quantitative programs

- **SPSS** – sophisticated and user-friendly (www.spss.com)
- **SAS** – often an institutional standard, but many feel it is not as user-friendly as SPSS (www.sas.com)
- **Minitab** – more introductory, good for learners/small data sets (www.minitab.com)
- **Excel** – while not a dedicated stats program it can handle the basics and is readily available on most PCs (Microsoft Office product)

Qualitative programs

Absolutely essential: here is an up-to-date word processing package

Specialist packages include:
- **NU*DIST, NVIVO, MAXqda, The Ethnograph** – used for indexing, searching and theorizing
- **ATLAS.ti** – can be used for images as well as words
- **CONCORDANCE, HAMLET, DICTION** – popular for content analysis
  (all above available: www.textanalysis.info)

- **CLAN-CA** popular for conversation analysis (http://childes.psy.cmu.edu)

(Continued)

Box 11.3 (Continued)

Step 2 Log in your data

Data can come from a number of sources at various stages throughout the research process, so it's well worth keeping a record of your data as it's collected. Keep in mind that original data should be kept for a reasonable period of time; researchers need to be able to trace results back to original sources.

Step 3 Organize your data

This involves grouping like sources, making any necessary copies and conducting an initial cull of any notes, observations, etc. not relevant to the analysis.

Step 4 Screen your data for any potential problems

This includes a preliminary check to see if your data is legible and complete. If done early, you can uncover potential problems not picked up in your pilot/trial, and make improvements to your data collection protocols.

Step 5 Enter the data

This involves systematically entering your data into a database or analysis program, as well as creating codebooks, which can be electronically based, that describe your data and keep track of how it can be accessed.

Quantitative data

Codebooks often include: the respondent or group; the variable name and description; unit of measurement; date collected; any relevant notes

Data entry: data can be entered as it is collected or after it has all come in. Analysis does not take place until after data entry is complete. Figure 11.2 depicts an SPSS data entry screen

Qualitative data

Codebooks often include: respondents; themes; data collection procedures; collection dates; commonly used shorthand; and any other notes relevant to the study

Data entry: whether using a general word processing program or specialist software, data is generally transcribed in an electronic form and is worked through as it is received. Analysis tends to be ongoing and often begins before all the data has been collected/entered

---

Box 11.3   *(Continued)*

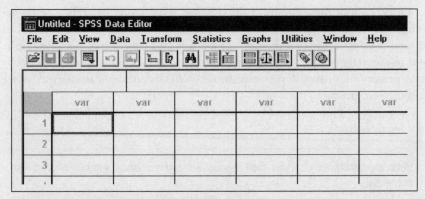

FIGURE 11.2   DATA ENTRY SCREEN FOR SPSS

Step 6   Clean the data
This involves combing through the data to make sure any entry errors are found, and that the data set looks in order.

Quantitative data
When entering quantified data it's easy to make mistakes – particularly if you're moving fast, i.e. typos. It's essential that you go through your data to make sure it's as accurate as possible

Qualitative data
Because qualitative data is generally handled as it's collected, there is often a chance to refine processes as you go. In this way your data can be as 'ready' as possible for analysis

---

STATISTICS – THE KISS (KEEP IT SIMPLE AND SENSIBLE) APPROACH

*'Doctors say that Nordberg has a 50/50 chance of living,
though there's only a 10 percent chance of that.'*

– Naked Gun

It wasn't long ago that 'doing' statistics meant working with formulae, but personally, I don't believe in the need for all real-world researchers to master formulae. Doing statistics in the twenty-first century is more about your ability to use statistical software than your ability to calculate means, modes, medians and standard deviations – and look up *p*-values in the back of a book. To say otherwise is to suggest that you can't ride a bike unless you know how to build one. What you really need to do is to learn how to ride, or in this case learn how to run a stats program.

Okay, I admit these programs do demand a basic understanding of the language and logic of statistics. And this means you will need to get your head around (1) the nature of variables; (2) the role and function of both descriptive and inferential statistics; (3) appropriate use of statistical tests; and (4) effective data presentation. But if you can do this, effective statistical analysis is well within your grasp.

Now before I jump in and talk about the above a bit more, I think it's important to stress that …

> Very few students can get their heads around statistics without getting into some data.

While this chapter will familiarize you with the basic language and logic of statistics, it really is best if your reading is done in conjunction with some hands-on practice (even if this is simply playing with the mock data sets provided in stats programs). For this type of knowledge 'to stick', it needs to be applied.

Variables

Understanding the nature of variables is essential to statistical analysis. Different data types demand discrete treatment. Using the appropriate statistical measures to both describe your data and to infer meaning from your data requires that you clearly understand your variables in relation to both cause and effect and measurement scales.

Cause and effect
The first thing you need to understand about variables relates to cause and effect. In research-methods-speak, this means being able to clearly identify and distinguish your dependent and independent variables. Now while understanding the theoretical difference is not too tough, being able to readily identify each type comes with practice.

DEPENDENT VARIABLES   These are the things you are trying to study or what you are trying to measure. For example, you might be interested in knowing what factors are related to high levels of stress, a strong income stream, or levels of achievement in secondary school – stress, income and achievement would all be dependent variables.

INDEPENDENT VARIABLES   These are the things that might be causing an effect on the things you are trying to understand. For example, conditions of employment might be affecting stress levels; gender may have a role in determining income; while parental influence may impact on levels of achievement. The independent variables here are employment conditions, gender and parental influence.

One way of identifying dependent and independent variables is simply to ask what depends on what. Stress *depends* on work conditions or income *depends* on gender. As I like to tell my students, it doesn't make sense to say gender depends on income unless you happen to be saving for a sex-change operation!

Measurement scales

Measurement scales refer to the nature of the differences you are trying to capture in relation to a particular variable (examples below). As summed up in Table 11.1, there are four basic measurement scales that become respectively more precise: nominal, ordinal, interval and ratio. The precision of each type is directly related to the statistical tests that can be performed on them. The more precise the measurement scale, the more sophisticated the statistical analysis you can do.

NOMINAL   Numbers are arbitrarily assigned to represent categories. These numbers are simply a coding scheme and have no numerical significance (and therefore cannot be used to perform mathematical calculations). For example, in the case of gender you would use one number for female, say 1, and another for male, 2. In an example used later in this chapter, the variable 'plans after graduation' is also nominal with numerical values arbitrarily assigned as 1 = vocational/technical training, 2 = university, 3 = workforce, 4 = travel abroad, 5 = undecided and 6 = other. In nominal measurement, codes should not overlap (they should be mutually exclusive) and together should cover all possibilities (be collectively exhaustive). The main function of nominal data is to allow researchers to tally respondents in order to understand population distributions.

ORDINAL   This scale rank orders categories in some meaningful way – there is an order to the coding. Magnitudes of difference, however, are not indicated. Take for example, socio-economic status (lower, middle, or upper class). Lower class may denote less status than the other two classes but the amount of the difference is not defined. Other examples include air travel (economy, business, first class), or items where respondents are asked to rank order selected choices (biggest environmental challenges facing developed countries). Likert-type scales, in which respondents are asked to select a response on a point scale (for example, 'I enjoy going to work': 1 = strongly disagree, 2 = disagree, 3 = neutral, 4 = agree, 5 = strongly agree), are ordinal since a precise difference in magnitude cannot be determined. Many researchers, however, treat Likert scales as interval

TABLE 11.1 MEASUREMENT SCALES

	Nominal	Ordinal	Interval	Ratio
Classifies	✓	✓	✓	✓
Orders		✓	✓	✓
Equidistant units			✓	✓
Absolute zero				✓

because it allows them to perform more precise statistical tests. In most small-scale studies this is not generally viewed as problematic.

INTERVAL   In addition to ordering the data, this scale uses equidistant units to measure difference. This scale does not, however, have an absolute zero. An example here is date – the year 2006 occurs 41 years after the year 1965, but time did not begin in AD1. IQ is also considered an interval scale even though there is some debate over the equidistant nature between points.

RATIO   Not only is each point on a ratio scale equidistant, there is also an absolute zero. Examples of ratio data include age, height, distance and income. Because ratio data are 'real' numbers all basic mathematical operations can be performed.

Descriptive statistics

Descriptive statistics are used to describe the basic features of a data set and are key to summarizing variables. The goal is to present quantitative descriptions in a manageable and intelligible form. Descriptive statistics provide measures of central tendency, dispersion and distribution shape. Such measures vary by data type (nominal, ordinal, interval, ratio) and are standard calculations in statistical programs. In fact, when generating the example tables for this section, I used the statistics program SPSS. After entering my data, I generated my figures by going to 'Analyze' on the menu bar, clicking on 'Descriptive Statistics', clicking on 'Frequencies', and then defining the statistics and charts I required.

Measuring central tendency

One of the most basic questions you can ask of your data centres on central tendency. For example, what was the average score on a test? Do most people lean left or right on the issue of abortion? Or what do most people think is the main problem with our health care system? In statistics, there are three ways to measure central tendency (see Table 11.2): mean, median and mode – and the

TABLE 11.2 CENTRAL TENDENCY FOR 'AGE OF PARTICIPANTS'*

Data related to age of participants in a local youth group	
Raw data	12, 12, 10, 9, 12, 15, 11, 12, 11, 11, 15, 16, 17, 12, 13, 13, 14, 11, 10, 9, 9, 8, 13, 14, 12, 14, 15, 13, 13, 10, 9, 13, 14, 13, 9
N (no. of cases)	35
Mean (average)	12.11
Median (midpoint)	12
Mode (most common value)	13

*Figures generated with SPSS.

example questions above respectively relate to these three measures. Now while measures of central tendency can be calculated manually, all stats programs can automatically calculate these figures.

MEAN   The mathematical average. To calculate the mean, you add the values for each case and then divide by the number of cases. Because the mean is a mathematical calculation, it is used to measure central tendency for interval and ratio data, and cannot be used for nominal or ordinal data where numbers are used as 'codes'. For example, it makes no sense to average the 1s, 2s and 3s that might be assigned to Christians, Buddhists and Muslims.

MEDIAN   The mid-point of a range. To find the median you simply arrange values in ascending (or descending) order and find the middle value. This measure is generally used in ordinal data, and has the advantage of negating the impact of extreme values. Of course, this can also be a limitation given that extreme values can be significant to a study.

MODE   The most common value or values noted for a variable. Since nominal data is categorical and cannot be manipulated mathematically, it relies on mode as its measure of central tendency.

Measuring dispersion

While measures of central tendency are a standard and highly useful form of data description and simplification, they need to be complemented with information on response variability. For example, say you had a group of students with IQs of 100, 100, 95 and 105, and another group of students with IQs of 60,

239

TABLE 11.3   DISPERSION FOR 'AGE OF PARTICIPANTS'*

Data related to age of participants in a local youth group	
Raw data	12, 12, 10, 9, 12, 15, 11, 12, 11, 11, 15, 16, 17, 12, 13, 13, 14, 11, 10, 9, 9, 8, 13, 14, 12, 14, 15, 13, 13, 10, 9, 13, 14, 13, 9
N (no. of cases)	35
Range (spread of the data)	8 to 17 = 9
Inner quartile range (spread between 25th and 75th %)	10 to 14 = 4
Variance (spread around the mean)	4.93
Standard deviation (sq root of variance)	2.22

*Figures generated with SPSS.

140, 65 and 135, the central tendency, in this case the mean, of both groups would be 100. Dispersion around the mean, however, will require you to design curriculum and engage learning with each group quite differently. There are several ways to understand dispersion, which are appropriate for different variable types (see Table 11.3). As with central tendency, statistics programs will automatically generate these figures on request.

RANGE   This is the simplest way to calculate dispersion, and is simply the highest minus the lowest value. For example, if your respondents ranged in age from 8 to 17, the range would be 9 years. While this measure is easy to calculate, it is dependent on extreme values alone, and ignores intermediate values.

QUARTILES   This involves subdividing your range into four equal parts or 'quartiles' and is a commonly used measure of dispersion for ordinal data, or data whose central tendency is measured by a median. It allows researchers to compare the various quarters or present the inner 50% as a dispersion measure. This is known as the *inner-quartile range*.

VARIANCE   This measure uses all values to calculate the spread around the mean, and is actually the 'average squared deviation from the mean'. It needs to be calculated from interval and ratio data and gives a good indication of dispersion. It's much more common, however, for researchers to use and present the square root of the variance which is known as the standard deviation.

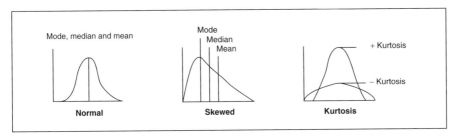

FIGURE 11.3 SHAPE OF THE DATA

STANDARD DEVIATION   This is the square root of the variance, and is the basis of many commonly used statistical tests for interval and ratio data. As explained below, its power comes to the fore with data that sits under a normal curve.

Measuring the shape of the data

To fully understand a data set, central tendency and dispersion need to be considered in light of the shape of the data, or how the data is distributed. As shown in Figure 11.3, a normal curve is 'bell-shaped'; the distribution of the data is symmetrical, with the mean, median and mode all converged at the highest point in the curve. If the distribution of the data is not symmetrical, it is considered skewed. In skewed data the mean, median and mode fall at different points.

Kurtosis characterizes how peaked or flat a distribution is compared to 'normal'. Positive kurtosis indicates a relatively peaked distribution, while negative kurtosis indicates a flatter distribution.

The significance in understanding the shape of a distribution is in the statistical inferences that can be drawn. As shown in Figure 11.4, a normal distribution is subject to a particular set of rules regarding the significance of a standard deviation. Namely that:

- 68.2% of cases will fall within one standard deviation of the mean
- 95.4% of cases will fall within two standard deviations of the mean
- 99.6% of cases will fall within three standard deviations of the mean

So if we had a normal curve for the sample data relating to 'age of participants' (mean = 12.11, s.d. = 2.22 – see Boxes 11.2, 11.3), 68.2% of participants would fall between the ages of 9.89 and 14.33 (12.11–2.22 and 12.11+2.22).

These rules of the normal curve allow for the use of quite powerful statistical tests and are generally used with interval and ratio data (sometimes called parametric tests). For data that does not follow the assumptions of a normal curve (nominal and ordinal data), the researcher needs to call on non-parametric statistical tests in making inferences.

Table 11.4 shows the curve, skewness and kurtosis of our sample data set.

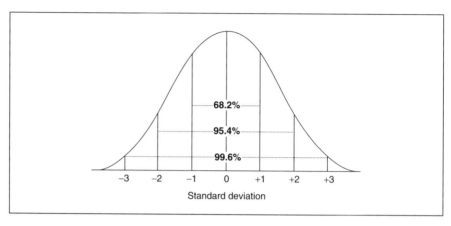

FIGURE 11.4 AREAS UNDER THE NORMAL CURVE

TABLE 11.4 SHAPE OF THE DATA FOR 'AGE OF PARTICIPANTS'*

Data related to age of participants in a local youth group	
Raw data	12, 12, 10, 9, 12, 15, 11, 12, 11, 11, 15, 16, 17, 12, 13, 13, 14, 11, 10, 9, 9, 8, 13, 14, 12,14, 15, 13, 13, 10, 9, 13, 14, 13, 9
N (no. of cases)	35

Histogram
(distribution)

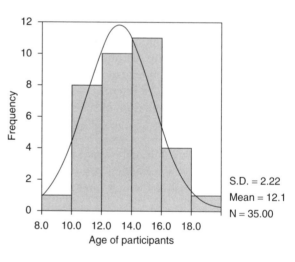

S.D. = 2.22
Mean = 12.1
N = 35.00

Skewness (symmetricality)	0.070
Kurtosis (flatness)	−0.562

*Figures and histogram generated with SPSS.

Inferential statistics

While the goal of descriptive statistics is to describe and summarize, the goal of inferential statistics is to draw conclusions that extend beyond immediate data. For example, inferential statistics can be used to estimate characteristics of a population from sample data, or to test various hypotheses about the relationship between different variables. Inferential statistics allow you to assess the probability that an observed difference is not just a fluke or chance finding. In other words, inferential statistics is about drawing conclusions that are statistically significant.

Statistical significance

Statistical significance refers to a measure, or 'p-value', which assesses the actual 'probability' that your findings are more than coincidental. Conventional p-values are .05, .01, and .001, which tells you that the probability your findings have occurred by chance is 5/100, 1/100, or 1/1,000 respectively. Basically, the lower the p-value, the more confident researchers can be that findings are genuine. Keep in mind that researchers do not usually accept findings that have a p-value greater than .05 because the probability that findings are coincidental or caused by sampling error is too great.

Questions suitable to inferential statistics

It's easy enough to tell students and new researchers that they need to interrogate their data, but it doesn't tell them what they should be asking. Box 11.4 offers some common questions which, while not exhaustive, should give you some ideas for interrogating real-world data using inferential statistics.

**Box 11.4   Questions for Interrogating
Quantitative Data using Inferential Statistics**

- **How do participants in my study compare to a larger population?**
  These types of question *compare a sample with a population*. For example, say you are conducting a study of patients in a particular coronary care ward. You might ask if the percentage of males or females in your sample, or their average age, or their ailments are statistically similar to coronary care patients across the country. To answer such questions you will need access to population data for this larger range of patients.

(Continued)

Box 11.4   *(Continued)*

- **Are there differences between two or more groups of respondents?**
  Questions that *compare two or more groups* are very common and are often referred to as 'between subject'. I'll stick with a medical theme here ... For example, you might ask if male and female patients are likely to have similar ailments; or whether patients of different ethnic backgrounds have distinct care needs; or whether patients who have undergone different procedures have different recovery times.
- **Have my respondents changed over time?**
  These types of question *involve before and after data* with either the same group of respondents or respondents who are matched by similar characteristics. They are often referred to as 'within subject'. An example of this type of question might be, 'have patients' dietary habits changed since undergoing bypass surgery?'
- **Is there a relationship between two or more variables?**
  These types of question can *look for either correlations (simply an association) or cause and effect*. Examples of correlation questions might be, 'Is there an association between time spent in hospital and satisfaction with nursing staff?' or, 'Is there a correlation between patient's age and the medical procedure they have undergone?' Questions looking for cause and effect differentiate dependent and independent variables. For example, 'Does satisfaction depend on length of stay?' or, 'Does stress depend on adequacy of medical insurance?' Cause and effect relationships can also look to more than one independent variable to explain variation in the dependent variable. For example, 'Does satisfaction with nursing staff depend on a combination of length of stay, age and severity of medical condition?'

(I realize that all of these examples are drawn from the medical or nursing fields, but application to other respondent groups is pretty straightforward. In fact, a good exercise here is to try to come up with similar types of question for alternative respondent groups.)

Selecting the right statistical test

There is a baffling array of statistical tests out there that can help you answer the types of question highlighted in Box 11.4. And programs such as SPSS and SAS are capable of running such tests without you needing to know the technicalities of their mathematical operations. The problem, however, is knowing which test is right for your particular application. Luckily, you can turn to a number of test selectors now available on the Internet (see Bill Trochim's test selector at www. socialresearchmethods.net/kb/index.htm) and through programs such as MODSTAT and SPSS.

But even with the aid of such selectors (including the tabular one I offer below), you still need to know the nature of your variables (independent/ dependent); scales of measurement (nominal, ordinal, interval, ratio); distribution shape (normal or skewed); the types of questions you want to ask; and the types of conclusions you are trying to draw.

Table 11.5 covers the most common tests for univariate (one variable), bivariate (two variable) and multivariate (three or more variable) data. The table can be read down the first column for univariate data (the column provides an example of the data type, its measure of central tendency, dispersion and appropriate tests for comparing this type of variable to a population). It can also be read as a grid for exploring the relationship between two or more variables. Once you know what tests to conduct, your statistical software will be able to run the analysis and assess statistical significance.

Presenting quantitative data

When it comes to presenting quantitative data, there can be a real temptation to offer graphs, charts and tables for every single variable in your study. So the first key to effective data presentation is to resist this temptation, and actively determine what is most important in your work. Your findings need to tell a story related to your aims, objectives and research questions.

Now when it comes to how your data should be presented, I think there is one golden rule: *it should not be hard work for the reader*. Most people's eyes glaze over when it comes to statistics, so your data should not be hard to decipher. You should not need to be a statistician to understand it. Your challenge is to graphically and verbally present your data so that meanings are clear. Any graphs and tables you present should ease the task for the reader. So while you need to include adequate information, you don't want to go into information overload. Box 11.5 covers the basics of graphic presentation, while Box 11.6 looks at the presentation of quantitative data in tabular form.

TABLE 11.5 SELECTING STATISTICAL TESTS

Univariate	Bi/Multivariate		
	NOMINAL	ORDINAL	INTERVAL/RATIO (Assumption of normality – if not normal use ordinal tests)
NOMINAL 2 point scale: gender – 1 = female 2 = male	Compare 2 or more groups: **Chi squared**	Compare 2 groups: **Mann–Whitney** 3 or more groups: **Kruskal– Wallis**	Compare 2 or more groups: **ANOVA followed by t-test**
3 point scale: religion – 1 = Catholic 2 = Protestant and 3 = Jewish Central tendency: **Mode** Dispersion: **Frequency** Compare sample to population: **Chi squared**	Compare within same group over time: 2 pts: **McNemar test** 3+ pts: **Cochran's Q**	Compare within same group over 2 times: 2 pts: **Wilcoxon signed rank test** 3+ pts: **Cochran's Q** 3 or more times (2+ pts): **Freidman's test**	Compare within same group over times (2+ pts): **ANOVA followed by t-test**
	Relationship with other variables: Yes/no: **Chi squared** Relationship Strength: 2 pts: **Phi** 3+ pts: **Lambda**	Relationship with other variables: Yes/no: **Chi squared** Relationship Strength: 2+ pts: **Lambda**	Relationship with other variables: Yes/no: **Pearson's product moment correlation** Relationship Strength: **F-test** With 2 or more independent and 1 dependent variable: **MANOVA** 2+ dependent variable and 3+ groups: **Multiple regression** or **Path analysis**
ORDINAL TV viewing – order of preference, 1 = sitcoms, 2 = dramas, 3 = movies, 4 = news, 5 = reality TV OR Likert scale 1 = strongly disagree, 2 = disagree, 3 = neutral, etc. Central tendency: **Median** Dispersion: **Interquartile range** Compare sample to population: **Kolmogrov Smirnov**		Relationship with other variables: Small sample <10: **Kendall's tau** Larger Sample: **Spearman's rho** With 1 variable as dependent: **Somer's d**	Relationship with other variables: **Jaspen's coefficient of multi-serial correlation** With the interval/ratio variable as dependent: **ANOVA**
INTERVAL/RATIO e.g. Interval – IQ score Ratio – real numbers, age, height, weight Central tendency: **Mean** Dispersion: **Standard deviation** Compare sample to population: **T-test**			Relationship with other variables – no dependent/independent distinction: **Pearson's product moment correlation** With 1 independent and 1 dependent variable: **Pearson's linear correlation** With 2 or more independent and 1 dependent variable: **Multiple regression** With 2 or more independent and 2 or more dependent variables: **Canonical correlation**

Box 11.5   *Graphs Aplenty*

The power of graphs

As they say, a picture is worth a thousand words, so a good graph can go a long way in communicating your findings.

Sample data

In order to run you through the most commonly used graphs in quantitative analysis, I mocked up a four-variable data set in SPSS using a hypothetical example of survey data from 60 students (30 males and 30 females) about to graduate from high school:

Gender 1 = female 2 = male	Grade point average (out of possible 4)	Plans after graduation 1 = voc/tech training 2 = university 3 = workforce 4 = travel 5 = undecided 6 = other	Importance of university 1 = not at all important to 7 = essential
1	3.10	2	7
2	2.60	3	2
1	1.30	3	2
2	3.60	5	6
2	1.50	1	1

etc. (60 cases in all)

Exploring 'Plans after graduation'

'Plans after graduation' is a nominal variable so bar and pie graphs tend to work well. The line graph, however, does not work because it's better suited to showing change over time – which is not what we're trying to do.

(Continued)

Box 11.5 (Continued)

Bar graph

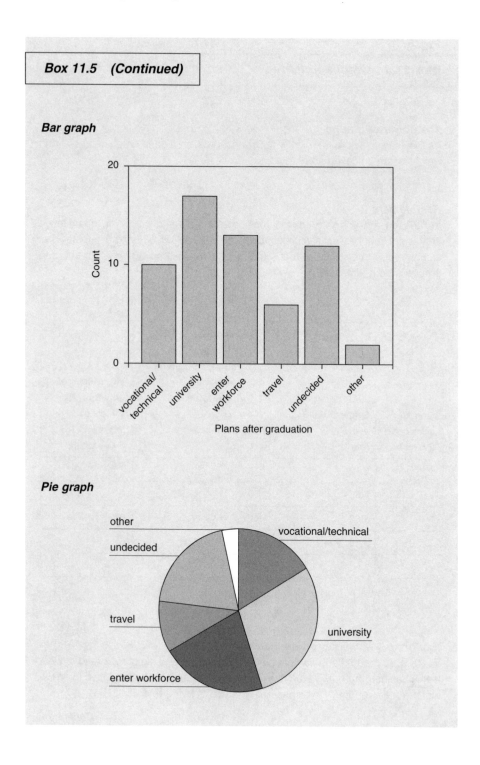

Pie graph

Box 11.5   (Continued)

Line graph

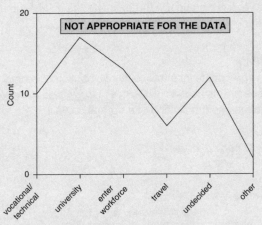

Plans after graduation

This type of graph would be better suited for data that showed something like changes in a student's GPA over their high school career (GPA would sit on one axis and year of study on the other).

Clustered bar graph

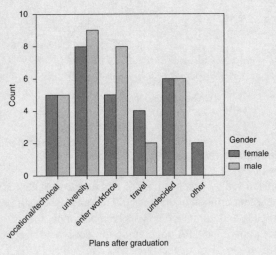

Plans after graduation

(Continued)

> ### Box 11.5   (Continued)

A clustered bar graph allows you to compare the distribution of a nominal variable for two or more groups. In this example, 'plans after graduation' is compared by gender.

Exploring 'GPA'

A histogram is appropriate for showing the distribution of interval and ratio data. Here we can see the distribution of 'GPA' (a ratio variable), complete with mean, standard deviation and the plotting of a normal curve.

Histogram with normal curve

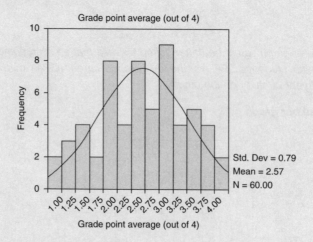

Exploring the relationship between 'GPA' and 'Importance of university'

In this example, a scatter graph is used to plot a *ratio* variable (GPA) against an *ordinal* variable (importance of university). The graph shows a positive correlation between GPA and perceived university importance, that is, while the relationship is not perfect, as GPA goes up so too does perceived importance. To find out the exact level of association you can run a Pearson's correlation, which shows a 0.773 correlation, significant at the .01 level.

Box 11.5   (Continued)

Scatter graph

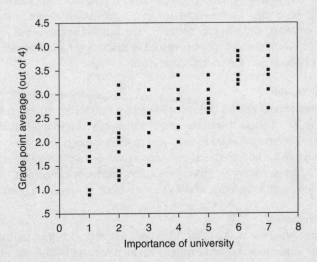

Importance of university

Generating the graphs

So how do you go about generating these types of graphs? Well there are two ways to do this and both involve sitting in front of a computer. The first is to have someone in the know show you what to do, and then practise it. The second is to sit down by yourself and have a play with a stats program. Most have great interactive online tutorials that can take you through the process from A to Z. While reading can give you familiarity, I truly believe that the best way to learn this kind of stuff is by doing.

Box 11.6   Generating tables

Presenting complexity with simplicity

Tables are generally more complex than graphs because they attempt to summarize the relationship between a number of variables. And because this summary

(Continued)

Box 11.6   (Continued)

can involve multiple statistical operations, statistics programs rarely spit tables out in a ready-to-use form. Now you can use an automatic table generator (you can find these on the Internet – one example is TableMaker at http://www.bagism. com/tablemaker), and this can certainly help, but the chances are you will still need to do some manual manipulation. The challenge here is walking the line between enough and too much information.

Rules of thumb

Your tables should not (a) give your readers a headache; (b) make their eyes glaze over; or (c) make them even more confused. While your tables don't have to stand alone (you will need to walk your readers through them) they should be something that the non-specialist can engage with and learn from. Your tables will be most effective if you can provide clear and adequate information, if you don't assume too much knowledge and if you keep them as simple as possible.

Some examples

Below are three examples taken from my own research into the process of giving up religion (see Applied Example 7.4 for more on the methods used in this study) (O'Leary 1997, 1999). Table 1 simply outlines the criteria I used to classify three distinct types of 'apostates' (people who have given up religious faith) and the percentage of my sample (n = 80) that fell into these categories. While this information is pretty self-explanatory and could've been presented in a non-tabular form, I thought the table allowed readers to get a quick sense of the distinctions I was trying to make.

Table 1   Apostate Classification and Distribution

Apostate type	Classification criteria
Anomic 30%	• A tone of: weariness; anger; irritated disgust, perhaps not with life, but at least with God or religion • A journey of reaction or rebellion
Egoistic 29%	• Empty, melancholic, depressive intellectualism • Confused detachment wherein religion becomes deconstructed to the point of irreconcilable doubt and emptiness
Postmodern 41%	• Without a reactionary basis, or a confused intellectualism • A willingness to expand the realms of spiritual possibility beyond immediate experience and frames of reference

Box 11.6   (Continued)

Table 2 is a bit more complex because it looks at the frequency distribution of these three apostate types by both gender and religion. It also shows that religion is significant, that is, the distribution is not even. You can't assume that your readers will know what this means so it is up to you to walk them through your table. An example of this type of walk-through is given below.

Table 2   Frequency Distributions for Demographic Variables by Apostate Type

	Anomic	Egoistic	Postmodern	Significance
Gender				
Female	50.0	45.8	46.9	
Male	50.0	54.2	53.1	
	100.0	100.0	100.0	
Religion				
Protestant	29.2	50.0	46.9	*
Catholic	70.8	50.0	53.1	
	100.0	100.0	100.0	

*Chi^2 test of significance $p < 0.05$.
All numbers are expressed as percentages.

As shown in this table, anomic, egoistic and postmodern apostates are as likely to be male as female. The results for religion, however, are somewhat more interesting. Egoistic and postmodern types are made up of similar proportions of Catholics and Protestants. Anomic apostates, however, are somewhat more likely to have a Catholic heritage.

The complexity of Table 3 is even greater because I attempt to compare certain characteristics of the apostates' journeys away from faith. In other words, I want to show if there is a statistically significant distinction between the three apostate types in relation to: how old they were when they first doubted their faith; how long the process took; whether it was still ongoing at the time of interview; and how intense the process was. The complexity of the table meant I definitely had to walk readers through it.

(Continued)

Box 11.6   (Continued)

Table 3   Mean Scores and Significance for Apostasy Profile Variables by Apostate Type*

	Anomic	Egoistic	Pomo	An-Eg	An-PM	Eg-PM
Age first doubt	20.88	19.58	16.94		*	
Process length	4.42	10.83	5.62	*		*
Process ongoing	0.08	0.35	0.15	*		*
Intensity	0.70	0.42	0.32	*	*	

*One way ANOVA (LSD) $p < 0.05$

The figures in this table point to varying and distinct patterns of disaffiliation for each apostate type. Anomic apostates generally complete an intense and relatively short journey away from faith. For the egoist, however, the process is quite lengthy, lasting an average of almost eleven years, with one-third still moving away from religion at the time of interview. The journey for the egoistic group, however, is not as intense as that of the anomic contingent. Postmodern apostates, on the other hand, go through a relatively short and often finalized process of disaffiliation that begins earlier in life. The process of disaffiliation is not generally seen as intense.

A final word
Good tables do take time to construct, and if you struggle at the high end of word processing, creating tables can be extraordinarily frustrating. But if you can manage to create tables that are well constructed and well explained, they can be an exceedingly important and effective communication tool.

QUALITATIVE DATA ANALYSIS (QDA)

'Not everything that can be counted counts, and not everything that counts can be counted.'

- Albert Einstein

I'd always thought of Einstein as an archetypal 'scientist'. But I've come to find that he is archetypal only if this means scientists are extraordinarily witty, insightful, political, creative and open-minded. Which, contrary to the stereotype, is exactly what I think is needed for groundbreaking advances in science. So when Einstein himself recognizes the limitations of quantification, it is indeed a powerful endorsement for working with qualitative data.

Yes, using statistics is a clearly defined and effective way of reducing and summarizing data. But statistics rely on the reduction of meaning to numbers, and there are two concerns here. First, meanings can be both intricate and complex, making it difficult to reduce them to numbers. Second, even with such a reduction, there can be a loss of 'richness' associated with the process.

These two concerns have led to the development of a plethora of qualitative data analysis (QDA) approaches that aim to create new understandings by exploring and interpreting complex data from sources such as interviews, group discussions, observation, journals, archival documents etc., without the aid of quantification. But the literature related to these approaches is quite thick, and wading through it in order to find appropriate and effective strategies can be a real challenge. Many students end up: (1) spending a huge amount of time attempting to work through the vast array of approaches and associated literature; (2) haphazardly selecting one method that may or may not be appropriate to their project; (3) conducting their analysis without any well-defined methodological protocols; or (4) doing a combination of the above.

So while we know that there is inherent power in words and images, the challenge is working through options for managing and analysing qualitative data that best preserve richness yet crystallize meaning. And I think the best way to go about this is to become familiar with both the logic and methods that underpin most QDA strategies. Once this foundation is set, working through more specific, specialist QDA strategies becomes much easier.

Logic and methods

Given that we have to make sense of complex, messy and chaotic qualitative data in the real-world everyday, you wouldn't think it would be too hard to articulate a rigorous QDA process. But the analysis we do on a day-to-day basis tends to be at the subconscious level, and is a process so full of rich subtleties (and subjectivities) that it is actually quite difficult to articulate and formalize.

There is some consensus, however, that the best way to move from raw qualitative data to meaningful understanding is through data immersion that allows you to uncover and discover themes that run through the raw data, and by interpreting the implication of those themes for your research project.

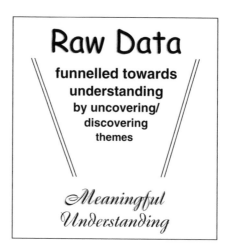

FIGURE 11.5   FUNNELLING DOWN TOWARDS MEANING

Discovering and uncovering

As highlighted in Figure 11.5, moving from raw data, such as transcripts, pictures, notes, journals, videos, documents, etc., to meaningful understanding is a process reliant on the generation/exploration of relevant themes; and these themes can either be discovered or uncovered. So what do I mean by this?

Well, you may decide to explore your data inductively from the ground up. In other words, you may want to explore your data without a predetermined theme or theory in mind. Your aim might be to *discover* themes and eventuating theory by allowing them to emerge from the data. This is often referred to as the production of *grounded theory* or 'theory that was derived from data systematically gathered and analyzed through the research process' (Strauss and Corbin 1998, p. 12).

In order to generate grounded theory, researchers engage in a rigorous and iterative process of data collection and 'constant comparative' analysis that finds raw data brought to increasingly higher levels of abstraction until theory is generated. This method of theory generation (which shares the same name as its product – grounded theory) has embedded within it very well-defined and clearly articulated techniques for data analysis (see readings at the end of the chapter). And it is precisely this clear articulation of grounded theory techniques that have seen them become central to many QDA strategies.

It is important to realize, however, that discovering themes is not the only QDA option. You may have predetermined (a priori) themes or theory in mind – they might have come from engagement with the literature; your prior experiences; the nature of your research question; or from insights you had while collecting your data. In this case, you are trying to deductively *uncover* data that supports predetermined theory. In a sense, you are mining your data for predetermined categories of exploration in order to support 'theory'. Rather than theory emerging from raw data, theory generation depends on progressive verification.

While grounded theory approaches are certainly a mainstay in QDA, researchers who only engage in grounded theory literature can fall prey to the false assumption that all theory must come inductively from data. This need not be the case. The need to generate theory directly from data will not be appropriate for all researchers, particularly those wishing to test 'a priori' theories or mine their data for predetermined themes.

Mapping themes

Whether themes are to be discovered or uncovered, the key to QDA is rich engagement with the documents, transcripts, images, texts, etc. that make up a researcher's raw data. So how do you begin to engage with data in order to discover and uncover themes in what is likely to be an unwieldy raw data set?

Well one way to look at it might be as a rich mapping process. Technically, when deductively uncovering data related to 'a priori' themes the map would be predetermined. However, when inductively discovering themes using a grounded theory approach the map would be built as you work through your data. In practice, however, the distinction is unlikely to be that clear, and you will probably rely on both strategies to build the richest map possible.

Figure 11.6 offers a map exploring poor self-image in young girls built through both inductive and deductive processes. That is, some initial ideas were noted, but other concepts were added and linked as data immersion occurred.

It's also worth noting that this type of mind map can be easily converted to a 'tree structure' that forms the basis of analysis in many QDA software programs, including NU*DIST (see Figure 11.7).

Delving into data

When it comes to QDA, delving into your data generally occurs as it is collected and involves: (1) reading and re-reading; (2) annotating growing understanding in notes and memos; (3) organizing and coding data; and (4) searching for patterns in a bid to build and verify theories.

The process of organizing and coding can occur at a number of levels and can range from highly structured, quasi-statistical counts to rich, metaphoric interpretations. Qualitative data can be explored for the words that are used; the concepts that are discussed; the linguistic devices that are called upon; and the nonverbal cues noted by the researcher.

257

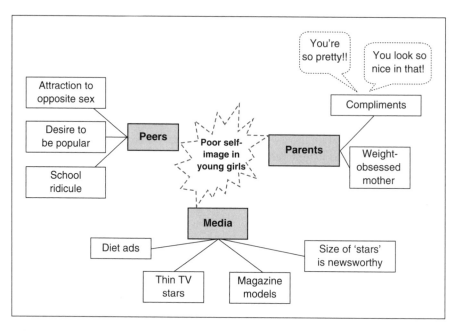

FIGURE 11.6 MAPPING YOUR THEMES

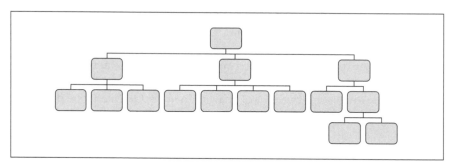

FIGURE 11.7 QDA 'TREE STRUCTURE'

EXPLORING WORDS Words can lead to themes through exploration of their repetition, or through exploration of their context and usage (sometimes called key words in context). Specific cultural connotations of particular words can also lead to relevant themes. Patton (2001) refers to this as 'indigenous categories', while Strauss and Corbin (1998) refer to it as 'in vivo' coding.

To explore word-related themes researchers systematically search a text to find all instances of a particular word (or phrase) making note of its context and meaning. Several software packages, such as DICTION or CONCORDANCE, can quickly and efficiently identify and tally the use of particular words and even present such findings in a quantitative manner.

EXPLORING CONCEPTS   Concepts can be deductively uncovered by searching for themes generated from: the literature; the hypothesis/research question; intuitions; or prior experiences. Concepts and themes may also be derived from 'standard' social science categories of exploration, for example power, race, class, gender etc. On the other hand, many researchers will look for concepts to emerge inductively from their data without any preconceived notions. With predetermined categories, researchers need to be wary of 'fitting' their data to their expectations, and not being able to see alternate explanations. However, purely inductive methods are also subject to bias since unacknowledged subjectivities can impact on the themes that emerge from the data.

To explore concepts, researchers generally engage in line-by-line or paragraph-by-paragraph reading of transcripts, engaging in what grounded theory proponents refer to as 'constant comparison'. In other words, concepts and meaning are explored in each text and then compared with previously analysed texts to draw out both similarities and disparities (Glaser and Strauss 1967).

EXPLORING LITERARY DEVICES   Metaphors, analogies and even proverbs are often explored because of their ability to bring richness, imagery and empathetic understanding to words. These devices often organize thoughts and facilitate understanding by building connections between speakers and an audience. Once you start searching for such literary devices, you'll find they abound in both the spoken and written word. Qualitative data analysts often use these rich metaphorical descriptions to categorize divergent meanings of particular concepts.

EXPLORING NONVERBAL CUES   One of the difficulties in moving from raw data to rich meaning is what is lost in the process. And certainly the tendency in qualitative data collection and analysis is to concentrate on words, rather than the tone and emotive feeling behind the words, the body language that accompanies the words, or even words not spoken. Yet this world of the nonverbal can be central to thematic exploration. If your raw data, notes or transcripts contain nonverbal cues, it can lend significant meaning to content and themes. Exploration of tone, volume, pitch and pace of speech; the tendency for hearty or nervous laughter; the range of facial expressions and body language used; and shifts in any or all of these, can be central in a bid for meaningful understanding.

Looking for patterns and interconnections

Once texts have been explored for relevant themes, the quest for meaningful understanding generally moves to the relationships that might exist between and amongst various themes. For example, you may look to see if the use of certain words and/or concepts is correlated with the use of other words and/or concepts. Or you may explore whether certain words or concepts are associated with a particular range of nonverbal cues or emotive states. You might also look to see if there is a connection between the use of particular metaphors and nonverbal cues. And of course, you may want to explore how individuals with particular characteristics vary on any of these dimensions.

Interconnectivities are assumed to be both diverse and complex and can point to the relationship between conditions and consequences, or how the experiences of the individual relate to more global themes. Conceptualization and abstraction can become quite sophisticated and can be linked to both model and theory building.

QDA software

It wasn't long ago that QDA was done 'by hand' with elaborate filing, cutting, sticky notes, markers, etc. But quality software (as highlighted in Box 11.3) now abounds and 'manual handling' is no longer necessary. QDA programs can store, code, index, map, classify, notate, find, tally, enumerate, explore, graph, etc., etc. Basically, they can: (1) do all the things you can do manually, but much more efficiently; and (2) do things that manual handling of a large data set simply won't allow. And while becoming proficient at the use of such software can mean an investment in time (and possibly money), if you're working with a large data set you're likely to get that time back.

Okay … if QDA programs are so efficient and effective, why are they so inconsistently called on by researchers working with qualitative data? Well, I think there are three answers here. First, is a lack of familiarity – researchers may not be aware of the programs, let alone what they can do. Second is that the learning investment is seen as too large and/or difficult. Third, researchers may realize, or decide, that they really don't want to do that much with their qualitative data; they may just want to use it sparingly to back up a more quantitative study.

My advice? Well, you really need to think through the pros and cons here. If you're working with a small data set and you can't see any more QDA in your future, you may not think it will pay to go down this path – manual handling might do the trick. But if you are (a) after truly rigorous qualitative analysis; (b) have to manage a large data set; or (c) see yourself needing to work with qualitative data in the future, it's probably worth battling the learning curve. Not only is your research process likely to be more rigorous, you will probably save a fair bit of time in the long run.

To get started with QDA software, I would recommend talking to other researchers or lecturers to find out what programs might be most appropriate for your goals and data. I would also have a look at relevant software sites on the Internet (see Box 11.3); there is a lot of information here and some sites even offer trial programs. Finally, I'd recommend that you take appropriate training courses. NU*DIST and NVIVO are both very popular and short course are often easy to find.

Specialist strategies

Up to this point, I've been treating QDA as a homogenous approach with underlying logic and methods, and I haven't really discussed the distinct disciplinary and paradigmatic approaches that do exist. But as mentioned at the start of this section, the literature here is dense, and a number of distinct approaches have developed over the past decades. Each has its own particular goals, theory and methods … and each will have varying levels of applicability to your own research. Now while I would certainly recommend delving into the approaches that resonate with you, it's worth keeping in mind that you don't have to adopt just one approach. It is possible to draw insights from various strategies in a bid to evolve an approach that best cycles between your data and your own research agenda.

Table 11.6 may not be comprehensive enough to get you started in any particular branch of qualitative data analysis, but it does provide a comparative summary of some of the more commonly used strategies. You can explore these strategies further by delving into the readings offered at the end of the chapter.

Presenting qualitative data

I don't think many books adequately cover the presentation of qualitative data, but I think they should. New researchers often struggle with the task and end up falling back on what they are most familiar with, or what they can find in their methods books (which are often quantitatively biased). So while these researchers may only have three cases, five documents, or eight interviews, they can end up with some pseudo-quantitative analysis and presentation that includes pie charts, bar graphs and percentages. For example, they may say 50% feel … and 20% think, when they're talking about a total of only five people.

Well this isn't really where the power of qualitative data lies. The power of qualitative data is in the actual words and images themselves – so my advice is to use them. If the goal is the rich use of words – avoid inappropriate quantification, and preserve and capitalize on language.

So how do you preserve, capitalize on and present words and images? Well, I think it's about story telling. You really have to have a clear message, argument or storyline, and you need to selectively use your words and/or images in a way

TABLE 11.6 COMPARING SPECIALIST QDA STRATEGIES

Content analysis 'To interpret meaning in speech and text'	• Can involve linguistic 'quantification' where words are units of analysis that are tallied • Can also refer to thematic analysis through coding
Discourse analysis 'To interpret language as it is situated in a socio-historic context'	• Rather than focus on simply what is said, discourse analysis explores language as it constitutes and embodies a socio-historic context tied to power and knowledge • Analysis necessarily involves data exploration that is 'critical'; in other words, challenges the dominant ideology
Narrative analysis 'To interpret the "stories" of individuals'	• Data collection and interpretation is often iterative with focus on story building • Metaphors seen as important
Conversation analysis 'To understand the structure and construction of conversation'	• Painstakingly transcribed conversations are explored for structural organization of speech • Turn taking between speakers and sequential ordering of utterances are of particular importance in understanding conversation
Semiotics 'To interpret the meanings behind signs and symbols'	• Involves identification of 'cognitive domains' – or the learning skills and mental processes used to make meaning • Attempts to deconstruct specific meanings in order to reconstruct understanding
Hermeneutics 'To interpret text in a dialogic fashion'	• Involves moving in and out of text using a 'hermeneutic spiral', or a process that cycles in on richer understandings by altering viewpoints • Focus on alternative perspectives – global *vs.* detailed/conventional *vs.* critical etc.
Grounded theory 'To generate theory directly from data'	• Highly inductive (analytic induction) • Use of 'constant comparative method' to explore each data source in relation to those previously analysed

that gives weight to that story. The qualitative data you present should be pointed, powerful and able to draw your readers in.

I think an example is the best way to get this across. To do this, I'll go back to my own study on religious disaffiliation. Now for this study, I actually conducted in-depth interviews with 80 'apostates' (those who had given up religious faith), so I was able to effectively quantify and present the data in tabular form (which I shared with you in Box 11.6 – also see Applied Example 7.4). But while this quantification definitely makes for a nice summary, it is the words and stories of the apostates themselves that is most compelling.

**Box 11.7   An Example of Qualitative
Data Presentation**

This example centres on the 'Egoistic Apostate', one of three types of apostate (apostates being individuals who have given up religious faith) identified in my own research on religious disaffiliation (O'Leary 1997, 1999). While I think the example here stands alone in terms of qualitative data presentation, you can refer to Box 11.6 (as well as Applied Example 7.4) for more context.

THE EGOISTIC APOSTATE

The common road
Egoistic apostates have a difficult time reconciling religion with the condition of the world or the condition of themselves. Processes of disaffiliation are inscribed with introspection, negative self-reflection and an emptiness that leads to a sense of disenchantment with God, religion and at times, the self. Apostasy tends to be an intense intellectual exercise in confusion and detachment. The following narrative captures the essence of egoistic disaffiliation:

> I was starting to have a really hard time, I think it was in year eight. My parents were fighting a fair bit, and ... God didn't seem to want to help. My life at times has not been easy ... I have been depressed, I have had some mighty lows and as a youth it was during these lows that I really doubted God. It's hard to believe in anything when you do not believe in yourself and I wanted to turn to God, but he didn't reach out. I often felt that God was not there for me ... It made me wonder whether he existed at all, I used to think about that all the time. Was he there? Did he just not care about me? (Interview No. 13)

Quite telling in this egoistic passage is a clearly articulated sense of disenchantment with both God and religion. The statements, 'God did not seem to want to help ...', '... he didn't reach out', show both disenchantment with familial religion, and painful internalization of God's rejection of a personal relationship. Focus is placed on the self, and there is clear indication of the emptiness associated with religious doubts.

For egoistic apostates, the process of disaffiliation tends to be an introspective journey of doubt and questioning arising from a very personalized sense of disappointment. The hallmark of the egoistic journey is a meditative and intellectual focus accompanied by a sense of alienated loss. The following narrative further illustrates the point:

(Continued)

Box 11.7   (Continued)

> I was sort of isolated as a child, I lived in a safe cocoon of ignorance, I didn't think that my parents really ... that I really ever felt that what they did or thought was right, but I didn't really know why. When I went to uni and met a few people that made me question things for the first time. All the inconsistencies that go along with the church. I had never really looked at religion objectively, I don't even think I looked at it at all. Anyway, it's depressing. I mean you just have to look at the opulence of the church as compared to that of the poor who they say they want to help, and you, ah, realize that there may be a problem with the idea of God. I really ... I had a hard time with that revelation, I mean I just think that, well that nothing makes sense. I just don't know. (Interview No. 67)

This passage clearly shows a sense of disenchantment with the notion of God and religion. The 'inconsistencies' of the church leave this egoistic apostate with an internalized sense of disenchantment. The hypocrisy perceived in the church leads to a loss of religion that is quite mournful. The statement, 'I really ... I had a hard time with that ...', shows a sense of lost confusion that is difficult to resolve; God and religion are thoughtfully considered to the point of vulnerable uncertainty.

Divergent paths

While lost and confused introspection is a common theme in egoistic journeys away from faith, the journey can still take somewhat divergent paths. For example, the depressed introspection that marks the egoistic respondent's journey can be associated with reactionary pain and anger:

> I was sixteen when I started to doubt the traditional church and a traditional God. There is just so much suffering in the world. How could there be a God who would allow so many people to die and, so many children to suffer? ... How could we make sense of the world if there is a God who is such a strong father, yet such an absolute bastard? God made no sense. Either he is mean and vindictive or there is no God. I myself think that there is no male God. No religion that I have ever heard of really captures the essence of this world. I was completely disenchanted with religion, and with what it tries to give me ... the more I looked, the more I realized that the Christian faiths were all bastions of greed and oppression. It is such a waste, on both a personal and social level. That's why I became an atheist. (Interview No. 38)

Box 11.7 **(Continued)**

For this respondent, egoistic disenchantment is the result of a resentful recognition of 'suffering in the world'. The perceived 'greed and oppression' of Christianity leads to both anger and alienation. For example, words such as 'mean', 'vindictive' and 'bastard' point to angry reactionism, while an egoistic sense of personalized alienation and emptiness is pointed to by the phrases, '[i]t is such a waste ...' and, 'I was completely disenchanted ...'. This respondent thus presents a simultaneous sense of mourning and anger.

Anger, however, is not the only construct associated with egoistic apostasy. Many egoistic journeys actually have a strong rational and logical component. In this case, disenchantment is coupled with a rational reflection on familial faith. The following narrative is indicative:

> I can't remember what exactly started me on the path, but I think that it is just all the problems in the world. Holy wars always spun me out. King Arthur and all that. I mean Holy–War isn't that an oxymoron? Anyway, I think I just gave up the notion of God, God first. There can be no God in this world, and then, I mean look at it. Old people handing money to preachers over the phone and people still going to war. I don't get it, never will, how can you not have some serious question of both religion and God, how can you not let it get to you? I mean I really let that worry me ... once I gave up on God, well then you can start to really see religion for what it is ..., it is a mess. Yeah, it may be hard, but once you think about it logically, what else can you do but let religion go? (Interview No. 68)

For this respondent, the egoistic, emotive components of the process appear to be tempered with a sense of logic. Egoism is present, particularly at the start of the apostatic journey. This egoism, however, has been negotiated with a less emotive plea to the intellect, that is, to 'think about it logically'.

Concluding remarks
A journey in which both God and religion are examined and deconstructed on a personal level with a relatively acute sense of disenchantment, loss, confusion and emptiness may best characterize egoistic apostasy. From this common ground, however, the journey can take various paths, including journeys tainted with angry reactionism, and journeys that incorporate a sense of rationality and logic.

SOME 'CONCLUDING' THOUGHTS

Drawing conclusions is all about clearly summarizing what your data reveals and then linking this back to your project's main questions, aims and objectives. If you really get in there and engage with your data (whether it's quantitative or qualitative) you are likely to discover that your findings and conclusions follow on quite naturally and logically from your analysis. All of your findings should arise from your data and should be pointing you (and when you present it, your readers) to your overarching arguments and final conclusion (the concluding remarks in Box 11.7 above serves as a short example).

To draw appropriate, relevant and significant conclusions you will need to:

- Consider your findings in light of current research 'literature'.
- Consider your findings in light of the limitations and methodological constraints of your study.
- Pull together all the significant/important findings of your study and consider why and how they are significant/important.
- Search for clarity, but don't force fit your findings to portray a world without ambiguity and complexity.
- Clearly link your findings to your research question, aims and objectives, and relevant theory.

As you draw together your conclusions, you may find that you have begun to conceptualize a bigger picture in a fairly sophisticated manner; and that sharing these thoughts, insights and ideas might be best communicated in the form of an original framework or model. In fact, while many studies into real-world problems culminate with recommendations (see Chapter 12), it's not unusual to see conclusions come together as a potentially useful new model for understanding and/or action.

FURTHER READING

I've tried to put together a diverse range of readings that are: fairly recent (unless seminal); practical and applied. Keep in mind that you really can't go past www.amazon.com when trying to find the latest books on virtually any topic. Not only is the search facility pretty good, but the information (especially for newer titles) generally includes an overall description, table of contents, editorial and customer reviews, and quite often a sample chapter.

Quantitative analysis

Bryman, A. and Cramer, D. (2005) *Quantitative Data Analysis with SPSS Release 12 for Windows.* London: Routledge.

Bryman, A. and Hardy, M. A. (eds) (2004) *Handbook of Data Analysis.* London: Sage.

Carver, R. H. (2003) *Doing Data Analysis with MINITAB 14.* Pacific Grove, CA: Duxbury Press.

Der, G. and Everitt, B. S. (2001) *Handbook of Statistical Analyses Using SAS.* Boca Raton FL: CRC Press.

Jefferies, J. and Diamond, I. (2001) *Beginning Statistics: An Introduction for Social Scientists.* London: Sage.

Salkind, N. J. (2003) *Statistics for People Who (Think They) Hate Statistics.* London: Sage.

Trochim, W. M. (2005) *The Research Methods Knowledge. Base.* http://www.socialresearchmethods.net/kb/index.htm

Qualitative analysis

Boyatzis, R. E. (1998) *Transforming Qualitative Information: Thematic Analysis and Code Development.* London: Sage.

Gibbs, G. (2003) *Qualitative Data Analysis: Explorations with NVivo (Understanding Social Research).* Buckingham: Open University Press.

Miles, M. and Huberman, A. (1994) *Qualitative Data Analysis: An Expanded Source Book.* Thousand Oaks, CA: Sage.

Silverman, D. (2001) *Interpreting Qualitative Data: Methods for Analysing Talk, Text and Interaction.* London: Sage.

Wolcott, H. F. (1994) *Transforming Qualitative Data: Description, Analysis, and Interpretation.* London: Sage.

Content analysis

Kripppendorf, K. (2003) *Content Analysis: An Introduction to Its Methodology.* London: Sage.

Neuendorf, K. A. (2001) *The Content Analysis Guidebook.* London: Sage.

Discourse analysis

Hoey, M. (2000) *Textual Interaction: An Introduction to Written Discourse Analysis.* London: Routledge.

Wood, L. A. and Kroger, R. O. (2000) *Doing Discourse Analysis: Methods for Studying Action in Talk and Text.* Thousand Oaks, CA: Sage.

Narrative analysis

Clandinin, D. J. and Connelly, F. M. (2004) *Narrative Inquiry: Experience and Story in Qualitative Research.* San Francisco: Jossey–Bass.

Riessman, C. K. (1993) *Narrative Analysis.* London: Sage.

Conversation analysis

Psathas, G. (1994) *Conversation Analysis: The Study of Talk-in-Interaction.* London: Sage.

Ten Have, P. (1999) *Doing Conversation Analysis: A Practical Guide.* Thousand Oaks, CA: Corwin.

Semiotics

Chandler, D. (2001) *Semiotics: The Basics.* London: Routledge.

Gottdiener, M., Lagopoulos, A. and Boklund-Lagopoulos, K. (eds) (2003) *Semiotics.* London: Sage.

Hermeneutics

Herda, E. (1999) *Research Conversations and Narrative: A Critical Hermeneutic Orientation in Participatory Inquiry.* New York: Praeger.

Van Manen, M. (1990) *Researching Lived Experience: Human Science for an Action Sensitive Pedagogy.* New York: State University of New York Press.

Grounded theory

Glaser, B. and Strauss, A. (1967) *Discovery of Grounded Theory.* Chicago: Aldine.

Strauss, A. and Corbin, J. (1998) *Basics of Qualitative Research: Techniques and Procedures for Developing Grounded Theory.* London: Sage.

Chapter Summary

- Effective data analysis involves: keeping your eye on the main game; managing your data; engaging in the actual process of quantitative and/or qualitative analysis; presenting your data; and drawing meaningful and logical conclusions.

- Analysis should be approached as a critical, reflective and iterative process that cycles between data and an overarching research framework that keeps the big picture in mind.

- Regardless of data type, managing data involves: familiarizing yourself with appropriate software; developing a data management system; systematically organizing and screening your data: entering the data into a program; and finally, 'cleaning' your data.

268

- Being able to do statistics no longer means being able to work with formulae. It's much more important for researchers to be familiar with the language and logic of statistics, and be competent in the use of statistical software.

- Different data types demand discrete treatment, so it's important to be able to distinguish variables by both cause and effect (dependent or independent), and their measurement scales (nominal, ordinal, interval and ratio).

- Descriptive statistics are used to summarize the basic features of a data set through measures of central tendency (mean, mode and median), dispersion (range, quartiles, variance and standard deviation), and distribution (skewness and kurtosis).

- Inferential statistics allow researchers to assess their ability to draw conclusions that extend beyond the immediate data. For example, if a sample represents the population; if there are differences between two or more groups; if there are changes over time; or if there is a relationship between two or more variables.

- Selecting the right statistical test relies on knowing the nature of your variables; their scale of measurement; their distribution shape; and the types of question you want to ask.

- Presenting quantitative data often involves the production of graphs and tables. These need to be (1) selectively generated so that they make relevant arguments; and (2) informative yet simple, so that they aid the reader's understanding.

- In qualitative data analysis there is a common reliance on words and images to draw out rich meaning; but there is an amazing array of perspectives and techniques for conducting an investigation.

- Qualitative data analysis creates new understandings by exploring and interpreting complex data from sources such as interviews, group discussions, observation, journals, archival documents, etc., without the aid of quantification.

- The methods and logic of qualitative data analysis involve uncovering and discovering themes that run through raw data, and interpreting the implication of those themes for research questions.

- Qualitative data analysis generally involves: moving through cycles of inductive and deductive reasoning; thematic exploration (based on words, concepts, literary devices and nonverbal cues); and exploration of the interconnections among themes. Qualitative data analysis software can help with these tasks.

- There are a number of paradigm- and discipline-based strategies for qualitative data analysis including: content, discourse, narrative and conversation analysis; semiotics; hermeneutics; and grounded theory.

- Effective presentation of qualitative data can be a real challenge. You will need to have a clear storyline, and selectively use your words and/or images to give weight to your story.

- Your findings and conclusions need to flow from analysis and show clear relevance to your overall project. Findings should be considered in light of: significance; current research literature; limitations of the study; and finally your questions, aims, objectives and theory.

12
Producing Research 'Deliverables'

*'It is of great importance that the general public be given
the opportunity to experience, consciously and intelligently,
the efforts and results of scientific research. It is not sufficient
that each result be taken up, elaborated, and applied by a few
specialists in the field. Restricting the body of knowledge to
a small group deadens the philosophical spirit of a people
and leads to spiritual poverty.'*

- Albert Einstein

RESEARCH AS COMMUNICATION

I often find longer quotes a bit hard to follow. Probably something to do with my own attention span (which they say makes any 5 year old with ADD look focused.) But I do find Einstein's words highly relevant, particularly in researching real-world problems where change oriented goals highlight the need for 'the general public … to experience … research'. In fact, Einstein's premise provides a framework for this entire chapter; for if we are to avoid 'restricting the body of knowledge to a small group', then research deliverables, that is, accounts and other outcomes, must be: (1) communicated effectively; (2) disseminated broadly; and (3) applied effectively in the real world.

For those struggling with the final phases of a research project, the take-home message here is about communication. You may think the ultimate goal in writing

271

up your project is simply reporting on what you did and what you found, but there's much more to it than this. The real goal of any 'reporting' is to provide engaging explanation and clear illumination – it's essential that your audience can see the consequence of your research journey. And while many research accounts are dry, turgid, dense, boring and even a bit 'holier than thou', this is exactly what you should try to avoid if you want your work to make a difference in the real world.

Producing 'deliverables'

What generally comes to mind when you think of research communication? The most common answer is research reports … and this is certainly a mainstay, particularly in the academic world. But I want to put on my consultant's hat for a moment and talk a bit about the concept of 'deliverables'; a word much more common in the consultancy world than the academic world … but a world I think has a place in researching real-world problems.

Now if you were to work as a consultant, you would find that clients generally want something useful and user-friendly. This is likely to include a well-written concise report (I haven't worked with anyone who wanted a 100+ page waffly academic thesis), but it can often include other types of 'deliverables' that help facilitate the move from knowledge to on-the-ground change. And while this is common practise in consultancy, the concept of 'deliverables' is extremely useful in most types of applied research.

Research deliverables, as an addendum to a research report, can include:

- *Recommendations* – a quite common type of deliverable. Effective recommendations not only cover what should happen, but how it might happen. This means recommendations should be contextually sensitive, relevant and practical. Rather than a hypothetical wish list, recommendations need to be achievable. One strategy here is to recommend incremental (small phased-in steps for change) and not just fundamental change.
- *Action plans* – often undertaken with stakeholders (and embedded in action research processes) the development of an action plan can be a natural follow on from research recommendations. The idea here is to clearly articulate a change process that will bring recommendations to fruition.
- *Procedures, protocols, guidelines, programmes* – also a step beyond recommendations, the production of deliverables such as procedures, protocols, guidelines and programmes sees researchers using the knowledge they have produced to develop usable practices and processes. Examples here might be standard operating procedures within industry, guidelines for healthy school canteens, or protocols for dealing with suspected cases of plagiarism.
- *Tools/kits* – similar to procedures and protocols, tools and kits are 'packages' that facilitate problem resolution and situation improvement. For example, say

you developed a questionnaire that an organization might require at a later time or in a different setting – the questionnaire itself can be a useful deliverable. A good example here is the *Community Toolbox* (http//ctb.ku.edu), which draws on researcher experiences to offer a host of information, examples, checklists, surveys and other resources for improving community health and development.

- *Prototypes/models* – in addition to on-the-ground change in one setting, the deliverable here can be an example (prototype or model) of what might be achieved by a similar organization facing a similar situation or problem that is willing to undergo a similar process. Action research often provides prototypes since change initiatives are embedded in its research processes.
- *Policy development* – unless you're collaborating with certain high profile stakeholders or perhaps a steering committee, you may not be in a position to write policy. Your recommendations, however, can be strongly policy oriented. For example, you may end up drafting a policy for discussion on school bullying, or offering recommendations for the development of a government policy on carbon dioxide emissions.
- *Education/awareness materials* – another genre of 'deliverable' is promotional materials that can improve education and increase awareness. This can include news stories, press releases, brochures, pamphlets, websites and anything else you think might have an impact.

Knowing and engaging your audience

The key to effective real-world problem research may be flexible modes of communication, but the key to effective communication is the ability to connect with your audience. And this starts with knowing who they are.

When researching real-world problems, your audience can be diverse and should certainly reach beyond the academic world. So before producing 'deliverables' you should ask:

- *Who am I writing for?* – writing should be a communication process *with* an audience, and this means writing with your audience in mind. Consider whether your audience will be community leaders, community members, managers, politicians, practitioners, academics etc. or whether your audience cuts across more than one of these groups. Also consider whether one particular deliverable will meet the needs of all your stakeholders.
- *What do they know?* – if you want to communicate effectively you need to start where people are – not over or under their heads. This means considering what your audience is likely to know about the topic at hand, as well as what they know about the research process. You need to 'add value' to what people already know without losing them in the process.

- *What will they find most useful?* – if you want your research to have an impact, utility is key. Not only should your research communication be readily understandable by your audience, it should also be something they will be able to use to facilitate on-the-ground change.
- *What are their expectations?* – I once worked with an academic consultant who insisted on giving clients what she knew they needed, not what they wanted or requested. And who knows, maybe she was right about what they needed. But the unwillingness to work *with* clients (who often felt patronized) limited acceptance of her research outcomes. Now for quite good reasons, you too may decide that clients' expectations are unrealistic, but this should be openly negotiated, rather than blatantly ignored.
- *How might they react?* – rarely are stakeholders neutral, they generally have vested interests, so it's worth considering how they might react to your findings and recommendations. Not that this should impact *what* you find/recommend, but it might effect *how* you present these findings and recommendations. Remember, the goal here is working towards tangible change, so it's smart to work in politically sensitive ways.

Knowing your audience is crucial, for without this knowledge it's difficult to engage interest. People are busy, and they generally don't have time to spend on things where the relevance to their own situation is unclear. If you want to get your message across, then that message needs to target your audience in a way that shows its significance and value.

Finding an appropriate structure and style

When it comes to finding a structure for writing up your research account and associated deliverables, the main things you should consider are acceptance and usefulness. Your research account is unlikely to be optimally useful if it's not presented in what your readers consider to be an acceptable format. But even if it is presented suitably, your report still needs to be as engaging, user-friendly and useful as possible. The main choice here is to go with a traditional format (useful for meeting requirements and expectations) or to go with something more alternative (a structure you believe will best get your message across).

The traditional format

When it comes to research reports, there is certainly a traditional structure that is recognized, accepted, expected and often advocated. This is the 'introduction, literature review, methods, findings, discussion, conclusion' format that dominates the literature. And it's quite easy to see why so many researchers adopt this. Not only does it tend to be expected, it also answers reader's questions in a sequence quite natural to the flow of a normal conversation. As shown in Table 12.1,

TABLE 12.1 THE 'TRADITIONAL' CONVERSATION

The questions	The answers that structure the chapters/sections of the conventional report
So tell me what your research is about?	Title Abstract Introduction • research question(s) • hypothesis (as appropriate)
And why did you choose this particular topic/question?	Introduction • rationale
What do you hope to achieve?	Introduction • aims and objectives
I really don't know much about this, can you fill me in?	Background • recent literature and prior research (the literature review) • theory (current and seminal as appropriate) • context (social, cultural, historic and geographic)
How exactly did you go about doing your research?	Research design/approach • methodological approach (framework) • methods (techniques/procedures) • limitations
And what did you find out?	Findings/Results/Emergent story • text, tables, graphs, charts, themes, quotes etc. Discussion • analysis, interpretation and meaning of findings
How would you explain the relevance/importance of what you've done?	Conclusion • implications • significance
What will you be able to offer to others as a result of this study?	Deliverables • recommendations • action plans • programmes, guidelines • kits/tools • models/prototypes • promotional materials

project-related questions and their respective answers readily fall into a traditional format.

While the traditional format may not suit every circumstance, it is a format that can limit the work readers need to do to make sense of your write-up, and therefore your research. It is also a format that allows some flexibility within it. For example, the voice you adopt and the emphasis you place on each section will vary according to your audience. For more academic works, you might be expected to engage heavily with past research accounts and theory, and explicate all aspects of method in a fairly formal manner. Funding agencies might also require formality, but want emphasis placed on conclusions and recommendations. Meanwhile bureaucratic management might want the heart of your report to be contained within a tight executive summary. Finally, for practitioners and community groups, emphasis might be best placed on issues and resolution strategies – presented in a tone that is as down-to-earth and unpretentious as possible.

Alternative formats

While the academic world and its requirements can be quite prescriptive, expectations within a workplace or community can be more open. Depending on the nature of you as researcher, the organization(s) you might be affiliated with, your research topic, your methods and your audience, you might find that an alternative structure best gets your message across.

Alternative structures for writing up your research report can be based on:

- *chronology* – describing how the events within your research project unfolded over time
- *theory-building* – describing how theory was inductively generated, and allowing that theory to build throughout your report
- *findings first* – providing readers with your conclusions up-front, and then describing how you got there

Any one of these formats might be better suited to both your story and your audience than the traditional structure. I think the main thing to consider here is whether your readers will be 'accepting'. If you decide to go with a structure that is new to your readers, you need to take great care that the logic of that structure becomes self-evident as your readers progress through your account. You don't want them to get 'lost' as you take them through your research project. Any structure you adopt should take your readers through a clear, coherent and hopefully compelling storyline.

THE WRITING PROCESS

Okay, we're now down to the nitty-gritty of writing. And trust me, you're not alone if you wish this whole research thing could happen without you needing to write it up. Regardless of the dimension or scope of the project, writing up is usually approached with a sense of apprehension and wariness – and in many ways this is justified. For one thing, you probably aren't too practised in the art of writing research reports, and secondly, research is often judged not by what you did, but by your ability to report on what you did.

So while there really is no way around it (to disseminate you generally need to write), there are quite a few practical strategies for negotiating the writing process in a way that improves the overall quality of the project, and makes the task less daunting. If you can make a start, craft a good story and are willing to draft and redraft, you can produce a research account with the potential to make a difference.

Box 12.1   The Perils of Writing!

It's not easy ...

> '*I always write a good first line, but I have trouble in writing the others.*'
>
> Molière (1622-73), French dramatist

> '*No pen, no ink, no table, no room, no time, no quiet, no inclination.*'
>
> James Joyce (1882-1941), Irish author

> '*Writing ... a combination of ditch-digging, mountain-climbing, treadmill and childbirth.*'
>
> Edna Ferber (1887-1968), US writer

> '*Let's face it, writing is hell.*'
>
> William Styron (b. 1925), US novelist

But then again ...

> '*Writing is a dreadful labour, yet not so dreadful as idleness.*'
>
> Thomas Carlyle (1795-1881), Scottish essayist and historian

---

Managing the task

So how do you make a start in the inevitable writing process? Well, I actually think the best advice is to avoid leaving it all until the very end. Write as you go. If you see writing as part and parcel of the research process rather than just an account of that process you will never have to face what looks like an insurmountable obstacle.

Process or product

Traditionally, research has been a three-step process: (1) write and submit a research proposal; (2) conduct the research; (3) write up the report. But writing can be a more integrated part of the research journey. For example, if you formulate even your most initial ideas in written form, you will have begun to produce notes for the first draft of your 'introduction' and 'methods'; and annotating your sources can lead to preliminary drafts of your 'literature review'. These sections can then be redrafted as you go through the process of data collection. Similarly, preliminary analysis, note taking and writing throughout data collection will provide you with a good start on 'findings'.

Keep in mind that even if you're a procrastinator and you're not that keen on writing as you go, it is a highly attractive option compared to facing the daunting prospect of having to start your writing from scratch when you complete your data collection and analysis.

Writing as analysis

As well as a head start on report production, 'writing as you go' can actually be part of the analysis process. Very few people can formulate finalized ideas in their heads without committing them to paper. Ideas almost always evolve as you write, so writing throughout the research process can be crucial in moving from simple descriptions through to broader synthesis and on to significant, relevant, logical and coherent storylines. In fact, writing and rewriting can be the key to bringing storylines into focus.

Constructing your 'story'

So why am I using the word 'story'? Well I'm using it because good stories grab reader interest, hold that interest, have a strong plot, take readers on a journey, and lead them to logical, yet sometimes surprising, conclusions. The other implication of stories is that people simply won't read them if they're boring, tedious, long-winded, pretentious, etc. Yes, your write-up needs to report on your research, but it should do more … it should unfold, it should engage and it should tell an interesting story.

Now as the author of that 'story', there are several things you need to do:

1. *Think of your research account as a 'conversation'* – now I realize conversations are two-way, but you can apply this even in writing. You may not be there to see or hear a response, but you should be trying to engage your readers in

a conversation. In fact, if you can give relevant information, predict questions and respond to inquiries, your writing will become 'interactive'. Remember, very few people have the ability to stay interested and focused on dry and turgid writing – they need to be mentally, intellectually and/or emotionally involved.

2. *Become familiar with the craft* – very few authors are not avid readers. One of the most effective things you can do is find 'good' examples of what you intend to write. These examples may not be prototypes, but they can certainly give you some sense of the shape of your end product.

3. *Find a voice* – there is likely to be a tension between 'engaging story telling' and 'take me seriously reporting', and this is a tension you'll have to negotiate based on you, your goals, your audience, and their expectations. The more you know about these elements, the better off you are in finding an effective voice. Now the generally rule in regards to writing in the first person has been to avoid it – this is so your research does not appear to be tainted with personal bias and subjectivities. But this convention is relaxing. While using first person to give your personal opinion is likely to be frowned upon, using 'I' to report on happenings and events is now more commonly accepted.

4. *Develop your structure* – decide on a structure and work up an appropriate outline for your write-up early on. The more you know about where you want to go, the easier it will be to set a course that can help you get there. Remember that your structure can always be modified as your thinking evolves.

5. *Craft the story line* – whether you opt for a traditional or alternative structure, your report will need to have a beginning, a middle and an end. It needs to engage your readers, pique their interest and take them through your research journey in a way that unfolds the story and logically leads to your conclusion. Also check to see if your story logically answers questions similar to those in Table 12.1. Ways to begin this process include: writing a creative working title; constructing one or more draft outlines; and writing a one-page abstract.

6. *Be ready to make convincing arguments* – it is essential that you write purposefully. The quality and credibility of your write-up is largely dependent on your ability to construct logical and convincing arguments. You need to convince, reason and argue your points. And of course, you need to be able to back up your arguments with appropriate references and data.

7. *Write/construct your first draft* – you can think about it, and you can keep thinking about it, but it won't happen unless you do it. If you've constructed writing as part of the research process rather than its product, the bones of your first draft will be there for you to put together and flesh out. If, however, you've followed the 'write-up after' approach, you'll need to gather your notes and put it all down on paper.

8. *Get appropriate feedback* – reader expectations can vary widely, so don't wait until the last minute to find out that your approach is inappropriate. Be sure

to pass a draft of your write-up to someone who either: (a) has some experience in research; or (b) has some insights into reader expectations.

9. *Be prepared to redraft* – this should be an expectation. In fact, as discussed below, very few people can get away with submitting a second draft, let alone a first.

From first to final draft

Whether your decision making processes see you go for formal or casual, traditional or alternative, dry or sensational, there is a common denominator. No matter what format, style or voice you adopt, your final work needs to be polished and professional. If you want people to take your message seriously, if you want action and change to be a result of your work, then you simply cannot come across as an amateur. Your authority can actually be enhanced or destroyed by not only the quality of your research, but by its presentation. Bottom line? Be ready to draft and redraft.

Now as you work through various drafts, you'll be tightening up different aspects of your writing (see Box 12.2). But you can approach this in any number of ways. Some like to work sentence by sentence in a slow and diligent fashion, while others don't want to break a stream of consciousness; they try to get new ideas down on paper all at once, to be cleaned up later on. As long as you find a process that works for you, there is nothing wrong with developing your own approach. It is the end result that counts.

Box 12.2 offers a number of checklists for helping you get to a quality end product. While it may seem somewhat tedious, almost all good writers do go through some variation of this process (see Box 12.3).

Box 12.2   Checklists for the Redrafting Process

Reworking the first draft
It would be nice if your first draft were it. But it rarely works that way. When you step back and take stock, you're likely to find that the process of writing itself has evolved your ideas; and that your thoughts have moved beyond what you initially managed to capture on paper. As you work through your first draft ask yourself:

☑ Is this making sense? Does the logic flow? Do I need to alter the structure?
☑ Am I using a 'voice' I am comfortable with?
☑ Do I need to incorporate more material/ideas – or are sections really repetitive?

Box 12.2   *(Continued)*

☑   Am I happy with my overall argument, and is it coming through?

☑   Does each chapter or section have a clear and obvious point or argument?

☑   Have I sought and responded to feedback?

Reworking the second draft

Once you're happy with the overall ideas, arguments, logic and structure, it's time to fine tune your arguments and strive for coherence and consistency. In doing this, ask yourself:

☑   How can I make my points and arguments clearer? Do I 'waffle on' at any point? Am I using lots of jargon and acronyms? Should I incorporate some/ more examples?

☑   Do I want to include some/more diagrams, photos, maps etc.?

☑   Is the structure coherent? Are there clear and logical links between chapters/sections?

☑   Is there consistency within and between chapters/sections? Do I appear to contradict myself at any point? Is my voice used consistently throughout the work?

☑   Is the length on target?

☑   Have I sought and responded to feedback?

Moving towards the penultimate draft

Being ready to move towards a penultimate draft implies that you are reasonably happy with the construction and logic of the arguments running throughout and within your document. Attention can now be turned to fluency, clarity and overall readability. Ask yourself:

☑   Are there ways I can further increase clarity? Are my terms used consistently? Have I got rid of unnecessary jargon?

☑   Are there ways I can make this read more fluently? Can I break up my longer sentences? Can I rework my one-sentence paragraphs?

☑   Are there ways I can make this more engaging? Can I limit the use of passive voice? Do I come across as apologetic? Are my arguments strong and convincing?

☑   Am I sure I have protected the confidentiality of my respondents/ participants?

(Continued)

Box 12.2   (Continued)

☑ Have I guarded against any potential accusations of plagiarism? Have I checked and double checked my sources, both in the text and in the references or bibliography?

☑ Have I written and edited any preliminary and end pages, namely title page, table of contents, list of figures, acknowledgements, abstract, preface, appendices and references?

☑ Have I thoroughly checked my spelling and grammar?

☑ Have I done a word count?

☑ Have I sought and responded to feedback?

Producing the final draft

You'd think that if you did all the above, your final document would be done. Not quite; you now need to do a final edit. If it's a large work and you can fund it, you might want to consider using a copy editor. It's amazing what editorial slip-ups someone with specialist skills can find, even after you've combed through your own work a dozen times. Some things you may want to ask prior to submission are:

☑ Have I looked for typos of all sorts?

☑ Have I triple-checked spelling (especially those things spell checkers cannot pick up like typing 'form' instead of 'from').

☑ Have I checked my line spacing, fonts, margins, etc.?

☑ Have I numbered all pages, including preliminary and end pages sequentially? Have I made sure they are all in the proper order?

☑ Have I checked through the final document to make sure there were no printing glitches?

Box 12.3   *I wish I could write like you ...*

When I published my first book, I had several students say things like, 'It sounds like you're talking to me,' 'I wish I had an easy, natural style like that.' Well I definitely take that as a compliment, but let me tell you a little about my 'easy, natural style.'

> **Box 12.3   (Continued)**

Take this chapter, particularly its introduction, as an example. I sat down to start this chapter a couple of weeks ago, and I'd say it took about four or five attempts before I found a start I was happy with (and this is just the quote and first two paragraphs). Now once I was settled that this was the way I would start, I must have re-written that section three or four times – sentence by sentence – until I was pretty satisfied. Only then did I move on to the next section.

On my next writing day, I began by re-reading that first bit, and realized it was getting there, but not quite there – so I re-wrote it two or three more times … only at this stage did I feel it was beginning to sound easy and natural – so I left it. So as I sit and type, that's where it's up to, but that's not the end of the process. When I finish the entire chapter next week, I will review it again, make more modifications, and when happy, give it to a reader who is tough, but whose opinion I respect. Undoubtedly he will have comments, and I will take them into consideration and modify the text as I see fit.

Now because this is the last chapter, the next step is to look at all the chapters in context to make sure the whole thing nests together well. Again more modification is a distinct possibility. I will then do a copy edit and send it off to my publisher. Done? Not quite … from here Sage publishers will help me with more reviews (and possible modifications), professional copy editing, and layout and design – and this is what you will eventually see …

If only an easy and natural style came easily and naturally!

RESEARCH DISSEMINATION AND UTILIZATION

A tremendous amount of effort needs to go into the conduct of rigorous and credible problem-based research. So the last thing you want to do is go through the whole research process and have absolutely nothing come of it. But unfortunately this can actually be the rule rather than the exception. An unbelievable amount of research into real-world problems ends up as nothing more than reports sitting somewhere on a shelf.

But of course, for research into real-world problems to achieve its goals, broad dissemination and effective utilization are imperative. Without them you have nothing more than academic waffle (and don't we have enough of that out there already!). If your goal is to have an influence on areas such as professional development, practice, programmes, policy, or pervasive cultures, your research must be disseminated to stakeholders in user-friendly ways that optimize utilization.

Disseminating outcomes

Conducting a research project, even if it's done well, in no way assures wide dissemination. Take for example the PhD thesis, probably the most prestigious piece of academic research writing there is. Sadly, it can also be the most poorly disseminated. Most theses are read by the author, a reviewer or editor, the supervisor or supervisory panel, and examiners. At the high end, that's about seven or eight people. Not a lot of dissemination for a work that usually takes four or more years. Now this doesn't mean that research dissemination won't happen, but it does remind us that broad dissemination requires creativity and flexibility in message delivery. You need to go beyond an academic model.

This is particularly true when researching real-world problems. Because (a) getting your message out is crucial, and (b) you often need to engage a diverse audience, it's well worth considering a range of dissemination options. Such options include:

- *Informing the community* – options here include presentations to town or council meetings, articles for local newspapers, talking on local radio, addressing community action groups, speaking to parent teacher associations, etc. And remember, the last thing you want here is dry and boring!
- *Enlightening the workplace* – options here include workplace presentations, articles for professional journals and trade magazines, and presentations at trade shows and conferences. Again a stiff academic presentation is probably not going to grab attention. You need to highlight pressing issues, significant findings and compelling conclusions.
- *Presenting at 'academic' conferences* – as much as this will allow you to disseminate your work, academic conferences are also great places for networking and making contacts in the research/practice world. Conferences can give heightened profile to both you and your work.
- *Getting published* – beyond articles for local papers, or articles in trade and practitioner publications, you can also consider publishing for an academic or broad general audience. Academic publishing generally means traditionally structured articles in refereed journals. Now while this does offer a high level of prestige (and can definitely help you if you want to pursue further education), it can be difficult to get journal articles accepted, and dissemination can be rather limited. Another option is to write a non-fiction book that appeals to the general populace (for example, there are plenty of high-selling titles based on research into stress, bullying, globalization, etc.). The work you'll need to do to get this off the ground can be tremendous, but so is the potential for extraordinarily wide dissemination.

Facilitating utilization

Okay, last section of the last chapter of the book, and in many ways this section brings us full circle. Now you might be thinking that facilitating research utilization is something you do at the end of your research process. And yes, there are some steps you can take to motivate the use of your findings after the research process is complete. But working towards effective utilization is really something that needs to happen throughout the entire life cycle of your research project. If your goal is to make a difference, then consideration of how this difference might occur should be integrated into planning and decision making throughout your project.

Effective research utilization requires:

- *Relevant, meaningful questions* – the premise here is that you're asking timely questions that have significance for an organization, an institution, a group, a field etc. Research that centres on questions that can lead to tangible situation improvement is likely to have the political support necessary for actioning real change.
- *Stakeholder involvement* – the stronger the relationship with key stakeholders, the more likely that your research findings can influence decision making processes. At a minimum, you'll need to insure that key decision makers are considered in the planning and conduct of your project. But at the other end of the spectrum you can work collaboratively with stakeholders thereby increasing their sense of ownership over findings and their potential to bring about change.
- *Political nous* – related to stakeholder involvement, but somewhat more strategic, political nous means knowing who should be a part of the process and how their support can best be solicited. If you can get the right people on side, your research is that much more likely to end up going somewhere.
- *Integrity and rigour in methods* – if you want decisions to be based on evidence or 'data', then there needs to be faith in that data. Decision makers and key stakeholders must be confident that the conduct of your research has occurred with integrity and rigour.
- *Credible, relevant and significant findings* – findings that are likely to lead to on-the-ground change are those whose credibility, relevance and significance are clear. Now while it's true that findings that validate assumptions and expectations can lead to high levels of utilization, unexpected results can also lead to change. The trick here is being aware of any potential resistance that may need to be overcome.
- *Feasible recommendations* – I think this is important because impractical recommendations really are a waste of time. Recommendations need to sit within the realm of possibility. In addition to being achievable, it will help if your recommendations are economical, cost-effective and in line with organizational/personal goals.

- *Tangible deliverables* – if you offer something tangible that is both practical and useful for driving change, then you're certainly facilitating the utilization process. The more practical your outcomes can be, the better the chance of their making a difference on the ground.
- *Effective written and verbal communication* – as this chapter stresses, it's all about communication. Think about your audience and do your best to grab their interest and share a compelling, undeniable 'story' with them.
- *Wide dissemination* – finally get the message out there. Dissemination can take many forms and should **not** be restricted to formal written research accounts.

THE FINAL WORD

So, you've reached the end of the journey – or at least the end of this book. Hopefully, your research journey will continue. So what last words of wisdom do I have for you? Well, I don't think I'll take that on by myself … In fact I think I'll leave that to Albert Einstein – he's a bit more qualified than me.

Einstein on continuing the journey …
'The important thing is not to stop questioning …'

Einstein on overcoming challenges …
'In the middle of difficulty lies opportunity …'

Einstein on the sometimes confusing research process …
'If we knew what it was we were doing, it would not be called research, would it?'

Einstein on the joys of being a professional researcher …
'If I had only known, I would have been a locksmith.'

I wish you all the best in your quest to research real-world problems. You never know what contribution you might make to a better world!

FURTHER READING

The writing process
There are two types of readings related to the writing process. First are readings that address the topic explicitly, such as those I have cited below. Second are readings that act as examples. If you know what 'product' you are trying to produce, finding a few effective examples can offer a world of learning.

Arnold, J., Poston, C. and Witek, K. (1999) *Research Writing in the Information Age.* Boston: Allyn & Bacon.

Booth, W. C., Colomb, G. C. and Williams, J. M. (2003) *The Craft of Research.* Chicago: University of Chicago Press.

Evans, D. and Gruba, P. (2002) *How to Write a Better Thesis.* Melbourne: Melbourne University Press.

Strunk, W. Jr and White, E. B. (1999) *Elements of Style.* Boston: Allyn & Bacon.

Dissemination and utilization

While books dedicated to research dissemination and utilization are not easy to find, these topics are often embedded in research methods texts, particularly those texts that are practitioner oriented. Examples of texts that cover the topic include:

Clarke, A. (1999) *Evaluation Research: An Introduction to Principles, Methods and Practice.* London: Sage. (See Chapter 7: Evaluation Utilization)

Dempsey, P. A. and Dempsey, A. D. (2000) *Using Nursing Research: Process, Critical Evaluation, and Utilization.* Philadelphia: Lippincott. (See Chapter 13: Utilizing the Results of Research)

Majchrzak, A. (1984) *Methods for Policy Research.* London: Sage.

Patton, M. Q. (1996) *Utilization-Focused Evaluation: The New Century Text.* London: Sage.

Chapter Summary

- The key to the production of effective research 'deliverables' is engaging communication, useful outcomes and broad dissemination in the real world.

- In addition to research accounts, research deliverables can include: recommendations; action plans; procedures, protocols, guidelines and programmes; tools and kits; prototypes and models; policy; and education and awareness materials.

- To write effectively you need to know your audience … including who they are, what they know, what they are likely to find useful, what their expectations are, and what reactions they may have to your work.

- Your write-up can follow a standard structure that follows the introduction, literature review, methods, findings, then conclusion format; or it can follow an alternative structure that may better suit a particular project's aims and objectives. While alternative structures can allow for more creative expression, the standard format gives readers what they tend to expect.

- Preparing research accounts and deliverables often involves a relatively unpractised form of writing that can be intimidating, so it's well worth 'writing as you go'.

- Your research write-up should unfold as an interesting story. As the author of that story you need to: think of writing as a conversation; become familiar with the craft; find a voice; develop a structure: create a storyline; make convincing arguments; and get down to the business of writing and rewriting.

- Moving from first to final draft is a multi-stage process that sees you working systematically through the development of: logic and argument; coherence and consistency: fluency and readability; and finally copy editing.

- Once your project is complete you are likely to want broad dissemination. Options here include community forums, workplace presentations, academic conferences and publications.

- If you: construct meaningful questions; involve stakeholders; have political nous; ensure rigour in methods; produce credible findings, feasible recommendations and tangible deliverables; communicate effectively; and disseminate widely, you are likely to reach the ultimate goal of having your study effect change.

Bibliography

Abbott, P. and Sapsford, R. (eds) (1997) *Research into Practice: A Reader.* Buckingham: Open University Press.

Angrosino, M. V. and Mays de Perez, K. A. (2000) 'Rethinking Observation: From Method to Context', in N. K. Denzin and Y. S. Lincoln (eds), *Handbook of Qualitative Research.* Thousand Oaks, CA: Sage. pp. 673–702.

Arnold, J., Poston, C. and Witek, K. (1999) *Research Writing in the Information Age.* Boston, MA: Allyn & Bacon.

Babbie, E. (2000) *Practice of Social Research.* Belmont, CA: Wadsworth.

Bakeman, R. and Gottman, J. M. (1997) *Observing Interaction: An Introduction to Sequential Analysis.* Cambridge: Cambridge University Press.

Barrentine, L. B. (1999) *An Introduction to Design of Experiments: A Simplified Approach.* Milwaukee, WI: ASQ Quality Press.

Beitler, M. A. (2003) *Strategic Organizational Change.* Dayton, OH: Ppi Publishing.

Bell, J. (2000) *Doing Your Research Project: A Guide for First-Time Researchers in Education and Social Science.* Buckingham: Open University Press.

Berg, B. L. (2000) *Qualitative Research Methods for the Social Sciences.* Boston, MA: Allyn & Bacon.

Berk, R. A. and Rossi, P. H. (1999) *Thinking about Program Evaluation.* Thousand Oaks, CA: Sage.

Best, S. J. and Krueger, B. S. (2004) *Internet Data Collection.* Thousand Oaks, CA: Sage.

Bickman, L. and Rog, D. J. (1998) *Handbook of Applied Social Research Methods.* Thousand Oaks, CA: Sage.

Blaikie, N. (2000) *Designing Social Research.* Cambridge: Polity Press.

Blaxter, L., Hughes, C. and Tight, M. (2001) *How to Research.* Buckingham: Open University Press.

Booth, W. C., Colomb, G. C. and Williams, J. M. (2003) *The Craft of Research.* Chicago: University of Chicago Press.

Boud, D. and Feletti, G. (1998) *The Challenge of Problem-Based Learning.* London: Kogan Page.

Bowling, A. (2002) *Research Methods in Health: Investigating Health and Health Services.* Buckingham: Open University Press.

Boyatzis, R. E. (1998) *Transforming Qualitative Information: Thematic Analysis and Code Development.* London: Sage.

Brear, M., Powis, B., O'Leary, Z. and Davidson, D. (2004) 'Evaluating Community Participation in a Healthy Islands Setting: Towards Evidence Based Decision Making', *Health Promotion Journal of Australia*, 15 (2), pp. 137–41.

Bryman, A. and Cramer, D. (2005) *Quantitative Data Analysis with SPSS Release 12 for Windows.* London: Routledge.

Bryman, A. and Hardy, M. A. (eds) (2004) *Handbook of Data Analysis.* London: Sage.

Burns, R. (2000) *Introduction to Research Methods.* French's Forest NSW, Australia: Longman.

Cameron, E. and Green, M. (2004) *Making Sense of Change Management: A Complete Guide to the Models, Tools and Techniques of Organizational Change.* London: Kogan Page.

Campbell, D. T. and Stanley, J. C. (1966) *Experimental and Quasi-Experimental Designs for Research*. Dallas, TX: Houghton Mifflin.

Carver, R. H. (2003) *Doing Data Analysis with MINITAB 14*. Pacific Grove, CA: Duxbury Press.

Cavana, R. L., Delahaye, B. L. and Sekaran, U. (2000) *Applied Business Research: Qualitative and Quantitative Methods*. New York: John Wiley and Sons.

Chandler, D. (2001) *Semiotics: The Basics*. London: Routledge.

Charles, C. M. and Mertler, C. A. (2001) *Introduction to Educational Research*. White Plains, NY: Longman.

Chen, H. (1999) *Theory Driven Evaluations*. Thousand Oaks, CA: Sage.

Christensen, L. B. (2000) *Experimental Methodology*. Boston, MA: Allyn & Bacon.

Clandinin, D. J. and Connelly, F. M. (2004) *Narrative Inquiry: Experience and Story in Qualitative Research*. San Francisco: Jossey–Bass.

Clarke, A. (1999) *Evaluation Research: An Introduction to Principles, Methods and Practice*. London: Sage.

Coghlan, D. and Brannick, T. (2004) *Doing Action Research in Your Own Organization*, 2nd edn London: Sage.

Converse, J. and Presser, S. (1986) *Survey Questions: Handcrafting the Standardized Questionnaire*. Newbury Park, CA: Sage.

Cornwall, A. and Pratt, G. (eds) (2004) *Pathways to Participation: Reflections on Participatory Rural Appraisal*. Warwickshire: ITDG Publishing.

Creswell, J. W. (1998) *Qualitative Inquiry and Research Design: Choosing Among Five Traditions*. London: Sage.

Creswell, J. W. (2002) *Research Design: Qualitative, Quantitative and Mixed Methods Approaches*. London: Sage.

Crombie, I. K. and Davies, H. T. O. (1996) *Research in Health Care: Design, Conduct and Interpretation in Health Services Research*. Chichester: John Wiley & Sons.

Crotty, M. (1998) *The Foundations of Social Research: Meaning and Perspective in the Research Process*. St Leonards: Allen and Unwin.

Cryer, P. (1996) *The Research Student Guide to Success*. Buckingham: Open University Press.

Daly, J., Kellehear, A. and Gliksman, M. (1997) *The Public Health Researcher: A Methodological Guide*. Oxford: Oxford University Press.

Daly, J., McDonald, I. and Willis, E. (eds) (1992) *Researching Health Care: Designs, Dilemmas, Disciplines*. London: Routledge.

Dempsey, P. A. and Dempsey, A. D. (1996) *Nursing Research: Text and Workbook*. Boston, MA: Little, Brown and Company.

Dempsey, P. A. and Dempsey, A. D. (2000) *Using Nursing Research: Process, Critical Evaluation, and Utilization*. Philadelphia: Lippincott.

Denscombe, M. (1998) *The Good Research Guide: For Small-Scale Social Research*. Buckingham: Open University Press.

Denzin, N. K. and Lincoln, Y. S. (eds) (1998) *Strategies of Qualitative Inquiry*. Thousand Oaks, CA: Sage.

Denzin, N. K. and Lincoln, Y. S. (eds) (2000) *Handbook of Qualitative Research*. Thousand Oaks, CA: Sage.

Der, G. and Everitt, B. S. (2001) *Handbook of Statistical Analyses Using SAS*. Boca Raton, FL: CRC Press.

Egan, G. (1994) *The Skilled Helper: A Problem Management Approach to Helping*, 5th edn. Pacific Grove, CA: Brooks/Cole.

Estrella, M. (ed.) (2000) *Learning from Change: Issues and Experiences in Participatory Monitoring and Evaluation.* Sterling, VA: Stylus Publishers.

Evans, D. and Gruba, P. (2002) *How to Write a Better Thesis.* Melbourne: Melbourne University Press.

Fals Borda, O. and Rahman, M. A. (1991) *Action and Knowledge: Breaking the Monopoly with Participatory Action Research.* New York: Intermediate Technology/Apex.

Fetterman, D. M. (1997) *Ethnography: Step-by-Step.* London: Sage.

Fielding, N. (1997) 'Qualitative Interviewing', in N. Gilbert (ed.), *Researching Social Life.* London: Sage. pp. 135–53.

Finnegan, R. (1996) 'Using Documents', in R. Sapsford and V. Jupp (eds), *Data Collection and Analysis.* London: Sage. pp. 138–51.

Fontana, A. and Frey, J. H. (2000) 'The Interview: From Structured Questions to Negotiated Text', in N. K. Denzin and Y. S. Lincoln (eds), *Handbook of Qualitative Research.* Thousand Oaks, CA: Sage. pp. 645–72.

Fowler, F. J. Jr (2001) *Survey Research Methods.* London: Sage.

Freire, P. (1970) *Pedagogy of the Oppressed.* New York: Herder & Herder.

Galvan, J. L. (1999) *Writing Literature Reviews: A Guide for Students of the Social and Behavioral Sciences.* Glendale, CA: Pyrczak Publications.

Geertz, C. (1977) *The Interpretation of Cultures.* New York: Basic Books.

Gilbert, N. (ed.) (2002) *Researching Social Life.* London: Sage.

Glaser, B. (1992) *Basics of Grounded Theory Analysis: Emergence versus Focus.* Mill Valley, CA: Sociology Press.

Glaser, B. and Strauss, A. (1967) *Discovery of Grounded Theory.* Chicago: Aldine.

Gottdiener, M., Lagopoulos, A. and Boklund-Lagopoulos, K. (eds) (2003) *Semiotics.* London: Sage.

Greenwood, D. and Levin, M. (1998) *Introduction to Action Research: Social Research for Social Change.* Thousand Oaks, CA: Sage.

Grills, S. (ed.) (1998) *Doing Ethnographic Research.* London: Sage.

Groves, R. M., Fowler, F. J., Couper, M. J., Lepkowski, J. M., Singer, E. and Tourangeau, R. (2004) *Survey Methodology.* New York: John Wiley & Sons.

Gubrium, J. F. and Holstein, J. A. (2001) *Handbook of Interview Research: Context and Method.* London: Sage.

Gupta, K. (1998) *A Practical Guide to Needs Assessment.* San Francisco, CA: Pfeiffer.

Habibie, H. (2003) '*Participatory Action Research to Improve the Livelihood of Rural People through Livestock Production in South Sulawesi*, Indonesia'. PhD thesis. Richmond: University of Western Sydney.

Hall, D. and Hall, I. (1996) *Practical Social Research: Project Work in the Community.* London: Macmillan.

Hammersley, M. and Atkinson, P. (1995) *Ethnography: Principles in Practice.* London: Routledge.

Hammersley, M., Foster, R. and Gomm, R. (2000) *Case Study Method: Key Issues, Key Texts.* London: Sage.

Hart, C. (2000) *Doing a Literature Review.* London: Sage.

Hart, C. (2001) *Doing a Literature Search.* London: Sage.

Hart, E. and Bond, M. (1995) *Action Research for Health and Social Care: A Guide to Practice.* Buckingham: Open University Press.

Hedrick, T. E., Bickman, L. and Rog, D. J. (1993) *Applied Research Design: A Practical Guide.* London: Sage.

Hock, R. and Price, G. (2004) *The Extreme Searcher's Internet Handbook: A Guide for the Serious Searcher*. Medford, NJ: Cyberage Books.

Hoey, M. (2000) *Textual Interaction: An Introduction to Written Discourse Analysis*. London: Routledge.

Holder, I. (2000) 'The Interpretation of Documents and Material Culture', in N. K. Denzin and Y. S. Lincoln (eds), *Handbook of Qualitative Research*. Thousand Oaks, CA: Sage. pp. 703–16.

Hood, S., Mayall, B. and Oliver, S. (eds) (1999) *Critical Issues in Social Research: Power and Prejudice*. Buckingham: Open University Press.

International Labour Organization (2005) *Facts on Safe Work*. Geneva: ILO. http://www.ilo. org/public/english/bureau/inf/download/wssd/pdf/health.pdf

Jablon, J. R., Dombro, A. L. and Dichtelmiller, M. L. (1999) *The Power of Observation*. Florence, KY: Thomson Delmar Learning.

Jefferies, J. and Diamond, I. (2001) *Beginning Statistics: An Introduction for Social Scientists*. London: Sage.

Kellehear, A. (1993) *The Unobtrusive Researcher: A Guide to Methods*. St Leonards: Allen and Unwin.

Kemmis, S. and McTaggart, R. (2000) 'Participatory Action Research', in N. K. Denzin and Y. S. Lincoln (eds), *Handbook of Qualitative Research*. Thousand Oaks, CA: Sage. pp. 379–99.

Kimmel, A. J. (1988) *Ethics and Values in Applied Social Research*. Newbury Park, CA: Sage.

Kolb, D. A. (1984) *Experiential Learning: Experience as the Source of Learning and Development*. Englewood Cliffs, NJ: Prentice-Hall.

Kripppendorf, K. (2003) *Content Analysis: An Introduction to Its Methodology*. London: Sage.

Kumar, S. and Chambers, R. (2003) *Methods for Community Participation: A Complete Guide for Practitioners*. Warwickshire: ITDG Publishing.

Kvale, S. (1996) *InterViews: An Introduction to Qualitative Research Interviewing*. Thousand Oaks, CA: Sage.

Layder, D. (1998) *Sociological Practice: Linking Theory and Social Research*. London: Sage.

Lee, R. M. (2000) *Unobtrusive Methods in Social Research*. Buckingham: Open University Press.

Levy, P. S. and Lemeshow, S. (1999) *Sampling of Populations: Methods and Applications*. New York: Wiley-Interscience.

Lewin, K. (1946) 'Action Research and the Minority Problems', *Journal of Social Issues*, 2, pp. 34–6.

Lincoln, Y. S. and Guba, E. G. (1985) *Naturalistic Inquiry*. Beverly Hills, CA: Sage.

Locke, L. F., Spirduso, W. W. and Silverman, S. J. (1999) *Proposals That Work: A Guide for Planning Dissertations and Grant Proposals*. London: Sage.

Lofland, J. and Lofland, L. H. (2003) *Analyzing Social Settings: A Guide to Qualitative Observation and Analysis*. Belmont, CA: Wadsworth.

Lohr, S. L. (1998) *Sampling: Design and Analysis*. Pacific Grove, CA: Brooks/Cole.

Majchrzak, A. (1984) *Methods for Policy Research*. London: Sage.

Mansoor, A. F. Kazi (2003) *Realist Evaluation in Practice: Health and Social Work*. London: Sage.

Martin, D. W. (2003) *Doing Psychology Experiments*. Belmont, CA: Wadsworth.

McCreadie, K. and O'Leary, Z. (2005) 'The Sale of Out of Date Foods in the Republic of Palau', *Pacific Health Dialog*, March, 11, p. 1.

McNiff, J. and Whitehead, J. (2002) *Action Research: Principles and Practice*. London: Routledge.

Middlewood, D. (1999) *Practitioner Research in Education: Making a Difference*. London: Sage.

Miles, M. and Huberman, A. (1994) *Qualitative Data Analysis: An Expanded Source Book.* Thousand Oaks, CA: Sage.

Miller, G. and Dingwall, R. (eds) (1997) *Context and Method in Qualitative Research.* London: Sage.

Millroy, W., Preissle, J. and LeCompte, M. (1992) (eds), *The Handbook of Qualitative Research in Education.* New York: Academic Press. pp. 470–505.

Morse, J. M. (1998) 'Designing Funded Qualitative Research', in N. K. Denzin and Y. S. Lincoln (eds), *Strategies of Qualitative Inquiry.* Thousand Oaks, CA: Sage. pp. 56–85.

Morton-Cooper, A. (2000) *Action Research in Health Care.* Oxford: Blackwell Science.

Murray, L. and Lawrence, B. (2000) *Practitioner-Based Enquiry: Principles for Postgraduate Research.* London: Falmer Press.

Neuendorf, K. A. (2001) *The Content Analysis Guidebook.* London: Sage.

Ogden, T. E. and Goldberg, I. A. (eds) (2002) *Research Proposals: A Guide to Success.* New York: Academic Press.

O'Leary, Z. (1997) 'Re-imagining Apostasy'. PhD thesis. Richmond: University of Western Sydney.

O'Leary, Z. (1999) *Reaction, Introspection and Exploration: Diversity in Journeys out of Faith.* Kew, Victoria: Christian Research Association.

O'Leary, Z. (2001) 'Conversations in the Kitchen' in A. Bartlett and G. Mercer (eds), *Postgraduate Research Supervision: Transforming (R)elations.* New York: Peter Lang.

O'Leary, Z. (2004) *The Essential Guide to Doing Research.* London: Sage.

Oppenheim, A. N. (1992) *Questionnaire Design, Interviewing and Attitude Measurement.* London: Pinter.

Patton, M. Q. (2001) *Qualitative Research and Evaluation Methods.* Thousand Oaks, CA: Sage.

Patton, M. Q. (1996) *Utilization-Focused Evaluation: The New Century Text.* London: Sage.

Payne, J. (1999) *Researching Health Needs: A Community-Based Approach.* London: Sage.

Peavey, F. (2005) *Strategic Questioning.* San Francisco: Crabgrass. http://www.crabgrass.org

Phillips, E. M. and Pugh, D. S. (2000) *How to get a PhD: A Handbook for Students and Their Supervisors.* Buckingham: Open University Press.

Pickett, J. P. et al. (eds) (2000) *The American Heritage Dictionary of the English Language,* 4th edn. Boston, MA: Houghton Mifflin.

Pratt, B. and Loizos, P. (1992) *Choosing Research Methods: Data Collection for Development Workers.* Oxford: Oxfam.

Prior, L. (2003) *Using Documents in Social Research.* London: Sage.

Psathas, G. (1994) *Conversation Analysis: The Study of Talk-in-Interaction.* London: Sage.

Punch, K. (1998) *Introduction to Social Research.* London: Sage.

Rahman, A. (ed.) (1994) *People's Self-Development: Perspectives on Participatory Action Research: A Journey Through Experience.* London: Zed Books.

Rao, P. S., Rao, R. S., Poduri, S. R. S. and Miller, W. (2000) *Sampling Methodologies with Applications.* New York: Lewis Publishers, Inc.

Reason, P. (ed.) (1989) *Human Inquiry in Action: Developments in New Paradigm Research.* London: Sage.

Reason, P. and Bradbury, H. (2001) *Handbook of Action Research: Participative Inquiry and Practice.* London: Sage.

Reed, J. and Proctor, S. (eds) (1995) *Practitioner Research in Health Care: The Inside Story.* London: Chapman and Hall.

Richardson, L. (2000) 'Writing: A Method of Inquiry', in N. K. Denzin, and Y. S. Lincoln (eds), *Handbook of Qualitative Inquiry.* Thousand Oaks, CA: Sage. pp. 936–48.

Riessman, C. K. (1993) *Narrative Analysis*. London: Sage.

Robson, C. (2000) *Real World Research*. Oxford: Blackwell.

Root, M. (1993) *Philosophy of Social Science: The Methods, Ideals and Politics of Social Inquiry*. Oxford: Blackwell.

Rossi, P. H. (1999) 'Evaluating Community Development Programs: Problems and Prospects', in R. F. Ferguson and W. T. Dickens (eds), *Urban Problems and Community Development*. Washington, DC: Brookings. pp. 521–67.

Rossi, P. H., Freeman, H. E. and Lipsey, M. W. (1999) *Evaluation: A Systematic Approach*. Thousand Oaks, CA: Sage.

Rossman, G. and Rallis, S. (2003) *Learning in the Field: An Introduction to Qualitative Research*. Thousand Oaks, CA: Sage.

Rubin, H. J. and Rubin, I. S. (2004) *Qualitative Interviewing: The Art of Hearing Data*. Thousand Oaks, CA: Sage.

Rudestam, K. E. and Newton, R. R. (2001) *Surviving Your Dissertation: A Comprehensive Guide to Content and Process*. London: Sage.

Sagor, R. (2004) *The Action Research Guidebook: A Four-Step Process for Educators and School Teams*. Thousand Oaks, CA: Corwin Press.

Salkind, N. J. (2000) *Exploring Research*. Englewood Cliffs, NJ: Prentice-Hall.

Salkind, N. J. (2003) *Statistics for People Who (Think They) Hate Statistics*. London: Sage.

Schensul, J. and LeCompte, D. (eds) (1999) *The Ethnographer's Toolkit*, 7 vols. London: Sage.

Schuman, H. and Presser, S. (1996) *Question and Answers in Attitude Surveys: Experiments on Question Form, Wording and Context*. San Diego: Academic Press.

Senge, P. M. (1994) *The Fifth Discipline: The Art and Practice of the Learning Organization*. New York: Doubleday/Currency.

Sharp, J. A. and Howard, K. (2003) *The Management of a Student Research Project*. Aldershot: Gower.

Silverman, D. (ed.) (1997) *Qualitative Research: Theory, Methods and Practice*. London: Sage.

Silverman, D. (2001) *Interpreting Qualitative Data: Methods for Analysing Talk, Text and Interaction*. London: Sage.

Singleton, R. and Straits, B. C. (1999) *Approaches to Social Research*. New York: Oxford University Press.

Smith, S., Willm, D. G. and Johnson, N. A. (eds) (1997) *Nurtured by Knowledge: Learning to Do Participatory Action-Research*. New York: Apex Press.

Stake, R. E. (2000) 'Case Studies', in N. K. Denzin and Y. S. Lincoln (eds), *Handbook of Qualitative Research*. Thousand Oaks, CA: Sage. pp. 435–54.

Strauss, A. and Corbin, J. (1998) *Basics of Qualitative Research: Techniques and Procedures for Developing Grounded Theory*. London: Sage.

Stringer, E. (1999) *Action Research*. Thousand Oaks, CA: Corwin Press.

Strunk, W. Jr and White, E. B. (1999) *Elements of Style*. Boston, MA: Allyn & Bacon.

Tamplin, S., Davidson, D., Powis, B. and O'Leary, Z. (2005) 'Issues and Options for the Safe Destruction and Disposal of Used Injection Materials', *Waste Management*, 25 (1).

Tashakkori, A. and Teddlie, C. (eds) (2002) *Handbook of Mixed Methods Social and Behavioral Research*. London: Sage.

Tavers, M. (2001) *Qualitative Research through Case Studies*. London: Sage.

Ten Have, P. (1999) *Doing Conversation Analysis: A Practical Guide*. Thousand Oaks, CA: Corwin.

Thomas, J. (1993) *Doing Critical Ethnography*. Newbury Park, CA: Sage.

Thompson, S. K. (2002) *Sampling*. New York: John Wiley & Sons.

Tortu, S., Goldsamt, L. A. and Hamid, R. (eds) (2001) *A Practical Guide to Research and Services with Hidden Populations*. Boston, MA: Allyn & Bacon.

Trochim, W. M. (2005) *The Research Methods Knowledge Base*. http://www.socialresearchmethods. net/kb/index.htm

Van Manen, M. (1990) *Researching Lived Experience: Human Science for an Action Sensitive Pedagogy*. New York: State University of New York Press.

Verhaag, B. (1997) *Blue Eyed: A Program about Discrimination and Prejudice*. Munich: Denkmal-film.

Wainer, H. (2000) *Drawing Inferences from Self-Selected Samples*. Mahwah, NJ: Lawrence Erlbaum Assoc.

Webb, E. J., Campbell, D. T., Schwartz, R. D. and Sechrest, L. (1966) *Unobtrusive Measures: Nonreactive Research in the Social Sciences*. Dallas, TX: Houghton Mifflin.

Webb, E. J., Campbell, D. T., Schwartz, R. D., Sechrest, L. and Grove, J. B. (1981) *Nonreactive Measures in the Social Sciences*. Dallas, TX: Houghton Mifflin.

Whyte, W. F. (ed.) (1991) *Participatory Action Research*. Newbury Park: Sage.

Willis, P. and Neville, B. (eds) (1996) *Qualitative Research Practice in Adult Education*. Ringwood, Victoria: Davis Lovell Publishing.

Winter, R. and Munn-Giddings, C. (2001) *A Handbook for Action Research in Health and Social Care*. London: Routledge.

Wisker, G. (2001) *The Postgraduate Research Handbook: Succeed with your MA, MPhil, EdD and PhD*. Hampshire: Palgrave.

Witkin, B. R. and Altschuld, J. W. (1995) *Planning and Conducting Needs Assessments: A Practical Guide*. London: Sage.

Witkin, B. R. and Altschuld, J. W. (1999) *From Needs Assessment to Action: Transforming Needs into Solution Strategies*: London: Sage.

Wolcott, H. F. (1994) *Transforming Qualitative Data: Description, Analysis and Interpretation*. London: Sage.

Wood, L. A. and Kroger, R. O. (2000) *Doing Discourse Analysis: Methods for Studying Action in Talk and Text*. Thousand Oaks, CA: Sage.

World Health Organization Regional Office for the Western Pacific (1995) *Yancuca Islands Declaration*. Manilla: WHO Regional Office for the Western Pacific.

World Health Organization Regional Office for the Western Pacific (1999) *Regional Guidelines for the Development of Healthy Workplaces*. Manilla: WHO Regional Office for the Western Pacific.

Yin, R. K. (2002) *Case Study Research: Design and Methods*. Thousand Oaks, CA: Sage.

Zuber-Skerritt, O. (ed.) (1996) *New Directions in Action Research*. London: Falmer Press.

Index

296

Exodus of 2ND Gen Latino youth
— Myth or fact?
✓ Reasons
-
✓ Can/are parents' influence a factor?